Dictionary of

GODS AND GODDESSES, DEVILS AND DEMONS

Dictionary of
GODS AND GODDESSES, DEVILS AND DEMONS

Manfred Lurker

Routledge & Kegan Paul
London and New York

First published in German in 1984 as
Lexikon der Götter und Dämonen
by Alfred Krämer Verlag, Stuttgart

This translation first published in 1987 by
Routledge & Kegan Paul Ltd
11 New Fetter Lane, London EC4P 4EE

Published in the USA by
Routledge & Kegan Paul Inc.
in association with Methuen Inc.
29 West 35th Street, New York, NY 10001

Set in 9/10 Ehrhardt
by Columns Ltd., Reading
and printed in Great Britain
by Cox & Wyman Ltd., Reading

Library of Congress Cataloging in Publication Data

Lurker, Manfred.
Dictionary of gods and goddesses, devils and
demons.
Translation of: Lexikon der Götter und Dämonen.
1984.
Bibliography: p.
1. Mythology – Dictionaries.   2. Demonology –
Dictionaries.   I. Title.
BL303.L8713   1987   291.2'1'0321   86–21911

British Library CIP Data also available

ISBN 0-7102-0877-4 (c)
ISBN 0-7102-1106-6 (p)

Contents

Preface

A basic element in all religions is the awareness, both intellectual and emotional, of man's dependence on non-human powers: powers which we conceive as personal, and vis-à-vis which we normally stand in a reciprocal relationship. Gods and demons are the forms taken by these powers, their hypostatizations, as it were, in the shape of light and darkness, sun and moon, fire and water, bird and snake. The divine can reveal itself in all the phenomena of nature, just as the demonic can. But it is not only from without that the numinous presents itself to man: it can arise spontaneously in religious experience as an 'exponent of feeling' (Wilamowitz-Moellendorf), and it can be divined as 'a dark abyss . . . which is not accessible to our reason' (Rudolf Otto). The images generated in the human mind are, then, representative of stages reached in man's understanding and in his knowledge of himself; in a certain sense, indeed, every divine image has traits which identify it as a self-projection of mankind. As ideal beings, the gods are what man would like to be; but they are also what he, in his spatio-temporal imperfection, cannot be.

Every religion has its own conventions and symbols which serve to express the functions, the aspects and the spheres of competence of the members of its pantheon. And this means that the conscious and unconscious nexus of conventions specific to any one religion is hardly, if at all, accessible to believers in another religion, or to those who believe in no religion at all. Thus, even for the ancient Greeks the animal gods of the Egyptians were shocking and revolting. And modern man, proud as he is of his reason and logic, fares no better when he is called upon to recognize an authentic view of God in the often and – in the most literal sense – obscure rites and images of an alien religion.

Above all, we must not fail to recognize that

the concepts 'god' and 'demon' are by no means evenly weighted in the various religions. The innumerable deities of Hinduism and Buddhism carry about as much significance as angels or saints do in monotheistic religions. There are mortal gods, gods who die (like Balder and Osiris) and demonic beings whom death cannot touch (for example, the Devas). The border-line between gods and demons is fluid (see Asura, or the Nymphs); and with the Christianization of a people, its erstwhile deities can be devalued to the status of devils (as in the case of Pan or Dabog) or accepted into the corpus of Christian saints (for example, Brigit Köndös). From the largely anonymous mass of spirits, gods and demons are distinguished by being more sharply and individually characterized, as shown, for example in the bestowal of names upon them.

The present reference work offers a conspectus of all the more important supernatural beings who have acquired 'personality' in this sense, both in the pantheons of the classical cultures and in the world religions of today; and the religious systems of the so-called 'primitive' races are also given their due place. Any attempt at an exhaustive survey of all the names, functions, symbols and attributes in this field was excluded from the outset: the mass of material is such that even several volumes could hardly cope with it. Heroic figures in saga and legend have been included only where this is justified by their subsequent deification: thus, Aeneas and Heraklés are included, while the Celtic King Arthur and the Germanic hero Siegfried are not. The same goes for founders of religions, and for saints: the reader will find Buddha and Lao-zi in these pages, but neither Muhammad nor Zarathustra. Mythological detail has been intentionally cut to a minimum. There is no entry for Christ: for various reasons, adequate treatment of this figure lies outside the scope of the present work. The reader's attention is directed particularly to the two appendices, in which the individual gods and demons are classified from various points of view.

The illustrations serve only to lighten the text, and are not intended to be in any way a scientifically exact iconography. It should be borne in mind that in the case of certain cultures it is hardly possible to find suitable matter for illustrative purposes and that certain peoples and religions have a pronounced antipathy to images and representation of any sort.

Manfred Lurker
Oberkirch, May 1984

Note on transcription and pronunciation

1 *Greek and Latin* English forms in general currency are used instead of their Greek or Latin equivalents: thus, Jupiter for Iup(p)iter, Centaurs, Nymphs, etc. Apart from these special cases, Greek and Latin names are taken as in the original German text, with changes in spelling where necessary. Head-words in the original text carry stress-marks based on: H. Hunger, *Lexikon der griechischen und römischen Mythologie*, 6th edn, 1969. These are retained.

2 *Sanskrit and Vedic* Standard transcription is used for Sanskrit and Vedic names, based on Macdonell, *Sanskrit-English Dictionary*, OUP, 1924. The distinction between the dental series: t, d, n, s; the retroflex series: ṭ, ḍ, ṇ, ṣ; and the palatal series: c, j, ñ, ś, has been retained. Here, ṣ and ś are both pronounced as *sh*; ṭ, ḍ, ṇ are the same sounds as are heard in English t, d, n; t, d, n are their continental counterparts (as in Italian); ñ is the Spanish ñ.

3 The *sh* sound where it otherwise occurs – particularly in ancient Near Eastern and Egyptian names – is transcribed as š. This letter also represents *sh* in the two Baltic languages, Lithuanian and Latvian. In Yoruba, *sh* is represented by ṣ.

4 *Chinese* For Chinese names the modern pinyin romanization has been used, though tone marks have been disregarded; x is something like the *sh* in *sh*ip, q is like the *ch* in *ch*eese; p, t, k are heavily aspirated; b, d, g are not voiced.

5 Wherever it occurs, ž is pronounced as j in French '*j*ournal'.

6 In Aztec and Maya names, c before e and i = s; before a, o, u = k.

Dictionary of Gods and Goddesses, Devils and Demons

A

Aatxe (Basque, 'young bull') Evil spirit in the shape of a bull which, the Basques believe, leaves its cave on stormy nights, and which may often assume human form. Under the name Etsai (i.e. devil) it instructs its devotees in its arts.

Abaddon (Hebrew, 'downfall', 'ruin') In the Old Testament, the word refers to the underworld, the place of destruction: e.g. Job 26:2; 28:22). In the Apocalypse, it means the angel of hell, the lord of the plague of locusts (Revelation 9: 7-11). Known in Greek as Apollyon, i.e. destroyer.

Abat(t)ur A mythical figure of the Mandaeans. At the last judgment it weighs souls and/ or their deeds. The name derives from Persian and is construed as meaning 'bearer of the scales'.

Abellio A Gallic local deity, known from inscriptions in the Garonne valley. He has been interpreted as a god of apple-trees.

Abgal (Apkallu) Seven Sumerian spirits deriving from the Abzu (→ Apsu) and subject to Enki. It is probable that they reflect legendary antediluvian kings. Some of the Abgal are conceived as fish-men.

Abhiyoga Generic name of the servile gods in Jainism; they help the supreme gods (→ Indra) to create rain and darkness.

Abora The supreme being worshipped by the Canary Islanders on the island of Palma. The god sat in heaven and caused the stars to move.

Abraxas (variants Abrasax, Abraxis) Occult theonym used in Graeco-Oriental gnosticism. In Greek values, the letters add up to 365, corresponding thus to the number of days in the year. The hebdomad of letters was associated with the seven planets. Abraxas stones were used as amulets and usually show the god with the torso and the arms of a man, the head of a cock and serpent legs. In scientific literature he is also known as Angnipede = 'snake-feet'.

Abu Sumerian god of vegetation. According to one tradition he was born from the skull of → Enki, an image of the emergence of plants from the earth's surface.

Abundantia Roman goddess personifying abundance (*abundantia*). She lived on in the Lady Habonde (Abundia) of French popular belief, who visits people's houses by night bringing prosperity.

Acala 'The Immovable', a divinity in Indian Buddhism. As 'Protector of the Teaching' his image stands before temples to ward off those hostile to the Buddhist doctrine. He has three eyes and six arms, and he grinds his teeth. His weapons include the sword, the thunderbolt (Vajra), the axe and the noose.

Acaviser → Lasas

Achelóos Greek river-god bearing the same name as the river which runs into the Ionian Sea. The son of → Okeanos and of → Tethys. The myth tells how Acheloos fought the hero

Heraklés for possession of the Deinaeira, taking the form first of a snake, then of a bull. He married the muse Melpomene, and the → Sirens were supposed to be his daughters. Under the name Achlae, Acheloos is attested in Etruria from the sixth century BC onwards, and is represented as heavily bearded and with the horns of a bull.

Achilleus (Latin, Achilles) Hero of Greek legend. The young Achilleus had been dipped by his mother → Thetis in the water of the Styx to make him invulnerable, but the water did not touch the heel by which she held him (hence 'Achilles' heel'). In the Trojan War he was slain by Paris. Achilleus was venerated as a hero throughout Greece. In the Black Sea area he had divine status, and was known from the Hadrian era onwards by the epithet Pontarchos = ruler of the sea.

Acoran The supreme being, worshipped by the inhabitants of Gran Canaria in the Canary Islands. Temples to him were erected in remote mountain places difficult of access, and these afforded inviolable asylum. A daily offering of milk was made to the god by maidens clad in white leather.

Adad (in Syria, Hadad) Babylonian god of weather and rain; the name is usually written with the cuneiform character for 'wind'. He was thought of as son of the supreme god → An. His epithets 'Dyke-warden of Heaven' and 'Lord of Abundance' identify him as the beneficent giver. If he withholds the rains, drought and famine ensue. His symbolical animal was the bull, his sign was a cluster of lightning flashes. An ancient hymn describes how heaven and earth rise before the god, who is also called Ramman (= thunder). The illustration (a seal motif) shows him in a robe adorned with astral signs and with a tall hat decorated on top with feathers; in his hand he holds the pincer-shaped bolts of lightning.

Adam(m)as The parental godhead of the Naassenes, a gnostic movement in Phrygia; conceived as a father-mother syzygy, the 'parents of the aeons'.

Adam Kadmon According to the Kabbala (a Jewish mystical movement) the first man, an emanation of absolute perfection. He is symbolized by the major axis of ten concentric circles, the Sephiroth or ten circles of creation. Thus, Adam Kadmon as primeval man symbolizes the universe. He is androgynous, and is seen in ancient Jewish mysticism as partaking in, or blending with God. The Bahir book (twelfth century) mentions the 'seven holy forms of God', all of which have correspondences in the limbs of the human body. Man thus exhibits the mystic structure of the godhead.

Adam Kasia ('the hidden Adam'), also known as Adam Qadmaia, 'the first Adam'. A god-like form postulated by the Mandaeans, which unites in itself microcosm and macrocosm. This form was regarded as, at one and the same time, the soul of the corporeal Adam and as the soul of every man. Adam Kasia is a redeemer, and is himself redeemed. Cf. in Jewish mysticism, → Adam Kadmon.

Adibuddha ('primeval Buddha') The concept is of a → Buddha who has existed from the beginning of time and who has created, through contemplative development of his Self, the five → Dhyāni-Buddhas. These are the Buddhas of contemplation, which then bring forth the five → Dhyāni-Bodhisattvas, from which the universe arises in a series of self-superseding acts of creation. Adibuddha is thus a kind of primeval or original creator. His epithet is Vajradhara ('bearer of the thunderbolt').

Aditi Indian goddess; her dominion is over the divine ordering of the world, and she is the mother of the → Adityas. In later tradition she appears as the personification of the earth; her bosom is its navel. The name 'Aditi' really means 'infinity', and the goddess is a form of the Great Mother who embraces all living and being. She is also a redeemer figure, as she is supposed to free those who believe in her from sickness, need and the stains of sin.

Adityas 'Progeny of Aditi' (→ Aditi) A Vedic grouping of seven or eight gods; at its head is → Varuṇa, often in association with → Mitra and → Aryaman. Martanda, the eighth son of Aditi, is seen as the divine fore-father of the human race. Like Aditi, the Adityas were believed to offer salvation from all ills. Post-Vedic literature postulates twelve Adityas in the role of twelve sun-gods, who are in turn connected with the twelve months of the year.

Adonis Originally a Phoenician-Syrian god (the Semitic word 'adon' means 'master'). He embodies vegetation scorched by the heat of the summer sunshine, and was worshipped in the mystic cults as a god who dies and is resurrected. According to Greek legend, he was born from a myrrh tree, into which his mother had been changed. He was the beautiful lover of → Aphrodíte. When he was killed by a boar while hunting, the goddess caused the Adonis rose to spring up from his blood, and she was able to secure his release from the underworld for six months in the year. The seeds of the so-called Adonis garden grow readily in a bowl or a box, and their blossoming and rapid withering were seen as symbolizing the life and death of the god. Adonis was taken over by the Etruscans under the name of → Atunis.

Adraste (or Andraste = she who is invincible) A goddess of war in ancient Britain, to whom

Queen Boudicca (AD 61) had captured Roman women sacrificed. A parallel is found in Gaul where the Vicontii had a goddess of war named Andarta.

Adrásteia ('the inescapable') Originally a Trojan-Phrygian mountain divinity who was also worshipped in Thrace and who appears in Greece from about 400 BC onwards as the guardian of righteousness and the goddess who avenges all wrongs; connected with → Nemesis. Whether there is any common Indo-Germanic connection with the Celtic-British → Adraste is not clear.

Adro A god of the Lugbara people who live on the shores of Lake Albert in East Africa. He lives with his wives and children on earth, preferably in rivers, and he makes himself known to humans in the shape of whirlwinds and grass fires. The celestial aspect of this earthly god is known as Adroa, a divinity in his own right, who created mankind in days gone by, but who now lives at infinite removal from us.

Aegir A north Germanic sea-giant, husband of → Ran. At a carousal for the Aesir (→ As), he had shining gold brought into the hall which was lit up as though by fire. It has been suggested that the gold represents the shimmering of tranquil seas without wind.

Aenéas To begin with, a Greek hero (Greek: Aineias) in the Trojan War, the son of King Anchises and the goddess → Aphrodíte, the mother of the gods from Mount Ida. The saga of his flight from the ruins of Troy became known to the Romans and the Etruscans in the sixth century BC; and soon thereafter he himself was honoured as a *heros*. For the Romans he was the embodiment of the old Roman virtue of *pietas* (piety, reverence for age and tradition) thanks to his having rescued his father (lamed by lightning) and the holy images, and taken them with him on his wanderings. The emperor Augustus believed that his family was descended from the son of the gods, Aeneas.

Aesculápius

The god of healing → Asklepiós, introduced into Rome during a plague in 293 BC. In his capacity as all-healer, he became one of the most popular gods of the early Empire. The emperor Marcus Aurelius had himself depicted as Aesculápius, bearing a caduceus as sceptre. In modern times the caduceus has become the symbol of the medical profession.

Aēšma Daēva

(*aēšma* = madness) The Parsee demon of lust and anger. His wrath is directed mainly against the cow, which occupies the central place among the creatures. Only by → Saošyant can he be finally overcome.

Aetérnitas

For the Romans the personification of eternity, both of the Empire and of the deified emperors. Symbolically represented by the phoenix perpetually arising from the ashes of its own burning, and the snake biting its own tail (Uroboros): both of these illustrating a process which has no beginning and no end.

Afi

God of rain and thunderstorms among the Abkhaz people who live in the western Caucasus. His name must not be uttered by women, who call him simply 'the one who is above'.

Agaš

(Avestan = 'evil eye') A demon of illness in Iranian religions: primarily a demon of those sins which are committed by means of the eye.

Agathós Daímon A good genius or guardian spirit in ancient Greek mythology. It was often imagined as a winged serpent which hovers invisibly round a man and brings good luck to his home.

Agdistis (Agditis) A hermaphrodite being in Phrygian mythology. It is descended from → Papas, made drunk by → Diónysos, and emasculates itself on waking from its drunken stupor. An almond tree grows from its sexual organs, and the fruit of this tree makes the daughter of the river-god → Sangarios pregnant. She gives birth to → Attis. Agdistis, now in its female aspect as a form of the Great Mother (→ Kybéle), falls in love with the beautiful youth Attis; when he is unfaithful to her, she makes him lose his reason.

Aglaia → Charites

Aglibol The moon-god of Palmyra (ancient Syria). He bears the sickle moon on his forehead – at a later date, on his shoulders. The name is sometimes explained as 'bull of Bol', which would suggest that the sickle was originally bull's horns. His cult spread via Greece to Rome.

Agni (etymologically connected with Latin *ignis* = fire) The Vedic god of fire. He carries the sacrificial burnt offering to the gods. There are two or three versions of his birth: on the one hand, he is said to be born from heaven, from the sun or from lightning, but then again he is born from an earthly source, from stone or from water, in which extinguished fire resides. As portrayed, he is reddish in hue, with a long beard and clothed in fire; in his hands he carries flames, a trident and a water-pot. He is said to be mounted on a ram or a male goat. In old texts Agni is described as the 'bull of the waters', that is to say, he makes the water pregnant: a symbolical reference to the cosmic process, in which (male) fire enters into (female) water. Agni is an intermediary between mankind and the gods, especially when he appears in the sacrificial fire.

Agnóstos Theós (Greek = 'the unknown god') It seems that altars to 'unknown gods' were set up in Athens. In his address to the men of Athens (Acts of the Apostles 17: 23) Paul uses the singular – 'To the unknown god' – but this seems to be a monotheistic adaptation. As far as the history of religion is concerned, there is no doubt that 'all gods' (Pantheon) were invoked and worshipped – gods who are not named but who are not nameless. An unknown or anonymous god is also attested in pre-Islamic Arabia, and votive inscriptions from Palmyra (second and third centuries AD) are addressed to him 'whose name is praised for ever and ever'. His epithets are 'Lord of the world' and 'the good one'.

Ah Bolom Tzacab In scholarly literature known also as god K or as 'the leaf-nosed god' because of the leaf-shaped ornament he wears in his nose. He was the Mayan god of agriculture, and was supposed to control rain and thunder.

Ahone The supreme deity of Indians who once lived in the Virginia area. He was so far removed from men, so remote, that they did little to honour him. In this, he differs from → Okeus.

Ahriman Middle Persian and modern Farsi version of the Avestan name Angru Mainyu ('evil spirit'), the name given by Zarathustra to → Ahura Mazda's adversary who counters every act of creation with an act of anti-creation. Ahriman is the embodiment of all evil; he inhabits an underground realm of eternal darkness, from which he brings smoke and blackness, sickness and death into the world. His symbolical creature is the snake. At the end of time, he will subside powerless into darkness. In Mithraism and

Zervanism Ahriman is venerated as a god; his rituals include the sacrifice of those animals which belong to the powers of evil. Cf. also → Arimanius.

Ahura Mazda Later Ormazd (old Persian = 'Lord of wisdom'). The name of the one true God preached by Zarathustra. Originally Ahura Mazda was conceived as ruling over the oppositional pair Spenta Mainyu and Angru Mainyu (→ Ahriman), but later he became conceptually identified with Spenta Mainyu. In the teaching of Zarathustra, light is made visible by Ahura Mazda and serves in his praise. Subsequently the paramount light, the sun, appears as the form of the god, and in the Avesta the sun and the moon are described as his eyes. Over against the world of truth and light which he has created, stands the anti-world of deception and darkness. By means of fire, Ahura Mazda can distinguish good from evil. On Achaemenian seals the god is depicted in a winged ring (the sun or the moon); sometimes his body projects upwards out of the ring. This type of representation was taken over from Assyria (cf. illustration to → Assur).

Ahurani 'She who belongs to Ahura', an Old Iranian water-goddess, to whom people prayed for growth, insight and progeny. Libation formed part of the ritual in her honour.

Aiakós A Greek god of the underworld, the son of Zeus and of Aigina. Because of his love of justice he was appointed judge of the dead. He is first mentioned by name in Plato.

Aíolos (Latin: Aeolus) The son of → Poseidon; in Greek mythology, the progenitor of the Aeolians, directed by → Zeus to rule the winds. It was he who gave Odysseus a bag containing contrary winds to speed the homeward journey.

Aión (Greek = time) The word may refer to an age or epoch in the history of the world, or to the god himself who personifies such an age. He is depicted in human form, entwined in serpents and with the head of a lion. He is often winged and sometimes shown standing in the Zodiac. He figures in the mysteries of Mithras, whose concept of Aion is of Persian origin (→ Zervan). The Lord of Time is also a primeval god (known as Aion to the Manichaeans), and he enters Greek thought in the shape of → Krónos, which in the course of further philosophical speculation, coalesces with its homonym → Chronos.

Airyaman Etymologically related to the Modern Persian *erman* = guest. The Old Iranian god corresponding to the Vedic → Aryaman. To begin with, he was a sort of collective deity whose duties included supervision of such social bonds and contracts as hospitality and marriage. He is the old Aryan god of marriage, but also appears in literature as a divinely ordained priest and doctor. At the end of time he will fish the souls of those temporarily damned out of hell by means of a net. Eschatologically he may coincide with → Sraoša.

Ai Tojon The creator of light among the Yakuts (in Siberia). He is conceived as a giant, double-headed eagle, which perches on the tip of the world-tree.

Aitu In Samoa, a portmanteau word for the lower order of gods who are called Atua in the Marquesas. Included here are, above all, the various tutelary gods of various families and villages, who appear in the shape of plants or animals. One Aitu known as Fe'e (= cuttlefish, squid) started out as a god of war but gradually took over the role of ruler over the kingdom of the dead. The Aitu often display demonic rather than godly characteristics. The word 'aitu' is also used in Maori, where it means not only 'deity' but also 'sickness' or 'misery'.

Aitvaras A Lithuanian household spirit which appears as a black cat or a black cock. When he flies in the sky he looks like a wavy line. He is a creature of the devil, which persuades the householder to sell his soul for a rich reward.

Aius Locútius (Latin = the speaker) A Roman nonce-god who is supposed to have given a warning of the approach of the Gauls (391 BC).

Ākāšagarbha ('whose origin is the ether') In Indian Buddhism, a → Bodhisattva with the characteristics of a celestial deity. He holds jewels in his hands, and his symbol is the sun. He appears in the Tibetan Books of the Dead as *Nam-mkhai snying-po*, yellowish in colour and furnished with sword and bell as attributes. In Japan he is known as Kokuzo, and is a personification of supreme knowledge of the absolute void (*śūnyatā*).

Aképhalos This is not really a proper name, but rather the designation of a 'headless' being which was regarded as a demon in antiquity. There were many of these: originally beheaded for criminal offences, they became ghosts or acolytes in magic practices. In Hellenistic Egyptian papyri dealing with magic, spells and incantations, the akephalos is even addressed as God; here we may perhaps see the influence of the myth of the dismembered → Osiris.

Aker

In ancient Egyptian texts his name is written with the determinant for 'Earth', and the god himself is an embodiment of the earth. He is represented as a narrow strip of land with either a human or a lion's head at the ends; later, this becomes two lions with their backs turned to each other, which bear the hieroglyph of the rising sun. One lion looks towards the west where the sun sets; the other faces east where the sun rises again from the realm of darkness. The two lions and hence the god they represent guard the entrance and the exit of the underworld.

Akerbeltz

('black billy-goat') In Basque popular belief, Akerbeltz is the representative of the god → Mari. In accordance with his name he is depicted as a black billy-goat. People who want their animals to do well turn to him for help. In earlier times, a black billy-goat was kept in the farm-steading to protect the herd from plague and sickness. In the sixteenth/seventeenth centuries he was venerated as a god by witches and wizards; sacrifices were made to him, and dance formed part of the ritual in his honour.

Akongo

The supreme god of the Ngombe who live in the Congo area. As creator, he bears the epithet 'he who forms'; that is, it is he who gave the world its shape.

Akşobhya

('the unshakable') One of the five → Dhyāni-Buddhas: probably an hypostasis of the historical → Gautama Buddha, with reference to his withstanding the (legendary) temptations of the satanic → Māra. Iconographically, he is represented as a Buddha clothed in the habit of a monk, and seated on a sun. He is celestially orientated on the east, and in Tantrism the eye of the Buddha, the element ether and the season of winter are attributed to him. In Tantric iconography he may be given six or eight arms; his main attribute is the *vajra*, the thunderbolt, and he rides on a pair of elephants. Several divinities emanate from Akṣobhya, including → Heruka, → Jambhala, Yamari.

Ala Earth-goddess of the Ibo people in East Nigeria. She represents the earth in its dual aspect – fecundity and death.

Alako A god of the Norwegian gypsies. His original name was Dundra, and he was sent down to earth in human shape by his father, the great God, to reveal their secret law and lore to the gypsies. When this was accomplished he returned to his own realm in the moon, and has ever since been known as Alako. The name is etymologically related to the Finnish word *alakuu* = waning moon.

Alalu The first among the heavenly kings according to the pantheon of the Hurrians who lived in North Syria in the second millennium BC. For nine years he occupied his divine throne before he was overthrown by Anu, the first of the gods. Alalu was called Hypsistos ('the highest') by the Greeks.

Alardi In the popular belief of the Ossetians in the Central Caucasus a spirit who on the one hand causes smallpox and, on the other, protects women. In folksong he is given the epithet 'the winged one'.

Alaunus A local Celtic name for the god → Mercurius. In the Mannheim area, Mercurius was given the epithet Alannus; near Salzburg, inscriptions have been found giving the form 'sacrum . . . Alounis'.

Albiorix ('King of the World')   Epithet, perhaps also a specific form of the Gallic war-god → Teutates.

Alcis   A divine pair of brothers in the belief of the East Germanic tribe of the Naharnavali (in Silesia?). According to Tacitus they were worshipped in a sacred grove, and they were never depicted. In the *interpretatio romana* they are identified with the heavenly twins → Castor and Pollux. The etymology of the word Alcis is not clear. It may be connected with the word *alces* which Caesar notes as meaning 'elk', and this would make the Alcis brothers elk or stag gods.

Alisanos (attested also in the form Alisanus)   A local god in Gaul, mentioned in inscriptions found in the Côte d'Or. The place-name Alesia may well be connected with him. Attempts have been made to identify him more closely as a mountain-ash god, or god of rowan trees.

Allah (Arabic, *al-ilah* = the God)   In the pre-Islamic period, the supreme deity, creator of the earth and giver of water. Interpreted monotheistically by Muhammad as the one true God, to whom it is incumbent upon men to submit (*islām* = submission). Allah is totally and essentially different from all that he has created: hence the prohibition of any attempt to portray him. The 'beautiful names' of God correspond to the epithets which are used to paraphrase Allah in the Qur'an: 99 names are known (hence the 99 beads in the Islamic rosary) but the 'greatest name', the name which will complete the hundred, is known to no mortal. In Islamic mysticism (Sufism) Allah is compared to a sun which sends forth its rays; his throne is a sign of his omnipotence and of his

remoteness from his creation. Since graphical representation of Allah is forbidden, it is only in calligraphy that he can be spiritually 'presented'.

Allat ('the goddess') Venerated in Central and North Arabia in pre-Islamic times. Herodotus records the Semitic name in the form Alilat. She was particularly revered in Ta'if where an idol to her, a white granite block, stood. She was supposed to be one of the three daughters of → Allah, and was associated with the planet Venus. Certain texts also seem to point to a solar connection.

Allekto → Erinyes

Almaqah Moon-god and tutelary god of the South Arabian kingdom of Saba. Members of the tribe of Saba called themselves 'the children of Almaqah'. He is symbolized by a cluster of lightning flashes and a weapon which looks like a slightly bent capital S. His symbolical animal is the bull, and in some texts he is referred to as 'Lord of the horned goats'.

Aloádes In Greek mythology the giant sons of Aloeus (or of → Poseidon) named Otos and Ephialtes. In their fight against the gods they try to storm Olympus; and they bind the god of war → Arés fast and hold him captive for 13 months. When → Ártemis throws herself between them in the shape of a hind, they kill themselves in their blind lust to hunt down the quarry. It is possible that the Aloades were pre-Hellenic gods, who were casualties in the struggle surrounding the introduction of the new religion of Zeus.

Alp (Alb) Old Norse *alfr*. The original designation of the mythical → Elben. In Germanic mythology, the Albs were unearthly beings, half god half dwarf: and here we may recall Alberich, the king of the dwarfs in the Nibelungensage, famed for his Tarnkappe which conferred invisibility, and the magic belt that gave him strength. In later years, the Albs came to be known as demonic beings which caused sickness and nightmares. In popular superstition the nightmare – a terrifying experience during sleep, followed by an equally terrifying awakening – is explained as induced by a threatening demon (→ Incubus, → Succubus). In Bavaria and Austria, the evil female demons known as Druden take the place of the Albs.

Alpan (also Alpanu, Alpnu) An Etruscan goddess, variously portrayed as winged or unwinged, belonging to the female demons known as → Lasas. She is naked except for a cloak which hardly conceals her body, she is richly bejewelled and wears light sandals. The evidence strongly suggests that she was a goddess of the art of love, but she also possesses traits that mark her as a goddess of the underworld.

Amaethon A Celtic god of agriculture in Wales, revered as the great ploughman. He belongs to the Welsh family of gods of the Don.

Amáltheia (in Latin Amalthéa) A nymph or, in other versions of the story, a she-goat which nourished the infant → Zeus with her milk, and was rewarded by being transferred to the heavens where she figures as Capella (Latin, = goat). A horn broken off from Amaltheia was transformed by Zeus into the cornucopia, the symbol of plenty.

Amaterasu (Japanese = 'shining from heaven') The sun-goddess of Shintoism, venerated in the shrine at Ise as the divine progenitor of the Japanese imperial family. Her epithet is Omikami: 'great and exalted divinity'. The myth tells how she arose together with the moon (god) when the god of heaven Izanagi washed his eyes on his return from the underworld. Angered by the atrocities committed by the storm-god → Susanowo, Amaterasu withdrew to a cave, and all light faded from the earth; but the other gods used a mirror to entice her back again.

Amaunet
One of the group of Egyptian gods known as the Ogdoad. She was seen as the Divine Mother presiding at the beginning of time, when she merged with → Neith. In inscriptions she is named as 'the mother who was the father'; that is to say, she needed no spouse. Within the Ogdoad, → Amun is allotted to her as partner. In the Ptolemaic era she was seen as the embodiment of the life-bringing north wind.

Amenominakanushi
(Japanese = Lord of the bright centre of heaven) The supreme heavenly divinity in Shintoism. In contradistinction to → Izanagi, he plays no part in myth, nor is there any record of a shrine or place of worship in his honour. Nevertheless he occupies first place in the list of gods: transcending all of them, he sits alone on a nine-fold layer of clouds (a symbolical reference to the nine heavens).

Amentet
Egyptian goddess of the west and of the lands lying in that direction. As the sun sets in the west (symbolizing the entrance to the underworld) Amentet is also the goddess of the necropolis where she receives the dead as they enter the Beyond.

Ameretāt
('non-death', 'life') In Old Iranian religion, Ameretāt belongs to the circle of Amešva Spentas, where she represents immortality. She is usually mentioned together with → Haurvatāt, whose dominion is over the waters, while Ameretāt rules the plant world. In the Yasna the two goddesses figure as the food and

drink of heaven. For the faithful, they represent the reward awaiting them after death. As abstract concepts they are both feminine, but when personified each can take on male gender. In the final sacrifice Ameretāt is united with her earthly symbol, the world of plants.

Ameša Spentas ('the holy immortals') In the religion of the Parsees, a collective title for the personifications of abstract concepts who serve → Ahura Mazda as his archangels. Five of the Ameša Spentas may well have arisen from elemental spirits via a process of reinterpretation: Aša (Avestan = truth) is symbolized by fire in the Gathas, Khšathra vairya ('desired realm') is the protector of metals, and is often represented as god of war; → Armaiti ('compliance, compliant thought/speech') is closely connected with the earth, while → Haurvatāt ('perfection') is associated with water, and Ameretāt ('immortality') with plants. To this original group of five, → Vohu Manah ('sound views') and → Sraoša ('obedience') were added as archangels after Zarathustra. On occasion, → Spenta Mainyu and even Ahura Nazda himself are mentioned as 'holy immortals'.

Amida Japanese form of → Amitābha, a dogmatic development of the eleventh/twelfth centuries. Amida is also given the Sanskrit name Amitāyuh ('immeasurable life'), a reference to the Buddha who possesses the properties of immeasurable light and life. In the Jōdo faith, teaching concerning Amida coalesces with the belief in Jōdo, the Pure Land. Thereafter, simple evocation of the name of Amida Buddha is enough to ensure release, provided belief is deep and genuine.

Amitābha (Sanskrit = immeasurable light; Chinese A-mi-t'o or O-mi-to) The most popular of the five → Dhyāni-Buddhas. He is enthroned in heaven as lord of the paradisical

land of Sukhavati, entry into which is vouchsafed to all who believe in him. His celestial direction is the west, his element is water and he is associated with the evening twilight. In iconography, he is represented as a red-coloured Buddha, both of his hands lie open in his lap in the pose of meditation. His ceremonial vehicle is a pair of peacocks, and he is symbolized by a lotus or an alms-bowl. The Amitābha cult reached China from India in the fourth – sixth centuries AD, and spread thence to Japan (→ Amida).

Amm The moon-god in pre-Islamic South Arabia. In the kingdom of Qataban he had the status of a tutelary national god, and the people of Qataban called themselves 'the children of Amm'. His lunar character is indicated by his epithet: 'he who waxes'. In addition, he acts as a weather god, and in this capacity he is symbolized by a cluster of lightning flashes.

Amma The divine creator in the religious system of the Dogon (in Mali). He created the universe in the form of a world-egg which was divided into two placentas: from these, the bisexual world arose. According to a different and occult tradition, the god raped the earth, whose sexual organ was an ant-hill.

Ammavaru A mother-goddess of the Telugu, a Dravidian people who live in east-central India. According to the myth, she existed before the coming to being of the four ages, that is, before the creation of the world. From an egg which she laid in the Sea of Milk arose the three gods → Brahmā, → Viṣṇu, and → Śiva. She rides on a jackal.

Ammit A female demon who plays a part in the Egyptian Day of Judgment. She was feared as 'devourer of the dead', and she had the head of a crocodile, the torso of a predatory cat and the buttocks of a hippopotamus. This monster lurked near the scales of justice waiting for the verdict to be given, whereupon she devoured the sinner.

Ammon

The god of the West Egyptian oasis of Siwa, and of its oracle site (Ammonium) which was celebrated in antiquity. The god was represented as a ram. Ammon is the Greek form of → Amun. After visiting the Siwa oasis, Alexander the Great regarded himself as a son of Zeus-Ammon, much as the Pharaohs were held to be sons of Amun-Re. North African rock drawings showing the ram bearing the disc of the sun are held to be outliers of the Ammon (Amun) cult.

Amoghapāśa

('unfailing noose') In Mahayana Buddhism, a form of → Avalokiteśvara. He is white in colour, has a face and eight arms, and stands with his feet close together on the moon. His main attribute is the noose (a hypostatization of compassion) with which he lassoes the faithful, much to their benefit.

Amoghasiddhi

('flawless perfection') In Buddhism, one of the five Dhyāni-Buddhas; he is green in colour and assigned to the northerly quarter. His vehicle consists of a pair of Garuḍas (mythological eagle-like birds), and his attribute is a double thunderbolt (*viśvavajra*). He is associated with the bodily eye, the rainy season and the element of water. In Tantrism he may · be represented with three faces and six arms.

Ámor

The Roman god of love, corresponding to the Greek → Éros. In Latin poetry Amor is also called Cupido (*cupiditas* = longing, lust, passion). In the Christian Middle Ages, a distinction was made between Amor or Amor Dei (= God) and Cupido (= the devil). In classical art, Amor was represented as a *puer alatus* (winged youth); his attributes are a bow and arrows and/or a torch. The story of Amor and Psyche has been popular since the early Hellenistic period. Here, Psyche, representing the caducity of human life on earth, is awakened by Amor's kiss to life eternal.

Amphitríte A goddess of the sea, possibly pre-Hellenic. In Greek mythology, she is the daughter of → Nereus, and the wife of → Poseidon. Accompanied by Nereids and Tritons she moves over the waters in a vessel made of mussels. It was only in association with Poseidon that she was made an object of worship.

Amun ('the hidden one') In the Pyramid texts he is already mentioned as a primeval god, in association with his wife → Amaunet. In Old Egyptian thought he was the moving agent in the invisible breeze; thus he was venerated as god of the wind and ruler of the air. From the eleventh dynasty onwards he is attested as god of Thebes. Here, he coalesces with the sun-god (→ Re) to become Amun-Re, and, as Thebes increased in power, he became king of the gods and tutelary god of the empire. In his capacity as primeval god of creation he is venerated in the shape of a goose; otherwise, the ram is his sacred animal, a reference to his function as god of fertility. After the fall of Thebes his cult prospered in Ethiopia and among the oasis dwellers (→ Ammon).

An (Anu) In Sumerian the name means 'above', 'heaven' and is written in the cuneiform character with the same sign as the word for 'God' (*dingir*). His consort is variously given as Ki (the earth) or the goddess Antum. An is the supreme god of the Sumerian pantheon, and the centre of his cult was at Uruk. In the Babylonian period his eminence as god of heaven is still stressed, but his role in religious observance is no longer an important one. In the main he is not favourably disposed towards human beings to whom he sends, for example, the demon → Lamaštu and the goddess of death → Māmitu.

Among the Hurrians, Anu was regarded as the successor of → Alalu.

Ana (or Anu) Celtic-Irish goddess of the earth and of fertility. She was said to be the mother of the gods. Two hills near Killarney in Munster are called after her Da Chich Anann: i.e. the two breasts of Ana.

Anahita ('the immaculate') Originally, a Semitic goddess related to → Anath, she was received into the pantheon of the Parsees as a goddess of fertility and of victory. She is pictured as a maiden in a mantle of gleaming gold, with a diadem and jewels. In iconography she wears a high crown, in her left hand she often carries a water-pot (in her capacity as goddess of water) and at her breast she carries a pomegranate blossom. The dove and the peacock are sacred to her. Temple prostitution formed part of her cult. In the Avestan calendar, the tenth day and the eighth month are dedicated to her. In Middle Persian tradition she is called Ardvi Sur, and in Asia Minor she was assimilated to the Great Mother. After the conquest of Babylonia by the Persians some traits of → Ištar as goddess of love and of the planets were transferred to Anahita.

Ananké Greek goddess of fate. As the personification of ineluctable necessity, of inevitability, she is even set above the gods. In Orphic teaching she is incorporeal but universally present. On occasion she fuses with the figure of → Adrásteia. In her capacity as 'she who guides the worlds', she is portrayed holding a spindle.

Anat(h) To begin with, a Phoenician-Canaanite goddess whose name is interpreted as meaning 'providence' or 'precaution'. She is the maiden sister of → Baal, but also on occasion his spouse. In the Ugarit texts, she wreaks terrible revenge on the god of death → Mot, on behalf of her dead brother. She was taken over by various peoples in Hither Asia as the goddess of nature and life, and contributed something towards the make-up of → Astarte and of → Atargatis. From the Ramessids onwards, Anat was also venerated in Egypt as a goddess of war; in this capacity her attributes include shield, spear and axe, and also a high crown with two ostrich feathers.

Anbay

A pre-Islamic god in south Arabia. His name may have been originally a regal plural and may be etymologically connected with the name of the old Mesopotamian god → Nabu ('the harbinger'). Anbay is an oracular god and 'Lord of justice'. In his capacity as 'spokesman' ('harbinger') he acts for the moon-god (→ Amm) who ranks above him in the pantheon.

Anezti

(Anedjti) God of the ninth nome of Lower Egypt, from whom → Osiris seems to have borrowed the crook and scourge as symbols of overlordship.

Aṅgiras

(aṅg = to say, announce, related to Greek angelos = angel) 'The seers descended from the gods' in the Veda and in Hinduism: 'sons of heaven' who by dint of sacrifice achieved immortality and the friendship of → Indra.

Ani

Etruscan god. On the bronze liver he is located at the exact north, that is to say, in the highest heaven. The name Ani may be etymologically connected with that of the Roman god → Janus. Whether two-visaged coins indicate an Etruscan *Ianus bifrons* is not certain: and equally doubtful is the claim that Ani comes from *ianus* ('buttress', 'arched gate') and is therefore connected with a sky-god (arch of heaven).

Anky-Kele

The god of the sea in the pantheon of the Chukchi people in north-east

Siberia. As lord of the (sea)creatures, and hence of the food supply, he has power of life and death over the human race.

Ánna Perénna

An ancient Roman goddess. During the class war between the patricians and the plebeians she is supposed to have saved the latter from famine. She was worshipped in a grove lying to the north of Rome, and every year on 15 March there was a popular open-air festival in her honour. It is possible that Anna Perenna is a derivation of the Earth Mother.

Anšar and Kišar

According to the Babylonian creation epic Enuma Eliš, the third generation of gods and the parents of the sky-god (→ An). The name Anšar is construed as meaning 'totality of heaven' or 'horizon of heaven'; Kišar would then be 'totality of earth' or 'earth horizon'. Similarity in sound led to the Assyrian national god → Assur being identified in the late Assyrian period with Anšar, and promoted to a position of supremacy over all the gods.

Antaíos

(in Latin Antaeus) According to Greek myth, the son of → Poseidon and the goddess of the earth → Gaia. The Greek word *antaíos* means 'he who meets'. The giant Antaíos lived in Libya; and everyone whom he met there he challenged to a wrestling match and killed. Herakles finally overcame him by picking him up from the ground, thereby severing Antaíos' dynamic contact with Mother Earth.

Anubis

Egyptian god of the dead, in the shape of a dog or a jackal; occasionally in human shape with a dog's head. It is not certain what the name means; the meaning 'little dog' has been suggested. At Assiut, Anubis was known by the epithet 'Lord of the cave mouth', i.e. the entrance into the city of the dead. As god of the dead he is

'Lord of the divine hall' and hence in charge of mummification, in which capacity he undertakes the ritual preparation of the corpse and its transfiguration. With the rise of → Osiris, Anubis was demoted *vis-à-vis* the new Lord of the Dead and put in charge of weighing the hearts at the last judgment. The Greeks gave the name Kynopolis to important centres of worship. In the *interpretatio graeca* Anubis was identified with → Hérmes.

Anuket (Greek form Anukis) Egyptian goddess of the Cataract area. Particularly venerated in Elephantine, she was also known as 'mistress of Nubia'. Her sacred animal was the gazelle.

Anunna (Sumerian = 'those who are of princely seed') Collective title for the pantheon of a given locality: e.g. the Anunna of Lagaš, or for the gods of heaven and earth. In Akkadian (the language spoken in Babylonia and Assyria) the loan-word Anunnaku denotes the lower gods in contra-distinction to the gods who dwell in heaven (→ Igigi).

Anyigba → Trowo

Apām napāt ('Grandchild of the waters')
In Old Iranian belief a 'god found in the water'. He is the giver of water to men, but he also acts in a military capacity. He is the hero who quells rebellious lands. His epithet is 'owner of swift steeds'. Vedic India had a god of the same name; according to the Rigveda he is golden in appearance and he distributes water. It is possible that → Poseidon as he appears on Bactrian coins is a mutation of the Old Iranian water-god.

Aparājita ('the unconquered') Belongs to the → Krodhadevatās of Indian Buddhism. He is white in colour, and decorated with snakes. He has three faces – white, black and red. In pre-Buddhist belief he seems to have figured as leader of the demons, and as such is trampled underfoot by → Bhūtadāmara.

Aparājitā ('the unconquered one (female))
A female deity in Indian Buddhism; she is yellow in colour and has one head and two arms, and is bedecked with jewels. Her countenance arouses terror, and she tramples → Ganeśa underfoot. She scatters all devilish beings (→ Māras) and unruly gods like → Brahmā are obliged to hold her sunshade over her head.

Aphrodíte Greek goddess of beauty and love, identified by the Romans with → Venus. Attempts to derive her name from the Greek word *aphros* = foam, date back to antiquity. On this interpretation, the goddess is 'she who is born of the foam'; or, as another of her names – Anadyomene – suggests 'she who arises from the sea'. Her cult is pre-Greek and probably

oriental in origin; certain rites associated with her, like the temple prostitution in Corinth, remind us of → Astarte. She was also known as Kypris and as Kythereia after the main shrines in her honour on Cyprus and Kythera. In coastal areas she was revered as Euploia – 'she who confers a good voyage'. Plato and others make a distinction between the 'heavenly' Aphrodite (Urania) and the goddess who 'belongs to the whole people' (Pandemos). According to Homer, Aphrodite was the daughter of → Zeus and Dione, married to → Hephaistos but in love with → Arés, a liaison from which → Éros was born. She also loved the beautiful → Adonis. Her attribute was the dove. Her aegis covered fertility in the plant world, and she was venerated in Athens as the goddess of gardens.

Apis (in Egyptian Hapi)   Holy bull worshipped in Memphis. He was originally a symbol of fertility, but in the course of time he acquired other characteristics; above all, he came to be identified with the 'glorious soul' of → Ptah.

After his death, Apis enters the god → Osiris, and the compound Osiris-Apis (in Grecianized form Serapis) is used to denote the ensuing *mixta persona*. Apis became a god of the dead. From the New Kingdom onwards he wears the disc of the sun as a head-dress. Apis-bulls were regarded as holy and were interred in subterranean burial chambers in the so-called Serapeum. Herodotus identifies Apis with → Epaphos.

Aplu An Etruscan god borrowed from the Greek pantheon (→ Apollon), latterly specified as god of thunder and lightning. He is pictured as naked except for a mantle which covers part of his body; on his head is a wreath of laurel and he holds in his hands a staff which usually ends in a laurel twig. The god figures in various myths, but there is no trace of a cult devoted to him.

Apo Katawan 'Master' or 'Father' Katawan: a god of the Hambal-Aeta, a negrito tribe in the Philippines. Sacrifice is made to him, and people pray to him.

Apóllon A Greek god, probably of Asia Minor origin. He fulfills several functions: as protector of cattle, he keeps wolves away (hence his name of Lykeios); as promoter of agriculture he gets rid of field-mice (Smintheus); and as a stone pillar standing in front of a house he protects both it and its inhabitants (Apollon Agyieus). He is a god of healing (with a snake as attribute) and a god of expiation, whose arrows bring sickness and death. Above all, however, he is the god of oracles, his most celebrated oracular shrines being Delphi and Delos. The laurel plant is sacred to him. As god of the muses Apollon Musagetes he is often represented with a lyre, and singing and music are in his gift. Finally, from the sixth century onwards he was demonstrably venerated as a sun-god. His epithet Phoebus ('the bright *or* pure one') was originally understood in a purely cultic sense, but it soon

31

acquired ethical connotations. The myth relates how he slew the Python dragon, only a few days after his birth. His parents were → Zeus and → Leto, his twin sister was → Artemis, and his son was the god of healing → Asklepios. Apóllon was the first Greek god to be introduced into Italy (Etruscan → Aplu). Augustus saw him as his personal tutelary god.

Apophis

An Egyptian monster, reptilian in nature, which lives in darkness and which threatens the sun-god in his daily journey across the heavens. Apophis is a rebel against divine and cosmic order. It is told in the hymns to the sun how the snake-demon is sliced with knives or pierced by a lance. In the late Egyptian period, Apophis came to be identified with → Seth.

Apsaras

Vedic water-spirits. As heavenly beings they are coupled with the musicians of the world of the gods (→ Gandharvas). They are fond of games of chance, and confer good fortune at the gaming table. According to the Atharva-veda, they can cause madness. It has been suggested that the name derives from Sanskrit *ap* = water and *sar* = to stream.

Apsu

(Akkadian; the Sumerian form is Abzu) Personification of the sweet-water ocean lying under the earth, which united with → Tiamat at the beginning of time. According to Sumerian myth, Abzu is the place where the goddess → Nammu formed the first men from clay. The Babylonian creation epic relates how Apsu is slain by the magic weapons of the goddess → Ea. It is in Apsu – that is to say, in the water – that Marduk is finally born.

Aralez

The ancient Armenians believed in the existence of these dog-like creatures gifted with supernatural powers. Their specific function was to lick the wounds of those killed or wounded in battle, who then recovered or were resurrected to new life. In the popular mind they were beneficent dog-like spirits who lived in heaven; at an earlier date they may well have been seen as god-like creatures of a menial order.

Aralo → Aray

Aramazd (from Old Persian → Ahura Mazda) The supreme deity of the ancient Armenians, creator of heaven and earth. He has a son → Mihr, and a daughter → Nana. He was taken over by the pre-Christian Georgians under the name of → Armaz. In the ascendancy of the Greek pantheon he was identified with → Zeus.

Arapacana A → Bodhisattva, one-faced, red or white in colour and resplendent like the full moon. He sits in meditative pose on a double lotus. In his right hand he wields a sword, in his left he holds a book which he presses to his breast.

Aray (also Ara) Old Armenian god of war, known as 'the beautiful'. Probably of common Indo-Germanic origin along with → Ares (originally a Thracian god). However, Aray also has certain characteristics of a dying god who rises again, which lends some support to the thesis that this Armenian god was identical with the Hittite god of the countryside who bore the same name. It is possible that this god lives on in Aralo, the Georgian god of agriculture.

Arduinna A local goddess in Gaul, named after the Ardennes. She was a goddess of hunting, and interpreted by the Romans as equivalent to → Diana. Her sacred animal was the boar.

Arebati Mythical sky-god of the Bambuti (Pigmy people on the Ituri in Congo). He is the ruler of the world, who created the first man by kneading his body from clay, covering it with a skin and pouring blood into the vessel thus formed. His epithet *afa* (= father) is to be understood in the same sense.

Arés (accented in Latin on first syllable: Áres) Greek god of war. Etymologically, his name is not entirely clear, but it probably means something like 'destroyer' or 'avenger'. He is accompanied by → Eris (dissension), Enyo (horror) and Phobos (fear). His original homeland was Thrace, and few temples were devoted to him in Hellas. He was not a popular god, and accordingly he is not often portrayed in Greek art. His parents were → Zeus and → Hera, and his mistress was → Aphrodíte. The war-like Amazons were supposed to be his daughters. The Romans identified Ares with their own god → Mars.

Arethusa → Kore-Arethusa

Aretia In Armenian belief, the earth, venerated as holy; spouse of Noah (properly an Old Testament figure), and mother of all living creatures.

Argaulídes → Kékrops

Árgos In Greek mythology a many-eyed giant entrusted by → Hera to keep guard on → Io; he was, however, lulled to sleep by → Hérmes and killed. His name has become proverbial for eyes which miss nothing.

Arhat (Sanskrit, 'he who is worthy of reverence') In Buddhism and Jainism a saint, one who has reached the highest stage of perfection possible on earth. In Hīnayāna Buddhism, the ideal figure who has reached the goal of self-deliverance, by means of asceticism and meditation; in Mahāyāna Buddhism, the → Bodhisattva who shows others the way to salvation and sacrifices himself for them, is more highly venerated. Essentially, the Arhat is a human being, but he is endowed with the heavenly eye which he uses to perceive the ebb and flow of beings in the different worlds. In the pantheon of Chinese Buddhism, the Arhats (called in Chinese *lo-han*) form a third class after the Buddhas and the Bodhisattvas, thus still occupying a higher position than the gods. In Jainism, the Arhats are removed in their perfection from all earthly desires and actions, and they are revered as 'supreme gods'.

Ariádne Originally a Minoan goddess; her Cretan name Aridela means 'she who shines in splendour'. Her death as described in Homer suggests a goddess of vegetation. In the myth, Ariadne is the daughter of the Cretan king → Minos and of → Pasiphae. She uses a ball of wool to help Theseus to find the way out of the mazes of the labyrinth. After her death, Ariadne was led out of the underworld by her husband → Dionysos and taken up to Olympus. Her crown was fixed by → Zeus as a constellation in the heavens (Corona Borealis).

Arimanius (Areimanios) A variant name for the Persian → Ahriman, found in classical writers. According to Herodotus, a god of the underworld, 'kakodaimon' in contrast to the good spirit. Plutarch says he is an embodiment of Hades and the darkness invoked by Persian magi. Later he came to be identified with the Egyptian god → Serapis (as god of the dead) as well.

Arinna Really the name of a Hittite town, after which this goddess was called 'Sun of

Arinna'. She was also known as Ariniddu, after her most important shrine. She is 'Queen of Heaven and Earth', she protects the kingdom and assists in its wars. Her cult symbol is the sun disc. She is often identified with the Hurrian goddess of heaven → Hebat. Husband of both is the weather-god.

Aristaíos An ancient Greek peasant god, protector of herds and the original bee-keeper. In Hellas he was ousted from favour by → Apóllon, as whose son he was subsequently regarded. In Kyrene (Libya) he continued to be venerated as the son of the goddess of the town.

Arma A Hittite moon-god, corresponding to the Hurrian → Kušuh. In hieroglyphic Hittat his determinant is a sickle moon (Lunula). On reliefs he wears the sickle moon on his pointed and horned cap. On his back he has a pair of wings.

Armaiti (also Aramati) Personification of 'compliant speech' (and thereby corresponding to the Vedic → Sarasvati) belonging to the → Ameša Spentas. In the Gathas, Armaiti is closely associated with the earth and offers nourishment to the cow. She is goddess of the earth and hence of fertility, and also of the dead who have 'gone into' the earth.

Ármány (Hungarian *ármányos* = cunning, insidious) The gloomy prospect facing the world was personified under this name in the Romantic movement in Hungary. First so used by Vörösmarty in 1825.

Armaz The supreme deity in pre-Christian Georgia; corresponds to the Armenian → Aramazd. His cult representation is described as clothed in golden armour, with a golden helmet and jewels. In his hand he carries a gleaming sword.

Arsnuphis (also Harensnuphis) Greek form of Egyptian divine name meaning 'the beautiful companion'. He is a Nubian god ('Foremost of Nubia') in the sense of the Egyptian → Šu; and he is also identified with the Nubian regional god → Dedun. He is often represented as a lion.

Arsū One of the most popular gods of Palmyra (ancient North Arabia). He is twin brother of Azizu (→ Azizos); together they represent the evening and the morning star, and are pictured in Palmyra as riding on camels or on horses.

Ártemis Greek goddess of the hunt, who can be shown to share in the functions of several other divinities. She is Queen of the wild beasts (*Potnia theron*) in which capacity she can be traced back to the Minoan period. Graphically, she is represented as winged and accompanied by lions, deer and birds. Mainly, however, she appears as the virgin huntress roaming the woods with her attendants, the → Nymphs. She can use her arrows – like her brother → Apóllon – to send peaceful death or sudden destruction. In anger she is terrible. Originally, human sacrifice was not unknown to her cult – we may recall the story of Iphigenia who was replaced on the altar by a hind. She was also the goddess of birth, and on Delos women sacrificed their hair to her in token of their devotion. She also appears as a goddess of vegetation and fertility (e.g. in the Peloponnese). In Asia Minor her cult overlapped that of the Great Mother (the many-breasted Artemis of Ephesus). Later, Artemis also came to be identified with the moon-goddess → Seléne. As bearer of light (Phosphoros) she had a temple in the harbour of Athens. The myth makes her the daughter of → Zeus and of → Leto.

Artio A goddess of forests and hunting venerated in north-east Gaul and by the Helvetii in Switzerland. Her attribute is a bear.

Aruna (1) → Kamrušepa

Aruna (2) ('reddish') In Indian religions the early dawn personified in the Purāṇas as the charioteer of the sun. He is counted among the → Ādityas.

Aryaman Belongs to the Vedic group of the → Ādityas. He is the personification of hospitality and appears in the Rigveda as founder of matrimony. The same god is found in Iran under the name of → Airyaman.

As (pl. Aesir) In Norse mythology, the race of gods inhabiting Asgard were called the Aesir. The name comes from Old Norse *ass* = stake, beam, and this might suggest that the oldest representations of these gods were carved stakes. At the head of the Aesir was → Odin, and they included → Thor, → Tyr, → Balder, → Heimdall, and the goddesses → Frigg, → Nanna, and → Sif. In the *History of the Goths* written by the historian Jordanes, the Aesir appear as deified ancestors (Gothic *ansis*). The dividing line between the Aesir and the other race of Germanic gods, the → Vanir, is not fixed.

Aš Egyptian god, described as 'Lord of Libya', dating from the very earliest times. He is represented either anthropomorphously or with a falcon's head. Later, he continued to be worshipped in oases in the Libyan desert, and took on some characteristics of → Seth. He is often shown with the head of one of the animals sacred to Seth.

Asag In Sumerian mythology a demon which dries up wells and covers the earth with sores into which it squirts poison. Originally seen as the agent bringing illnesses. Its Akkadian name is Asakku.

Asalluḫi (or Asariluchi) Sumerian god, assisting in the ritual of exorcism. The son of → Enki, to whom he reports the evil deeds of the demons.

Ašar Old Arabian equestrian god; known from a few inscriptions from Palmyra and some reliefs.

Asasel (Azazel) Hebrew proper name for a demon of the wilderness to whom a scapegoat is sent on the Day of Atonement. (Leviticus 16: 8-10). In the apocryphal book of Enoch, Asasel appears as the ringleader of the rebellious angels.

Ašera(t) Originally a goddess of the Semitic Amorites, similar in her functions as goddess of love and fertility to → Astarte, possibly even identical with her. She is usually shown naked. In the Ras Shamra texts she is described as the spouse of the supreme god → El, and is designated as 'Queen of the Sea' and 'Mother of the gods'. Her cult penetrated into Israelite territory (I Kings 15:13) and the images – also called *ašera* – mentioned in I Kings 14: 23 may have been those of her cult.

Ašertu A north-west Semitic goddess; the Hittite form of her name is Aserdus. She is identical with the Syrian-Ugaritic → Atirat. In a myth of Canaanite origin Ašertu is unfaithful to her husband Elkunirša when she tries to seduce the weather-god.

Ašnan (in Sumerian Emmer) Old Mesopotamian goddess of wheat, daughter of → Enki.

Asklepiós (in Latin, the accent is on *e*: Asklépios) Greek god of healing. His oldest known temple was at Trikka in Thessaly. It was

only from the fifth century BC onwards that his cult spread over the whole of Hellas, and he began to oust his father → Apóllon as a divine healer. Originally he may have been a snake-god; and when new votive shrines were being dedicated to him, a snake was involved in the ceremony as an incarnation of the god. He is usually pictured as a bearded man with his staff round which the sacred snake is entwined. The main centre of his cult was at Epidauros. His daughter was supposed to be → Hygíeia. Doctors in antiquity called themselves *asklepiades*. According to the myth, Asklepios learnt the art of healing from the wise Centaur Cheiron. He was particularly esteemed by the Romans (→ Aesculapius); in Hellenistic-Roman Egypt his name was transferred to → Imhotep.

Asmodaios (in Latin Asmodeus, in the Talmud Ašmedai) A demon (→ Aēšma Daēva) taken from Old Iranian religion by the post-exile Jews (Tobias 3: 8, 17). In rabbinic literature he becomes the chief of the evil spirits. In some ways, Asmodaios is reminiscent of the Assyrian → Pazuzu.

Aśokakāntā Sub-form of the Buddhist goddess → Marici. She rides on a pig and is golden-yellowish in colour. Sometimes she is pictured as standing on the moon above a lotus. She is clothed in white and she herself is bedecked with jewels; with her right hand she makes the *varada-mudra* gesture, indicating that certain wishes have been granted.

Asopós Boeotian river-god (after the river of the same name in central Greece). Son of → Poseidon. When → Zeus abducted one of his daughters, Asopos himself was struck by lightning.

Assur Originally the tutelary god of the town Assur; subsequently promoted to the rank of national god of Assyria. Etymologically the name is obscure. From the thirteenth century BC onwards, he gains the ascendancy over → Enlil, ousts him from the dominant role and takes over the epithets 'Great Mountain' and 'Father of the Gods'. From the ninth century BC onwards he is equated with → Anšar. Among his functions are the judicial office, otherwise reserved to the sun-god, and the conduct of war. In Assyrian art he is shown as a god standing in the winged disc of the sun and holding or bending a bow.

Aṣṭābhujā-Kurukulla (aṣṭābhujā = the eight-armed one) Special form taken by the Buddhist goddess Kurukulla. In the Sadhana texts she is described as having one head and eight arms, and as red in colour. She sits in meditation on the sun above a red lotus with eight leaves.

Astar (Ethiopic = sky, heavens) Often mentioned as god of heaven or sky-god in inscriptions dating from the time of the empire of Axum (Ethiopia, third to fifth centuries AD). The name is etymologically related to the South Arabian → ʿAttar.

Astarte (Aštarat)   Semitic goddess, associated mainly with Syria and Palestine. The Ugaritic form of her name is Attart; she appears in the Old Testament as → Asthoreth, and in Babylon as → Ištar. Her cult was that of an oriental goddess of love and fertility, and was accordingly marked by many excesses (temple prostitution). She is usually shown naked. When she was taken over by the Egyptians she began to figure more and more as a goddess of war, and spear and bow were her attributes. Among the Greeks, Astarte was identified with → Aphrodíte as the heavenly goddess of love. As in the case of other fertility goddesses, her sacred creature was the dove. According to Philon of Byblos, she donned a bull's head as a symbol of her ruling position, and there are other references to the horns assigned to her.

Asteria → Perses

Asthoreth   A goddess worshipped in the Palestine area, corresponding to the Syrian → Astarte. She was principally a goddess of love and fertility, though among the Philistines she was a goddess of war. Solomon paid occasional homage to her, and even had a temple erected in her honour near Jerusalem (I Kings 11:5; II Kings 23: 13). The plural form of her name is Astharoth, and this is used in conjunction with Baal as a collective name for the female divinities of the Canaanites (Judges 2: 13; I Samuel 12: 10). The biblical place-name Astharoth-Karnaim, i.e. 'Astharoth with the two horns', indicates that a horned goddess was visualized.

Astlik (from *astl* = star)   An Armenian goddess of astral nature, equivalent to the Old Mesopotamian → Ištar and to → Aphrodíte of the Hellenistic period: that is to say, she is seen mainly in the role of a goddess of love. With the coming of Christianity Astlik's status was reduced to that of progenitrix of fairies and nymphs.

Astō Vidātu (Avestan *ast* = bone) The
name may be roughly translated as 'disintegrator
of bodies'. Initially a minor demon, later promoted to the status of a god of death, whom no
mortal can escape. From the moment of generation on, all men should know that his noose is
already round their necks. For this reason, he has
the epithet *Marg* = death. In Middle Persian texts
he also appears as a chief representative of the
devil.

Asura In Indian Buddhism a group of
demons who once upon a time lived in heaven
but who were cast by the gods into the ocean.
The story of the struggle between the gods and
the Asura is a favourite theme in the Pali canon.
In the Vedic religion, the Asura (Vedic, *asu* =
life, life-force) were a primeval group of gods
who were superseded by the up-and-coming →
Devas. In the Atharvaveda and thereafter, the
name denotes only demons.

Asurakumāra ('Demon-princes') In
Jainism, the first group of the → Bhavanavāsin
gods. They belong to the uppermost regions of
the underworld; they are black in colour and their
clothing is red. Like the gods, they are able to
generate rain and thunder.

Aśvin (*aśvin* = having horses) Indian twin
gods equivalent to the → Dioskúroi. They appear
driving their horses in the morning sky, and they
are givers of honey. The fact that they are twins is
attested in the Rigveda. As divine healers they
can cure the sick and rejuvenate the old. At a
later period in Indian thought they are associated
with → Sūrya. As sons of → Dyaus, they are also
called *nāsatyas*.

Ataecina Old Hispanic goddess, venerated
in the region between the Tagus and the
Guadalquivir. Interpreted by the Romans as

equivalent to Proserpina. From inscriptions it is clear that she was regarded as a goddess of the underworld: one stele shows her holding a cypress branch.

Atargatis Syrian Mother Goddess (Dea Syria) who was also venerated in Asia Minor and in Greece during the Hellenistic-Roman period. The centre of her cult was at Bambyke (Hierapolis) in Syria. The name Atargatis is a compound of → Astarte and → Anat, whose functions she took over, particularly those relating to fertility. The male partner allotted to her was → Adad. Her throne was flanked by lions; the ear (of wheat) and the coping stone were her attributes. In Askalon she was worshipped under the name Derketo in mermaid form.

Áte Greek goddess of disaster; the embodiment of blind folly, benightedness, which stupefies man, mind and soul, and lands one in disaster. She was supposed to be a daughter of → Zeus.

Atea The primeval god of Polynesian tradition: the space in light which was in the beginning sexless but which then divided itself into the god → Rangi (heaven, sky) and the goddess Papa. These two are the parents of all the gods. A Tahitian myth relates that Atea was created as an initially female divinity by → Tangaroa.

Athená (or Athéne) Virgin tutelary goddess of Athens and Greek goddess of wisdom. Originally a Cretan-Minoan palace goddess, perhaps identical with a Cretan snake-goddess: the snake continued into later times to be associated with her (picture in the Parthenon). Her epithet *glaukopis* (= owl-eyed) hints at an earlier version in the shape of a bird. In Homer, Athena appears in two forms: as Promachos ('champion') she is goddess of battle and bearer of the terrible *aegis* (the breastplate with the head of Medusa); and as Ergane ('Craftsman') she acts as instructor in the handicrafts. In her capacity as a protective deity she bears the epithet Pallas; and the *palladion*, the icon named after her, was supposed to protect the city and its houses from harm. Regarding her birth, the myth tells how she sprang from the head of her father → Zeus. She forms no amorous attachment of any kind, and remains Parthenos – the virgin. The tale is told of how the gods competed with each other to see which of them could provide the most noble gift: Athená won the competition by giving Attica the olive-tree. But that was not all: she gave the peasant his plough, to women she gave the loom and she invented the flute. Thus, along with her role as goddess of war she is also a goddess of peace. The Romans equated her with → Minerva.

Atirat A West-Semitic goddess, described by the Babylonian king Hammurabi as 'daughter-in-law of the king of heaven' and 'queen of lasciviousness'. The name derives either from *atir* = friend, or from an Arabic word meaning 'brilliance, brightness'; if the latter derivation is correct, this would seem to point to a solar connection. In South Arabia, Atirat appears in association with the moon-god → Amm.

Átlas ('the bearer') Son of the Titan → Iapetós and the Oceanid Klymene; sentenced to carry the vault of heaven because he took part in the campaign against the gods. The equation with the mountain range in North Africa was known in antiquity; for example, it is to be found in Herodotus.

Atlaua Old Mexican water-god (Nahuatl *atl* = water) who is also associated with the 'arrow' (*atlatl*). He is 'Master of the waters'. When he takes his arrow in his hand, he will soar up like the Quetzal bird.

45

Aton In Ancient Egypt, primarily the designation of the visible disc of the sun, which was regarded as a manifestation of → Re. In the New Kingdom, the sun-disc was personified and under King Amenophis IV, who called himself Echnaton (i.e. 'he pleases Aton'), it was declared to be the one true god. Portrayals from this period show the sun-disc, whose rays are arms which end in hands bearing the loop of life. The monotheism associated with Aton was abandoned after the death of Echnaton.

Atri One of the deified bards, singers of sacred songs (→ Riṣis) in ancient India. His name, 'the devouring one', was an epithet of fire. We are told in the Rigveda that he discovered the sun which had been swallowed by a demon, and put it back into the heavens. According to the Purāṇas he is the father of → Soma.

Átropos → Moires

ʿAttar A god worshipped in South Arabia BC. In invocations of the divine trinity he takes pride of place. The planet Venus is allotted to him (the morning star); and he is a god of war and of protection in war, with the epithet 'he who is bold in battle'. In addition, he is the giver of water, vital for life, a function in which his services overlap those of the moon-god. The antelope is sacred to him, and one of his symbols is the spear-point. Outside South Arabia, ʿAttar may assume androgynous traits (as in Ugarit).

Attis Phrygian god of vegetation, lover of the Great Mother (→ Kybéle). In an older version of the myth he is a beautiful youth who is killed by a boar while hunting. The later version is the better known: according to it, Attis loses his reason in his desperate passion for Kybéle, and emasculates himself under a pine-tree. Spring flowers and trees grow up from the blood of the dying youth.

Attis mystery rites with sacramental partaking of food and *taurobolium* (baptism with bull's blood) were widespread throughout the Roman Empire. At the end of March the feast of the dying and resurrected god (symbolized by a pine-tree) was solemnized.

Atum Ancient Egyptian primeval god and creator of the world, venerated especially in Heliopolis. His name is construed as meaning 'he who is not yet completed', or perhaps 'the non-existent'. Before heaven and earth became separated he was the 'one lord'. In the Pyramid texts he appears as the primeval mountain, that is, the first substance to arise from primeval chaos. He may take the form of the scarab, the snake or (later) the ichneumon. Atum begat the first divine couple → Šu (breath of wind) and → Tefnut (humidity). In accordance with the solar syncretism of the Egyptians, Atum and → Re could be equated.

Atunis The Etruscan name of → Adonis, taken over by the Etruscans from the Greek pantheon in the fourth century BC. Represented only on mirrors, usually in association with → Turan; the two together corresponding to the Oriental-Mediterranean pair of the Great Mother and her son.

Aufaniae Celtic deities, known from votive inscriptions found in the Rhineland and in Spain. They seem to be matron-like figures.

Auróra For the Romans, the morning red and the goddess who raises it in the sky; cf. → Eos in Greece.

Auseklis (Latvian = morning star) A Baltic stellar god, subordinate to the moon but often represented as serving the sun. When marriages are held in heaven he forms part of the bridal cortege, and he is a willing helper in the heavenly bath-house. As a place associated with birth and with curative properties, the bath-house was particularly strongly endowed with vital forces.

Auxo → Horae

Avalokiteśvara (also Avalokita or Lokeśvara) In Buddhism, the most popular of all the → Bodhisattvas. He is regarded as an emanation of → Amitābha, and as the so-called → Dhyāni-Bodhisattva of the present age. The name is variously interpreted, with little agreement as to what it may mean: 'the lord who descends'; 'he who is enabled to reach the highest understanding'; 'master of light' (i.e., of the inner light, enlightenment). He is an embodiment of compassion, a main virtue in Buddhism. Out of compassion he descends to hell in order to redeem the souls who suffer there. Iconographically he is depicted in many ways. Usually he has two arms, but in the Tantric tradition he has four or six arms. One of his most significant attributes is the wreath of roses; another is the moon (→ Amoghapāśa, → Khasarpana). In his plaited crown he bears the portrait of Amitābha. When he is shown with ten or eleven faces, this is with reference to his universality. One of his most popular representations is as Cintāmaṇicakra-Avalokiteśvara: that is, he bears as attributes a jewel (*cintāmaṇi*) held before the breast, and a wheel (*cakra*). In China he has been transformed into the female deity → Guan Yin. In Japan he is known as K(w)annon and in Tibet as sPyan-ras-gzigs, as an incarnation of whom the Dalai Lama is regarded.

Awonawilona Creation god of the Zuñi (one of the Pueblo Indian tribes). He is the origin of all life; his epithet 'He-she' shows that he is held to be hermaphrodite. He created heaven/father and earth/mother by throwing balls of his skin on the primeval waters.

Ayiyanayaka (also Ayiyan)   A kind-hearted tutelary god of woodland and countryside venerated by the Dravidians and the Singhalese, tne protecting deity of the northern part of the island of Ceylon (Sri Lanka). According to one myth he was born as a golden statue from the right hand of → Viṣṇu. The god is still invoked today to protect crops and when there is danger of plague.

Ays   Among the Armenians this word means not only 'wind' but also the evil spirit which rushes along in the wind: it can penetrate into human beings and drive them crazy.

Aži Dahaka (Avestan *aži* = snake, cf. Modern Farsi *ažidahā* = dragon)   A mythical figure which reaches back into the very earliest Indo-Aryan times. It was a snake-like monster with three heads, initially preying on cattle and an enemy of all good men. Subsequently it was seen as the usurper of the Iranian kingdom and the embodiment of falsehood. Temporarily conquered, he will present himself as a threat once more at the end of time as an accomplice of → Ahriman, but then he will be defeated once and for all.

Azizos and Monimos   It is under these names that the morning star and the evening star were venerated in Syria; they were depicted as two boys with an eagle. The Neo-Platonist Iamblichos identified Azizos with → Arés. In Palmyra, the place of Monimos was taken by the god → Arsu.

B

Ba (1)   This Egyptian word means 'the ram', and it is the name of the ram-god of Mendes in the sixteenth nome of Lower Egypt. As a philoprogenitive god he was the object of veneration from women who wanted offspring. Ba the ram-god gradually turns into Ba (see next entry), a manifestation of → Re. In the Late Egyptian period, the god assumes the form of a billy-goat.

Ba (2) (pl: Baw)   Ancient Egyptian designation for a spiritual power which Horapollon identifies with Psyche. In the oldest religious texts, anonymous gods who make occasional appearances are written with the signs for Ba; and later the word becomes a synonym for the manifested form of a god. The Apis bull is the Ba of → Osiris, the star Sirius (Egyptian Sothis) is the Ba of → Isis, and the Pharaoh is seen as the 'living soul' of the sun-god → Re.

Ba (3)   Chinese goddess, a personification of drought. In some literary sources she is referred to as the daughter of the mythical Emperor → Huang-di.

Baal   Storm-god and god of fecundity of the West Semites, represented both in human shape and as a bull. The word *ba'l* means 'owner, lord' and can be a generic term for gods in general. Thus, it is applied to various local deities, as, for example, Baal-Sidon or Baal-Lebanon; the Baal of Tyros was known as → Melqart. → Baal-Hadad occupied a central position in Syria as a whole. Belief in Baal came with the Hyksos to Egypt, where the god is specifically depicted as wearing a conical cap with a long band and bull's horns. Soon afterwards, Baal was identified with → Seth.

Baal-Addir ('mighty Baal') Initially the god of the Phoenician town of Byblos, whence his cult spread to Punic (Carthaginian) Africa, whether as a god of fertility or of the underworld is a moot point. Among African troops in the Roman army he was identified with Jupiter Valens.

Baal-Biq'āh As 'lord of the plain' (between the Lebanon and the Anti-Lebanon) this was the deity after whom the town of Baalbek was named. Initially a weather-god (like → Baal-Hadad) he became in the Hellenistic period a sky- or sun-god, and was identified with Zeus. Under the Romans he was regarded as Jupiter Heliopolitanus (by then, Baalbek was called Heliopolis, sun-city).

Baal-Hadad Old Syrian god of storms and weather; the name means 'Lord of the thunder'. The Babylonian counterpart of Baal-Hadad was → Adad. As weather-god his epithet was 'cloud-rider', in his capacity as a warrior he was called 'Prince Baal' and in stories about his death and resurrection he was given the title 'prince and lord of the earth'. His symbol was the bull, the emblem of fertility. According to Ugaritic texts, Baal dwelt on the Sapan mountain and hence is also known as Baal Sapan. His chief enemies are → Jamm (sea) and → Mot (death). A stele at Ras Shamra shows the gods bearing in his hands a club and the symbol of lightning.

Baal-Hammon The earliest known reference to this god occurs in an inscription found at the Phoenician settlement of Zindsirli. The name is taken to mean 'lord of the censer altars'. He is known chiefly as the supreme god of Carthage, whence he was introduced to Malta, Sicily and Sardinia. In North Africa, he was revered mainly as a god of fertility, a role attested in the epithet given him in Roman times – Frugifer ('fruit-bearer'). The sacrifice of children played a part in his cult observances, both in

Sicily and in North Africa. Owing to the similarity between his name and that of the oasis god → Ammon, he was also regarded as an oracular god. The Greeks identified him with → Kronos, the Romans with → Saturnus.

Baal-Karmelos ('lord of Karmel') A Canaanite god revered on Mount Carmel. In I Kings: 18, 19 ff. it is related how the prophet Elijah challenged the priests of Baal to conjure up a burnt sacrifice without fire. This mountain god was also known to speak in oracles, and was still being venerated in Roman times, e.g. by the Emperor Vespasian.

Baal-Marqōd ('Lord of the dance') Old Syrian god, who had a shrine devoted to him in the neighbourhood of the modern city of Beirut. A curative well associated with him indicates that he was a god of healing. In Greek guise he appears on votive tablets as Balmarkos. In Roman parlance he was identified with → Júpiter.

Baal-Qarnain ('Lord of the two horns') A Punic god so called after two mountain peaks close to the Gulf of Tunis. He was represented as → Saturnus, and called Saturnus Balcarnensis. It seems likely that he was a local manifestation of → Baal-Hammon.

Baal-Šamēm (Baal-Sammin) The Phoenician name means 'Lord of Heaven', which would accordingly suggest a celestial deity. His cult was widespread (ancient Syria, North Mesopotamia, Cyprus, Carthage). He is represented on Seleucid coinage bearing a half-moon on his brow and carrying in one hand a sun with seven rays. The Romans called him Caelus (sky).

Baal Sapon Canaanite god, so called after Mount Sapon in Northern Palestine. In Ugarit he

was called Baal Sapan, and as the conqueror of the sea-god → Jamm he functions as the protector of mariners.

Baba (1) (Bau) Sumerian tutelary goddess of the city of Lagaš. Daughter of the sky-god → An, and spouse of the god of fertility → Ningirsu. Probably she was initially a Mother Goddess ('Mother Baba') and from Old Babylonian times onwards she was known as a goddess of healing ('female doctor of the black-headed'), and is often equated with → Gula. King Gudea praised her as 'mistress of abundance'.

Baba (2) In Hungarian popular belief, initially a being similar to a fairy who gradually took on the lineaments of a witch.

Baba-Yaga Witch in East European folk-tales, also known as Jezi-Baba. Sometimes she appears as a forest spirit, sometimes as the leader of a host of spirits, in which capacity she acquires demonic status. One White Russian tradition describes her as travelling through the air in an iron kettle with a fiery broom.

Babi A demon of darkness mentioned in the Egyptian Books of the Dead. He is probably represented in Greek incantational papyri by the name Bapho, a name used for → Seth. In Plutarch we find an associate of Seth – or perhaps Seth himself – named Bebon.

Bacab The gods of the four heavenly directions in Maya religion. Their names and their associated colours were: Kan (yellow), → Chac (red), Zac (white) and Ek (black).

Bacax A deity revered by the ancient Berbers; he was supposed to dwell in a cave at the

entrance of which sacrificial offerings were to be made.

Bácchus   Roman god of fertility and of wine. The Latin name is derived from the Greek Bákchos (→ Dionysos) whose cult was implanted in Rome at a comparatively early date. It was a secret cult, and its rites, the Bacchanalia, were marked not only by sexual excesses but by crimes of every description, so much so that from time to time the cult was prohibited. The most significant portrayal of Dionysiac mysteries is to be found in Pompeii.

Badb   (Bodb) Irish goddess of war. The battle-field is called after her 'land of Badb'. She was supposed often to take the form of a crow. At the mythical battle of Mag Tured it was she who decided the day.

Baga   Old Persian designation for God, etymologically connected with Sanskrit → *bhaga*. → Ahura Mazda is *baga vazraka*, 'the great god'; while → Mithra is simply called *baga*. In Parthian usage, the word *baga* could also signify a dynastic god.

Bagvarti   A goddess venerated by the Urartians, an ancient people who lived in what is now Armenia. She was the spouse of the Urartian tutelary god Ḥaldi.

Bahram   A Persian god, sometimes identified as the regent of the planet Mars, sometimes identical with → Verethragna as god of the wind.

Baiame   The supreme being in the religion of the Wiradyuri and Kamilaroi peoples in Australia. The name means 'creator' or 'the great one', and women refer to him as 'our father'. He created first himself and then all other things and beings. Baiame sits in heaven on a throne, he is invisible and is audible only in thunder. His son is → Daramulun.

Balarāma ('the powerful Rāma') A god of agriculture whose cult reaches back to the very earliest times in India. His attribute is the plough, and he was regarded as the elder brother of → Krisna.

Balder (Old Icelandic: Baldr; Modern Icelandic: Baldur) North German god; in the Edda he is described as handsome, brave and gentle, and of shining appearance. He is the son of → Odin and of → Frigg, and the benevolent opponent of the evil → Loki, who induces the blind → Hödur to shoot a branch of mistletoe at him, thus killing him (mistletoe being the only thing that could harm him). The etymology of his name is not clear, and there are accordingly several different interpretations of his function; thus he is variously seen as a god of light and as a god of vegetation – that is, as a god who dies and is resurrected. Again, he has been seen as a hypostatis of the war-god Odin, an interpretation depending on equation of his name with the Old Norse adjective *baldr* = courageous, bold.

Bali Indian demon: in the second world-age (*kalpa*) he ruled over all three worlds but had to yield sovereignty over earth and heaven to → Visnu. Ever since, he has been ruler of the underworld. According to the Mahābhārata, Bali, enemy of the gods, lives in the shape of an ass in a dilapidated hut.

Baltis An Ancient Arabian goddess venerated at Carrhae in north-west Mesopotamia. She was identified with the planet Venus.

Bandāra (more accurately, Bandāra deviyō) Originally, the title of high officials in the Singhalese kingdom, thereafter the designation of a group of gods superior to the → Yakṣas. Often chief local deities are called simply Bandāra. The group includes, among others, → Dādimunda.

Bangputys Lithuanian god of the sea, whose name means 'he who blows the waves'. In a folksong he is called simply 'god of the waves'.

Barastir (Barastaer)   The ruler of the world of the dead among the Ossetians (Caucasus). His function is to direct the dead souls, as they arrive, to their places in paradise or in the underworld.

Bardha ('the white ones')   In Albanian popular belief, whitish nebulous figures who dwell under the earth. They may be compared with the → Elves. To propitiate them, one strews cakes or sugar on the ground.

Baršamin Old Armenian god, possibly a sky-god. It seems likely that he was taken over from the Syrian pantheon, and is probably identical with → Baal-Šamēn.

Basajaun ('Lord of the forest')   A Basque spirit dwelling in the woods or in caves high up in the hills. He protects flocks and herds. In Basque tradition he plays the part of a cultural initiator who instructs mankind in the art of agriculture, and from whom they copy forging and working in wrought iron.

Bašāmum A god worshipped in ancient south Arabia. His name may come from Arabic *bašām* = balsam bush. This suggests that he was a god of healing, a hypothesis strengthened by the fact that one ancient text relates how he cured two wild goats or ibexes.

Bastet An Egyptian goddess, interpreted as a personification of ointment. At an early period she was visualized in the shape of a lion, and this led to her coalescence with the leonine → Sachmet. In line with the syncretism typical of Egyptian religion she was seen as the 'eye of → Re' and coupled with → Tefnut. From the New Kingdom onwards, Bastet is increasingly represented as having the head of a cat. Memphitic tradition makes her the mother of the god of embalming → Anubis. The centre of her cult was Bubastis, and hence we find even classical authors calling her Bubastis.

Bata Taurine god, tutelary deity of the seventeenth nome of Upper Egypt. He is known from the New Kingdom legend of the two brothers.

Baubo Initially, a personification, current in Asia Minor, of female fecundity. According to Orphic (Greek) tradition she is an old woman, who makes the grieving → Demeter laugh by showing her her pudenda. The obscene gesture is to be understood as a protective charm against the powers of death. As a demon, Baubo was visualized as headless or with her head placed between her legs. The name has been variously interpreted as meaning 'belly', 'hole', 'womb'.

Ba Xian ('The Eight Immortals') In Chinese popular belief there are many men and women whose way of life sets them far apart from others, so much so that they can lead a happy life on earth which never ends: these are *xian*. A particularly well known group of *xian* is formed by the 'Eight Immortals' who are partly historical personages, partly legendary in nature. Their symbols and attributes are in common use as lucky charms. Their names are: → Cao Guo-jiu, → Han Xiang-zi, → He Xian-gu, → Lan Cai-he, → Li Tie-guai → Lü Dong-bin, → Zhang Guo-lao, and → Zhong-li Quan.

Bebellahamon North Arabian (Palmyran) god in whom scholars have seen a variant of the Punic → Baal-Hammon.

Beelzebub (Beelzebul) The well-known derivation from 'baal-zebub', i.e. lord of the flies, is not proven; it is more probable that the name means 'Baal the prince', thus corresponding to the Phoenician concept of the god. He was a tutelary god in the land of the Philistines (II Kings 1:2). Rabbinical texts interpreted the name as meaning 'Lord of the dunghill'; the word *zabal* = to dung, is used in rabbinical literature as a synonym for idolatry. In the New Testament, Beelzebub is chief of the demons (Matthew 12: 24-27).

Befana In popular belief in north Italy, a female demon of midwinter. She brings presents – but she can also turn nasty and may turn up as a ghost. In some ways she reminds us of the → Bercht in German popular belief. The name Sefana (or Befania) comes from Epiphany, the feast of the Magi (6 January).

Beg-tse (Tibetan *beg-ce* = hidden shirt of mail) God of war in Lamaism. He is clad from head to foot in mail, and he carries a garland of human heads and a crown in the shape of a skull. He often appears under the name of lCam-srin.

Behanzin A fish-god venerated in Dahomey.

Behedti This god, who took the form of a crouching falcon, was venerated in the Egyptian town of Behdet (Edfu). Very early on he became a local form of the great falcon-god → Horus. The proper symbol of the solar deity is the disc of the sun, fitted with a pair of wings. Behedti also takes over the role of the king identified with Horus.

From the Middle Kingdom onwards, the sun-disc became a widespread symbol of protection.

Behemoth (Hebrew *behema* = animal) A designation of the hippopotamus (Job 40). In Jewish eschatology it figures as an apocalyptic beast; and in the Christian Middle Ages it was identified with → Satan, and patristic authority was invoked to prove it. Perhaps we may also see a relic of Behemoth in the allegedly secret figure of Baphomet, whose symbolic presence the Knights Templar are said to have venerated and kissed upon entry to the Order. If this is indeed so, then the name does service here as a cover-name for the true God.

Behēr Ethiopic sea-god, often named in conjunction with → Astar.

Bel (1) This Akkadian word means 'Master' and is a component in more than one divine name. In later times, the word Bel came to be used for the god → Marduk, and this applies to the Biblical passages involving his name as well (e.g. Jeremiah 46:1; Daniel 14: 3). In a Greek version of the Babylonian creation myth he is called Belos.

Bel (2) The supreme god of Palmyra, whose name was originally Bol (from Semitic Baal?); Bol seems to have turned into Bel (→ Bel) under Babylonian influence. He was a sky-god and his attributes included lightning flashes and an eagle. He formed a trinity along with the moon-god (→ Aglibol) and the sun-god (→ Yarhibol).

Belenus A Celtic god revered especially in the eastern Alpine area, though his cult extended into north Italy and south Gaul. The root *bel-* probably means 'shine', which would suggest that Belenus was a god of light. In Aquileia, the god was presented as → Apollon.

Bēletsēri A Babylonian goddess who figures as 'book-keeper' and 'clerk' of the underworld. As the underworld is circumscribed as 'steppe', she is also known by the epithet 'Queen of the steppe'. She is the spouse of the nomad god → Martu.

Belial Also Beliar ('the unholy one', 'the worthless one'). Wicked men are specifically described in the Old Testament as 'men of Belial' (2 Samuel 16: 7). In Psalm 18: 5 the word is used in the phrase 'floods of ungodly men' (*nachalei belial*), usually rendered in Catholic Bible translations as 'streams of the devil'. Satan, the devil, is clearly intended in the reference in 2 Corinthians 6: 15, and similarly in passages in the Qumran texts: Belial is the spirit (and the prince) of darkness.

Belili Old Mesopotamian goddess, probably a denizen of the underworld. She was a sister of the god of vegetation → Dumuzi. Several attempts have been made to derive the Biblical figure of → Belial from her.

Bellona (1) Cappadocian goddess (Asia Minor) who was given a role in the retinue of the Mother Goddess (→ Kybéle).

Bellóna (2) Roman goddess of war: more precisely, a personification of war. Her name comes from the Latin *bellum* = war. On occasion she figures as the spouse of → Mars.

Bendis Virgin, arms-bearing goddess of the Thracians; equated by the Greeks with → Artemis, sometimes with → Hekáte. Her cult was introduced into Athens in the time of Pericles.

Beng A gipsy name for the devil. He often engages God in a trial of strength, but is always beaten. He dwells in the woods and prefers to go about his shady business by night.

Benten In Japan, the Buddhist goddess of eloquence and music, patron saint of the geishas, and reckoned as one of the seven → Shichi-Fukujin, the gods of good luck. She is represented wearing a jewelled diadem and holding in her hands a stringed instrument. Her name is sometimes written as Benzaiten.

Bercht Perchta is an alternative form, and she is also called Frau Berta or Eisenberta. As a midwinter spirit she goes back to pre-Christian times in Germany; but with the coming of Christianity she became the personification of the night preceding Epiphany (6 January) called *perahtun naht* in Old High German. She appears in various guises: as Butzenbercht, the bringer of gifts, as 'Spinnstubenfrau' (spinning-room woman) who visits houses by night, and then again as 'stomach-slasher', 'bogey-woman'. Traces of the cult once surrounding her still survive: thus, in some Alpine districts it is customary to place food for her on the roof on Perchtentag (Epiphany). The → Perchten are called after her.

Berekyndai In Phrygia, the divine attendants of the Magna Mater (→ Kybéle).

Bes In ancient Egypt, a half-demonic half-divine figure which occurs also in the plural. The Bes has a grotesque face and a dwarfish body. To begin with, he carried a lion-skin on his back, of which only the ears and the tail survived into later times. His most important attributes are the Sanoose (a symbol of protection), knives as defensive weapons and musical instruments whose sounds scare off evil spirits.

Beset A female → Bes, belief in whom was particularly widespread in the time of the Ptolemies. The lion's tail is missing from her attributes; instead, she has a crown of feathers. Like Bes, her function is apotropaic.

Bestla In the Edda, the daughter of the giant Bolthorn, and the mother of the god → Odin. Her name is interpreted as meaning 'giver of bast', which would identify her as a goddess of the yew tree; alternatively as 'tree-bark', a reading which would made Odin a god born from a tree.

Bethel The word really means 'the house of God', but it is found as a divine name in Canaan. There is an identical place-name in the Old Testament (Genesis 31: 13) which has certainly nothing to do with the non-Biblical god. On the other hand, the reference in Jeremiah 48: 13 is probably to the god Bethel.

Bhaga (Sanskrit 'dispenser'; Iranian *baga* = god) In the Vedic religion, one of the → Ādityas. He is invoked as a giver of good fortune and prosperity, and in addition he is the god of marriage, to whom the month of spring is dedicated.

Bhagavān (Bhagwān: Sanskrit = the exalted one, the sublime one) In the Indian Bhagavata sect a designation for the supreme god, later identified with the god → Viṣṇu and with his incarnation → Kriṣṇa. Certain aboriginal tribes in India, like the Bhil, have taken over the Sanskrit word → Bhagwān, as the name of their highest god.

Bhagwān Supreme god of the Bhil people (in north-west Central India). Bhagwan was originally alone, but then he created the other gods and made them bearers of light. He is known by other names such as Parmesar ('the highest') and Andate ('Giver of corn'). He is also judge of the dead.

Bhairava (Sanskrit = the terrible one) This Indian god is regarded as an emanation of → Śiva having been born from the space between Śiva's eyebrows. He is endowed with four or six arms and a fierce visage with protruding canine teeth; he is festooned with snakes, and he carries a garland of skulls and a bowl full of blood. His sacred animal is the dog, and he often rides on one. Bhairava is regarded as a heavenly watchman, and it is customary to offer him small figures of dogs made out of sugar.

Bhaiṣajyaguru ('Master of medicine') A → Buddha of the healer's art, who makes his appearance as early as the fourth century AD. He is probably a deification of → Gautama Buddha in his capacity as medicine-man. His paradise lies in the east and is floored with lapis lazuli. In China he is called Yao-xi, in Japan Yaku-shi. He is usually shown holding in his right hand the bitter medicinal fruit of the myrobalan.

Bhavanavāsin One of the four main categories of gods in Jainism; they dwell in the upper regions of the underworld, in a place 'gleaming with jewels'.

Bhīma (Sanskrit = the terrible one) Several aboriginal Indian tribes have taken this name from Hindu mythology to designate a god who seems to be associated with sky and weather.

Bhṛkuti A female deity in the Buddhist pantheon. She has one head and four arms, she is yellow in colour and young. With her right hands she makes the gesture signifying that a wish has been granted, and holds a garland of roses; in her left hands she holds her attributes – the triple staff (the three staves bound together which a Brahman could carry to show he had renounced the world) and a waterpot. She is located on the moon and bears on her head the likeness of → Amitābha.

Bhūtadāmara ('Lord of the demons') One of the grim and terrible gods in Buddhism. He has one head and four arms; he is of dire appearance, and his three eyes are underlined in red. He is black in hue, but that does not prevent him from shining like a thousand suns. Eight snakes adorn him, and his crown is decorated with five skulls. It is his duty and function to hold all demons in check; and he even tramples on the god → Aparājita.

Bhūtas In India, a designation for demons who can assume the most varied assortment of shapes – horses, pigs, giants, etc.

Bia A child of the queen of the Greek underworld, → Styx, and the constant companion of → Zeus. His name (*bia* = power, strength) suggests that he may be no more than a hypostatization of the father of the gods.

Biegg-Olmai → Olmai

Bilwis (Middle High German *pilwiz*) In the earliest references to him, in texts from Bavaria and Austria, he appears as a nature spirit who uses a sort of missile to cure illnesses. At the end of the Middle Ages, however, there is a switch in meaning, and the erstwhile demonic creature turns into a magician, or even a female witch. Bilwis is also known in east Germany, where he appears as a man endowed with demonic powers and with sickles attached to his feet; at night he cuts narrow strips into corn-fields (hence

'Bilmesschneider', Bilmes-cutter), or chooses some other way to rob the farmer of part of his crops. Today, in popular belief, he is little more than a bogeyman.

Binbeal → Bunjil

Bisham → Shichi-Fukujin

Bochica Culture-hero of the Muisca Indians in Colombia. He gave his people laws and taught them handicrafts. His figure finally coalesced with that of the sun-god.

Bodhisattva In Buddhism a being (*sattva*) intent on achieving enlightenment (*bodhi*). The Chinese term is Pu-sa, the Japanese Bo-satsu. Bodhisattva is the → Buddha to be, whose compassion for humanity is so great that at times he renounces achievement of Buddhahood. Originally, this was taken to mean no more than the historical Buddha before his enlightenment, but in the sequel the number of Bodhisattvas became infinite thanks to the concept of 'future Buddhas'. They are heavenly beings who bring salvation (for example → Avalokiteśvara, and → Mañjuśrī), who are worshipped in ceremonial ritual and who are invoked in any and every case of need or distress. The eight 'great Bodhisattvas' are called Mahābodhisattvas. Iconographically the Bodhisattvas are shown robed as princes and bearing a five-leaved crown.

Boldogasszony (also known as Kis-boldogasszony or Nagyboldogasszony) Virgin goddess of the ancient Hungarians, 'the great and rich queen' whose milk is holy. She is the protector of mother and child. With the coming of Christianity, she was transformed into the figure of the Virgin Mary as the 'divine princess', the 'queen', the mother of the Hungarian people.

Bolla A demonic snake-like being in Albanian popular belief; called Bullar in South Albania. It is only on St George's day that it opens its eyes, and if it should then see a human being it will devour him. After twelve years the Bulla turns into the fearsome → Kulshedra.

Bonchor A god once worshipped by the ancient Berbers in what is now north Tunisia. He may possibly have corresponded to the Roman god → Jupiter.

Bor(r) In Germanic myth the son of → Bur, and father of the gods → Odin, → Vili and Ve. No cult of any kind was attached to him.

Boréas In Greek mythology, the personification of the harsh north wind. He surprises Oreithyia, the daughter of the King of Athens, at play and abducts her to his homeland in Thrace. When a Persian war fleet was decimated in a violent storm, Boréas achieved cult status in Athens and was duly worshipped.

Borvo A Gallic god. The root of his name (*bor*) is supposed to signify 'boil', 'bubble', and the god himself is associated with curative mineral springs.

Bragi (Old Icelandic *bragr* = the most distinguished) North German god of the art of poetry. He is first mentioned in late texts, and this has prompted the suspicion that he is in fact an historically attested Skald of the same name, who was subsequently promoted to mythological status. No cult seems to have been attached to his name; → Idun is mentioned as his wife.

Brahmā This is properly the masculine form of the Sanskrit word *brahman*, and it

designates the personification of → Brahman in
Indian religion. Originally, Brahmā was regarded
as the head of the → Trimūrti: he was creator
and director of the world, and he was the
supreme god of the Devadeva (the gods). He was
pictured with four heads and in his four hands he
holds the four Vedas, the holy scriptures of
ancient India. Among his other attributes are a
vessel containing water from the Ganges, and a
garland of roses; he rides on a Hamsa (i.e. a
goose) which becomes, by poetic licence, a swan.
His spouse is → Sarasvatī. In recent times, the
figure of Brahmā has lost much of its former
prestige. He is now god of wisdom and progenitor
of the Brahmins. An epithet used frequently in
connection with him is Kamalāsana – 'he who sits
on the lotus'.

Brahman (Sanskrit neuter noun)   Originally
this word designated the Vedic magic incantation
or sacred formula; then it came to mean the
power inherent in the utterance, the power which
enables the gods to perform their mythic functions and which enables the Vedic priests
(Brahmans) to undertake the sacred rites. Finally,
in the Upaniṣads, this holy power becomes the

omnipotent, indeed the creative principle, the original cosmic ground, the world-soul. One text describes Brahman as the 'wood' from which heaven and earth are built. In the Śatapatha-Brāhmaṇa, Brahman is construed as a personal and supernatural being.

Bress Irish god of fertility. According to the myth, he is a son of the King of Fomore, but is adopted by the → Tuatha De Danann. In the sequel, Bress himself becomes king and oppresses the Tuatha De Danann, until the latter win in a final decisive battle. Bress won freedom from the gods, thanks to his services in instructing the people of Ireland in the art of agriculture.

Bṛhaspati (also found as Brahmaṇaspati = Lord of prayer) Vedic god, who forwards the prayers of human beings to the gods. He is 'born from the great light in the highest heaven' and he drives darkness away with roars from his sevenfold mouth. In Vedic mythology he appears as the protector of cows, and as the regent of the planet Jupiter: in this latter capacity he is pictured as golden-yellow and bearing a staff, a garland of prayers (a prayer-ring) and a water-pot.

Brigantia A goddess (of victory?) known from inscriptions found in Britain. Her name is derived from the Celtic word *brig* (= hill, height), which is also the root of the name of the Brigantes, who lived in what is now Wales. The goddess may be connected with the Irish → Brigit, but this is not certain.

Brigit (Irish *brig* = power, authority) Daughter of the god → Dagda, and patroness of smiths, poets and doctors. She was associated with the ritual fires of purification, and the feast of *Imbolc*, on 1 February, was in her honour. Later, she was taken over by Christian hagiography and was venerated in Kildare as the holy

Brigit, who was supposed to tend the holy fire along with 19 nuns.

Britómartis A virgin goddess peculiar to Crete, who later on merged with the figure of → Artemis. The pre-Greek name was interpreted in late classical times as meaning something like 'sweet virgin'.

Buchis The holy bull venerated in the ancient Egyptian town of Hermonthis, near Thebes. He was supposed to be the 'living image' of the god → Month, though he also figured as the herald of the sun-god → Re. His brood-cows were regarded as holy in their capacity of 'those who gave birth to Re'. The bull was characterized by a white body and a black head.

Buddha (Sanskrit 'the awakened one', 'the enlightened one') The designation of one who has attained illumination or enlightenment

(bodhi), the highest aim in Buddhism. The Buddha can be recognized by 32 cardinal and 80 secondary bodily characteristics: e.g. on the sole of each foot is a wheel with a thousand spokes. The most important Buddha is the historical one (→ Gautama Buddha). Three or six Buddhas are supposed to have lived before him, and he will be followed by the fifth Buddha (→ Maitreya). No less than 54 Buddhas are mentioned in the 'Lalitavistara', and their number becomes infinite in later tradition. The five → Dhyāni-Buddhas form a special group. Once a Buddha has entered Nirvana he ceases to have any sort of relationship with the world and he can no longer be reached even by prayer. In Hinduism, Buddha is reckoned to be the ninth Avatāra of → Viṣṇu, he who introduces the present age of decadence. The Chinese name for Buddha is → Fo; the Japanese is Butsu.

Buddhakapāla ('Buddha-skull') A god in Tantrism, similar to → Heruka. He is of powerful build, bluish-black in colour, has one face and four arms, and is festooned with bones. As attributes he carries a knife, an hour-glass drum, a cudgel and a cranium. His female partner – his *prajñā* – is shown embracing him.

Budha In India, the regent of the planet Mercury. He is regarded as the son of the moon-god (→ Soma); he wears yellow garments and carries yellow garlands. His attributes are the sword, the shield and the club, and he rides on a lion.

Bukura e dheut ('the beauty of the earth') Old fairy-like creature in Albanian folk-lore and folk-tale. She is always ready to help, and so powerful that she can undertake tasks that would normally be the province of God or of an angel. Her castle is guarded by all sorts of weird and wonderful creatures. She often develops a demonic dimension and is then in touch with the underworld.

Bukuri i qiellit ('the beautiful one in heaven') A designation for God which is current in Christian circles in Albania. It goes back to ancient Illyrian times, when three gods divided themselves into heaven, ocean and underworld.

Bulaing Female divinity of creation in the religion of the Australian Karadjeri. She is an immortal being living in heaven, who has created all things and all creatures. The word *bulaing* is also used to denote the mythical serpents.

Buluga (also Puluga) The supreme god of the Negritos on the Andaman Islands. He is regarded as immortal, omniscient and invisible, he has created the world and mankind, and sees to it that his commandments are obeyed. His female counterpart, the supreme being of female sex, lives in the northern part of the archipelago; she is called Biliku. The wind is supposed to be Buluga's breath, and his voice is heard in the thunder.

Bumba Supreme being, creator and progenitor of the Boshongo, a Bantu tribe in Africa. In the beginning, he was alone; there was then nothing except darkness and water. Then Bumba was smitten by agonizing stomach pains, and he spat out the sun, the moon and, finally, living creatures. Mankind came last of all.

Bunjil (*Bundjil* = falcon) The supreme being of the Australian Kulin. This being formed the first humans, and it blew its breath into their mouths until they began to stir. It is not usual to refer to this being by name; usually it is called 'our father'. Its son is Binbeal, the rainbow. In the Karnai tribe, only initiates know of Bunjil's existence.

Bur(i) A mythical primeval being in the religious system of the Germanic tribes. He was the first man and the progenitor of the gods. He came forth from a salty block of ice when the primeval cow Audhumla licked it. His son is → Bor.

Burijaš A god of the Kassites who attacked Babylonia in the sixteenth century BC. He was called 'Lord of lands'.

C

God C A Maya god whose name is unknown. He was connected with the first day of creation (Chuen) and may well have been an astral deity (the Polar Star or Venus).

Cáca Roman goddess, sister of → Cácus.

Cácus Originally a pre-Roman god of fire, whose cult at the Palatine was ousted by the Greek hero Euandros. Cacus was then seen as the son of → Vulcanus: a fire-spitting fiend who lived in a cave on the Aventine Hill and slew passers-by.

Cagn Chief god of the Bushmen in South Africa. He was the first being, at whose command all things arose. He created the animals to serve man.

Cai-Shen The Chinese god of riches. He has been identified at different times with various historical personalities. He is said to have been a hermit endowed with supernatural powers; thus he was able to ride on a black tiger.

Cakravartin ('he who turns the wheel') An appellation for a world ruler in Indian Buddhism. His birth and his youthful years are closely similar to those of a → Buddha, and like a Buddha he has 32 cardinal characteristics on his body. He is the lord of the wheel (*cakra*) which symbolizes the Teaching. A Cakravartin can only be born when there is no Buddha on the earth. According to Jainist teaching, a Cakravartin has 14 'jewels' (*ratna*): first and foremost a wheel, then a fell (pelt), a staff, a sunshade, a jewel, a conch, a woman, a sword, a general, a housefather, a master-builder, a priest, a steed and an elephant.

Camaxtli Tribal god of the Chichimec. Originally an astral god, he became the Aztec god of hunting and of fate; on his body he bore the signs of the twenty days. In addition, he is the leader of warriors slain in battle or offered in human sacrifice, whose souls become stars in the eastern sky.

Cāmundā Hindu goddess, a manifestation of the terrible → Durgā. Her name seems to be derived from the names of two demons Canda and Munda, whom she is supposed to have slain. She is portrayed as black or red in colour, and she is often seated upon a demon. Her vehicle is an owl, and she prefers to frequent graveyards.

Candamius Old Hispanic god, whose name lives on in many place-names in central and north-west Spain. He was probably a mountain god who had celestial connections; he was claimed by the Romans as a variant of Jupiter.

Caṇḍaroṣaṇa (Candamahāroṣana = the angry and passionate one) One of the wild or unruly gods of Buddhism. He has one head and two arms, he squints, he has a big mouth with bared tusks. He carries a white snake as a sort of sacred cord, and he wears a tiger skin. His crown bears the image of → Akṣobhya. His right hand holds a sword; his left hand is placed over his heart and bears a snake. He is occasionally equated with → Acala.

Candra (Sanskrit, *candra* = the shining or lovely one) Indian moon-god. He is white in colour and wears white garments, and he drives a shining white chariot, which is drawn by ten white horses or by a white antelope. In later times,

Candra became merely another name for → Soma.

Cao Dai (Chinese Gao-tai = high terrace)
The supreme being in Caodaism, a syncretic religion which made its appearance in Vietnam as late as 1919. His symbol is an eye inscribed in a heart. He is regarded as creator and redeemer, and is identified both with Jehovah and with → Yu-huang Shang-di, the supreme god of Taoism.

Cao Guo-jiu
One of the 'Eight Immortals' (→ Ba Xian). Tradition has it that to him riches and honours were no more than dust. He is patron saint of actors. His attributes are a pair of board-like castanets.

Cariociecus
Old Hispanic war-god, identified by the Romans with → Mars.

Caruincho → Pariacaca

Castor and Pollux
The Latin names for → Kastor and Polydeukes.

Castur and Pultuce
The Etruscan version of the → Dioskúroi, the pair of heavenly twins whom the Etruscans took over from the Greeks (→ Kastor and Polydeukes). In the Etruscan setting, the Dioskúroi coalesced with an older pair of twin brothers, the Tindaridai ('scions of → Tin'). Their representation follows the classical iconographic model.

Cath (Cautha)
Etruscan sun-god, known also under the name of Usil (= sun?). He is uniquely represented as rising from the sea, bearing on his head the flaming disc of the sun; in each hand he holds a ball of fire.

Caturmahārājas (Chinese *tian wang*) In
Buddhist cosmogony these are the four great
kings who guard and control the four quarters of
the world; they correspond to the → Lokapālas of
Hinduism. They are enthroned on the invisible
and holy world-mountain of Meru, whence they
extend their protection to Buddhist truth
(*dharma*) in all parts of the world. To begin with,
they are regarded as benevolent beings, but with
the rise of Tantrism they turn into warlike and
menacing figures who inspire fear. The North is
guarded by → Vaiśravana, the West by the red →
Virūpākṣa, the South by → Virūdhaka, and the
East by → Dhṛtarāṣṭra.

Cautes and Cautopates Companions
of the god → Mithra, particularly associated with
him in the ritual slaughter of a bull. One has a
raised, the other a lowered torch; and this has led
scholars to see in them representatives of day and
night, the onset of spring and of autumn, life and
death. The etymology of the names is unclear.

Centaurs Fabulous creatures in Greek
mythology; wild and half-animal, they had a
human torso and the body of a horse. They dwelt
in thick forests and in the mountains, and seem to
have been nature demons of some kind. One of
the best known Centaurs was → Cheiron.

Ceres Old Italic goddess of agriculture, in religious observance closely connected with the earth goddess → Tellus. Ceres was supposed to be the daughter of → Saturn and of → Ops. She causes living things to emerge from her bosom, into which they are gathered again after death. Like the Greek → Demeter, she was also a goddess of fertility and of marriage. Her temple on the Aventine Hill was a central point for the plebs, the common people. Her feast, the Cerealia, was celebrated on 19 April.

Ceres Africana A North African goddess of the harvest, mentioned by Tertullian. She is also known as Ceres Punica. The Latin name hides an autochthonous fertility goddess.

Cernunnos A Celtic god who sits in the so-called Buddha attitude, his head adorned with a set of antlers. He is thus portrayed on the Gundestrup cauldron. His name has been taken to mean 'the horned one'. He seems to have been mainly concerned with fertility and with wealth, though he also seems to have been associated with the underworld. In a few cases he is portrayed with coins. Cernunnos may in fact be a pre-Celtic god (game preservation?).

Cghene Supreme being in the religious belief of the Isoko in south Nigeria. Cghene is regarded as the creator and father of all Isoko; he is utterly remote and inaccessible, and has neither temple nor priests. There is however a mediator between him and mankind – a post or stake, carved from a tree (Oyise).

Chac The rain-god of the Maya, corresponding to the Aztec → Tlaloc. In addition, he is one of the four gods who represent the four cardinal points or heavenly directions (→ Bacab). His cult centres on the sacred well at Chichen Itza.

Chalchihuitlicue (Chalchiuhtlicue = she who has the green cloak of jewels) Aztec goddess of flowing waters, the spouse of the rain-god → Tlaloc. She was also a goddess of vegetation, particularly concerned with causing the maize crops to flourish. Her attribute is a rattle on a stick; she has a watery-green shirt and coat which are adorned with water-lilies.

Charítes (Greek *charein* = to rejoice) In the beginning there was very probably only one Charis, the spouse of → Hephaistos. As a trinity, the Graces appear first in Hesiod, where they are named: Aglaia (splendour), Euphrosine (cheerfulness) and Thaleia (blossom). In mythology and in art they appear in the retinue of → Aphrodíte or of → Apóllon, and bring beauty and pleasure to mankind. The → Horai are closely associated with them. The → Gratiae correspond to the Charites in the Roman pantheon.

Cháron In Greek mythology the ferryman who rows the dead over the border river (Acheron, Styx) to the underworld, and delivers them at the entrance to Hades. He is paid by putting a coin (*obolos*) in the mouth of the dead person. Originally, Charon was a demon of death in the shape of a dog. He persists in modern Greek folklore as Charos, only now he rides a black horse which sweeps the dead along with it by means of its wooden saddle.

Charontes Male and female demons of death in the Etruscan religion; they are most frequently shown bearing hammers. The name is derived from → Charun.

Charun A male demon in the underworld of the Etruscans. His attribute is a hammer which he carries on his shoulder, or on which he supports himself. He has a nose like a vulture's, pointed animal ears and, often, snakes growing on his head instead of hair. Frequently he is shown with wings. Charun escorts the dead, and watches over the portals of graves. His name is connected with that of the Greek → Charon.

Chasca Coyllur
In pre-Columbian Peru, the god of flowers and protector of maidens.

Cheíron
(Chiron, Greek *cheir* = hand) Originally a Thessalian god of the art of healing. He owes his name to his skill with his hands. In Greek mythology he is the son of → Kronos, a wise → Centaur, well-disposed towards men, who instructs → Asklepiós in the curative skills. In his cave on Mount Pelion he reared many famous heroes (Achilles, for example) until finally he was struck by a poisoned arrow fired by → Herakles, and voluntarily renounced his immortality in favour of → Prometheus.

Cheng-huang
This Chinese designation was originally applied to chthonic gods and subsequently transferred to local gods, tutelary deities who are responsible for a district and its inhabitants. The Cheng-huang are terrestrial gods in that they supervise districts, look after law and order and ward off danger.

Chensit
Goddess of the twentieth nome of Lower Egypt, who took the form of the uraeus snake and was then associated with the tutelary deity → Sopdu. She may be portrayed bearing either the crown of → Hathor or the feather of → Maat, or both.

Chentechtai
This is the Grecianized form of the Egyptian appellation Chenti-cheti. To begin with, he was a crocodile god but soon took on the form of a falcon; he is also connected with → Kemwer, the black bull of Athribis. Finally he converges with → Osiris, so much so that he is referred to as 'Osiris who dwells in Athribis'.

Chenti-irti (Machenti-irti) A falcon-god venerated in the Egyptian city of Letopolis, who was identified with → Horus as far back as the Old Kingdom. His main characteristic is that, in correspondence with the myth of the lost lunar or solar eye, he is conceived as having no eyes. As a judge, he looks after law and order.

Chepre (Chepri) The appellation given to the scarab, the dung-beetle worshipped in Heliopolis in its aspect as primeval god. The scarab is then 'he who arose from himself', who came forth from the earth without any generative process. Very early on, he was taken as a manifestation of → Atum, and finally equated with → Re. The sun-god arises as Chepre, newly born from the underworld, and makes his appearance in the heavens. As a primeval god, Chepre can assume the shape of a snake; in human shape he is portrayed as bearing a scarab on his head.

Cherti A ram-god often mentioned on early Egyptian steles, who was venerated especially in the area of the town of Letopolis. In the Pyramid texts he is allotted the specific function of ferryman in the realm of the dead.

Cherubim (Kerubim, connected with the Assyrian word *karibu*) Hybrid creatures, half-animal half-human, who appear in the Old Testament. They are presented as guardians of the sacral points round which Jewish life and belief centre: the Tree of Life, the Ark of the Covenant, the temple; and they indicate the presence of God. In the vision of Ezekiel they form the living chariot of → Jahwe (Ezekiel 1: 5 f.) In the book of Revelations they are described as 'beasts' and they stand around the throne of God (Revelation 4: 6 ff.) They are 'full of eyes before and behind' and this identifies them as cosmic beings, the eyes symbolizing the stars. According to a Christian interpretation which goes back to Dionysius Areopagita, the Cherubim are a particular class of angels.

Cherufe A gigantic fabulous creature which eats men in the folk-lore of the Araucanian Indians who live in Chile and Argentina. It lives in volcanoes and feeds on young girls.

Chia Appellation of the moon, and the name of the moon-goddess of the Muisca Indians who live in what is today Colombia; she is also their progenitor. The ruler of Muikita (known under the name of Zipa) is regarded as the terrestrial representative of the moon.

Chicome coatl ('Seven snakes') Aztec goddess of foodstuffs; in particular, the giver of maize. Among her attributes are the maize cob and the ceremonial rattle (cf. → Chalchihuitlicue).

Chímaira (Greek = goat) A fabulous monster in Greek mythology: it has a lion's forequarters, the body is that of a goat (with a goat's

head) and the tail is replaced by a snake. Homer tells us that the Chimaira is native to the coast of Lycia, and it is possible that it was originally a demon symbolizing the Lycian 'earth-fire'. According to Vergil it lives at the entrance to the underworld. The monster was slain by the hero Bellerophon.

Chinna-mastā

('whose head is cut off': occurs also in the form Chinnamastakā) A terrifying goddess in Tantrism; she holds her own head in one hand, and the head's mouth opens to receive the blood that spurts from the gaping neck. The goddess is worshipped mainly in Bengal.

Chnubis

In Roman times a god combining Greek and Egyptian characteristics. He appears as → Agathós Daímon, and as a gnostic → Aión, and is portrayed as a snake with a lion's head which is usually surrounded by a halo of rays. Some connection between Chnubis and → Chnum is possible but not certain.

Chnum

(Chnumu) An Egyptian god in the shape of a ram; the name itself denotes a ram. He is portrayed as a man with a ram's head, the horns being horizontally aligned on each side. At Elephantine, Chnum was regarded as guardian of the source of the Nile and hence was donator of the life-giving waters. His main function is a creative one: he fashions the bodies of children on a potter's wheel and then introduces them into the mother's womb. Hence his epithet: 'the sculptor who gives life'. In the Hellenistic age, he played the part of a god of revelations, and he appears in the literature of necromancy as Haruer-Chnuph – i.e. as a variant of → Haroeris.

Chons

Egyptian moon-god, son of → Amun and of → Mut, with whom he forms the triad of Thebes. His name means 'he who fares through (the heavens)' – a reference to his lunar character. As 'Lord of time' he converges with → Thot, whose ibis head he sometimes adopts. He is usually represented as a young man in mummy posture with his legs close together, and with the crescent moon and the full moon on his head. In Thebes, Chons was equated with → Šu, and was regarded as bearer of heaven. One of his epithets is 'he who gives advice' (Greek Chespisichis). As Chons-Re he was seen as a form of the youthful sun-god, to whom one turned for protection against wild animals.

Chontamenti (Chonti-amentiu) Egyptian god of the dead. His name means 'he who is in the uttermost west': it is in the west that the sun goes down, and there too is the kingdom of the dead. The god is represented as a crouching dog or jackal. In the Pyramid texts we find a king wishing to be changed into Chontamenti so that he may be able to rule over the dead.

Chors A god of the eastern Slavs, known from his being mentioned in the so-called Nestor Chronicle along with other sources. He was probably a sun-god. The etymology of the name is not clear. He seems to have been a sort of hybrid with a dog's head and horns.

Chronos Personification of time, often coincident in the late classical period with the figure of → Aión. His portrayal as a bearded old man with sickle and hourglass was particularly popular in the Renaissance and the Baroque periods.

Cihuacoatl ('female snake') An earth- and mother-goddess venerated in the town of Colhuacan, often shown with a child in her arms. She it was who helped → Quetzalcoatl when the first man was being created. Sometimes she coincides with the figure of → Teteo.

Cinteotl (Centeotl)   Aztec god of maize, the most important plant in ancient Mexico. Cinteotl represents a specific aspect of → Quetzalcoatl.

Citipati ('Lord of the graveyard')   Graveyard demons in Buddhism, especially Tibetan Buddhism. They are represented as two dancing skeletons.

Coatlicue ('she who wears a skirt of snakes') Aztec goddess of earth and fire; she also appears as mother of the gods. Her statue in Mexico City shows, apart from the skirt of snakes, a head with two snakes and a necklace consisting of human hands and hearts: the latter in evidence of the need for human sacrifice if cosmic order is to be upheld. On her back hang 13 leather cords decorated with snails, symbolizing the mythical heaven. The goddess was made pregnant by a ball of down or an emerald, and gave birth to → Quetzalcoatl.

Concordia   Roman goddess, personification of concord. When civil disputes were settled, shrines were dedicated to her. She is portrayed – e.g. on coins – as bearing a cornucopia and a sacrificial bowl.

Confucius (Latin formation from Chinese *Kong-(fu)-zi*, 'Master Kong')   Chinese philosopher. In the year 174 BC one of the Han Emperors made sacrifice to him for the first time at his grave, which is still extant today. Not long afterwards, the first Confucian temple was erected. Finally, in a decree issued in the closing years of the Chinese Empire (in 1906) Confucius was placed on the same footing as the supreme deities of heaven and earth. Tradition has it that at his birth two dragons hovered over the home of his parents.

Consus ('he who gathers in') Roman god of the safely gathered harvest. He had an underground altar in a circus to the south of the Palatine Hill. By virtue of his chthonic character he was also connected with the dead.

Culsu A female demon of the Etruscans, who stands at the portal of the underworld. Her attributes include a burning torch and a pair of scissors (for cutting the thread of life?).

Cundā (also Candrā or Cunti) A female deity in Buddhism, an emanation of the Buddha → Vajrasattva, whose image she bears on her crown. She has one face, four arms, and she is white like the moon in autumn. One of her right hands is in the *mudrā* of donation, and one of her left hands holds a lotus on which a book lies. The other pair of hands are holding a bowl.

Curche Old Prussian god of fertility; he was also known as 'god of food and drink'.

Cyclops (Greek *Kyklopes* = 'round eyes') In Homer, man-eating giants with one single eye in their foreheads. In Hesiod, they are the sons of → Gaia, who forge thunderbolts for → Zeus. Later, they came to be regarded as helpmates of → Hephaistos, and denizens of volcanic areas.

D

God D No name is known for the Maya god thus designated in specialist literature. He appears as ruler of the night and the moon, and is portrayed as an old man with sunken cheeks. Sometimes he is shown carrying the shell of a sea-snail on his head – a symbol of birth and life.

Dabog A south Slavonic sun-god. The root *bog* can mean both 'riches' and 'god'. In the epic poetry of the Serbians, Dabog appears as ruler over the earth. He is mentioned among the gods, statues to whom were erected in Kiev, and in the 'Song of Igor' we are told that the Russians are 'Dabog's grandchildren'. Under Christian influence, Dabog was reduced to playing the part of → Satan. The Poles have an equivalent in Dazbog.

Dādimunda (or Devatā bandāra) One of the most popular gods of the Singhalese (Sinhala) people. To begin with, he was a god who looked after temples, then he became 'treasurer' (*devatā*) of the god → Upulvan, and finally he emerged as protector of Buddhism in Ceylon. He rides on an elephant, and there are many → Yakṣas in his retinue.

Daēnā This goddess, the daughter of → Ahura Mazda and of → Armaiti, is the personification of religion in the Old Iranian pantheon. The word *daēnā* means 'that which has been revealed'.

Daēvas (Daiwa; Middle Persian Dev) An appellation for the gods in the Indo-Aryan period (cf. Sanskrit → Deva, devi). For Zarathustra, the daēvas were, to begin with, simply the ancient gods, who were of no consequence in comparison with → Ahura Mazda; but later he came to regard them as fallen angels or as demons. They are black in colour and are active enemies of the true religion; they eat corpses and torture souls in hell.

Dagan (Hebraized form: Dagon) A west Semitic god of corn. His name means 'corn' but was confused by the Israelites with Hebrew *dag* = fish – hence the pictures of the fish-tailed god. In Ugarit, Dagan was regarded as father of Baal, and in the Old Testament he appears as the chief god of the Philistines (Judges 16: 23ff.). The Canaanites brought his cult to Mesopotamia, where he acquired → Šalas as consort; from certain texts we may deduce that he was also equated with → Enlil. Dagan occupied a special position in the religion of the Amorites in Mari.

Dagda An Old Irish god whose name means 'the good god'. He occupies a predominant position in the race of gods known as the → Tuatha De Danann. The epithet associated with him – Ollathir – can be translated as 'All-father'. He is the god of contracts, and is equipped with three attributes: an enormous club which slays but which can also restore life; a magic harp on which a melody for sleep, a melody for laughter and a melody for woe can be played; and a cooking-pot from which no one is turned away hungry.

Daho A Pyrenean deity in Roman times; what we know of his functions makes him comparable with → Mars.

Daikoku → Shichi-Fukujin

Daimon In the Greek pantheon, the divine instance which allotted us our individual fate. In Homer, the Olympic gods are called *daimones*; but from Hesiod onwards they are understood as beings intermediate between gods and heroes, who may have a beneficent or a malevolent influence on human destiny. Popular belief took them as personal guardian spirits. In Greek philosophy, *daimonion* came to mean the divine spark in man. Under Roman, oriental and early Christian influence, however, demons ended up as sinister and evil spirits.

Daityas In Indian belief, demonic enemies of the gods. They are the sons of the goddess → Diti banned by → Indra to dwell in the depths of the ocean because of her reluctance to perform sacrifice as due. In later tradition, Prahlāda, who was raised by → Viṣṇu to be king of the Daityas, exhibits the characteristics of a wise ascetic.

Dākinī Supernatural beings in Buddhism, who fly in the air. They are invested with specific magical powers, they can initiate novices into the secret learning of the Tantra, and they can be of assistance to a Yogin who wishes to further his spiritual insight. They appear as young girls hideously disguised or with the head of a lion or a bird, and with the face of a horse or a dog. They are also supposed to eat human beings.

Dakṣa In Indian thought, a deity bound up with the concept of the creative power. He is regarded as the son of the world creator → Prajāpati, from whose right thumb he is said to have arisen. He is also invoked as progenitor of the human race. According to one tradition, → Diti is his daughter.

Daktyloi (Greek *daktylos* = finger) In Greek tradition, demonic beings who discovered the art of working in metal. They may originally have had phallic significance. They are indigenous to Asia Minor and Crete, and form part of the retinue of the Magna Mater. A distinction is often made between right-hand *daktyloi*, who worked as smiths, and left-hand *daktyloi*, who were active as sorcerers and magicians.

Dala kadavara (also known as *garā yakā*) In the beginning probably, an elephant goddess of the Singhalese: *dala* = tusk. Later, after the introduction of Buddhism, it was believed that the now demonized god was a bringer of illnesses and misfortune. One way of keeping him off is to hold a ceremonial masked dance.

Damballa A divine being venerated on Haiti, whom all the other → Loa regard as their father. His sacred colour is white, and his symbolical creature is the snake. Accordingly, St John the Evangelist, who is portrayed with a snake (because of the legend of the beaker of poisoned wine), is regarded as a manifestation or variant of Damballa.

Damgalnunna (Damkina; in Greek form, also Daukē) Old Mesopotamian goddess, wife of → Enki, and mother of → Marduk. In Sumerian myths she often turns into the figure of the Mother goddess → Ninhursanga.

Damona Gallic goddess, often coupled with the god → Borvo. Her name means 'the big cow'.

Damu Sumerian god, son of the goddess of prosperity → Nin'insina. The centre of his cult was at Isin; one of his epithets was 'great priest of exorcism'.

Dana (also found as Ana) In Ireland the mother of the gods (→ Tuatha De Danann); in mythology she is hardly to be distinguished from → Ana.

Dānavas Half-divine half-demonic beings in Indian tradition. They were banished by → Indra to live in the ocean. The monster → Bali was one of their number.

Dáphne (Greek = laurel tree) Daughter of the river-god → Peneios. She was a beautiful nymph, who fled from → Apóllon when he was making advances to her. When Apóllon persisted in pursuing her, she was changed at her own wish into a laurel tree.

Daramulum Son of the Australian god of creation → Baiame. He rates as a mediator between his father and humankind, whose progenitor he is. In addition he was raised to the status of a lunar being. His name means 'one-legged'. Images of this god fashioned from clay are only shown at initiation ceremonies.

Da-shi-zhi ('the strongest') In Chinese Buddhism, a female Bodhisattva (→ Mahāsthamaprata). Through the power of love she was able to break out of the rule of Karma, thus opening a way for all creatures to escape from the cycle of rebirth. In art she is shown receiving souls in the shape of flowers in the heavenly paradise.

Datin A god often invoked in Thamudic (old north Arabian) inscriptions. Neither his name nor his function are clearly understood: it has been suggested that the name might mean 'he who seizes', or that the root meaning is 'fertility', 'abundance'.

Debata   Among the Toba-Batak in Sumatra, this word is used to denote both an individual god and divine power in general.

Decuma → Parcae

Dedun (Dewden)   Egyptian god, lord and giver of incense. To the monarch, Dedun brings the peoples and riches of southern lands. He was usually portrayed in human guise, but, like → Arsnuphis, he could also assume the form of a lion.

Deive   Lithuanian appellation for divinity; certain stones which were the object of veneration were called *deyves*. With the coming of Christianity, the word came to mean a heathen deity or a fairy of some kind.

Dema-deities   A.E. Jensen has proposed this label for a category of mythical primeval beings who are revered in primitive · planter-cultures as bringers of these cultures. They occupy a midway position between gods and men. It is to their death that men owe the first cultivable plants. In this connection, the myth of the maiden Hianuwele is particularly well-known. The word *dema* is taken from the language of the Marindanim who live in New Guinea.

Demeter (abbreviated form Deo)   Greek goddess of the earth and of fertility, daughter of → Kronos and of → Rheia. While searching for her daughter → Persephone, stolen from her by → Hades, she was well received in Attika, and showed her thanks by teaching the king's son Triptolemos how to organise his fields and planting. Her attribute is the ear of corn. Her epithet Melissa (= bee) indicates her maternal and nourishing function. According to Hesiod, her liasion with Iason produced Plutos, the god of

riches and the epitome of all the gifts of the earth. Her main feast was the Thesmophoria, a fertility rite from which men were excluded; here, living piglets, snakes and pine-cones (as phallic symbols) were thrown into Demeter's cave so that the generative power of the earth might be enhanced. The mysteries enacted in honour of Demeter at Eleusis took place in a shrine which was accessible only to initiates, who were bound by solemn vows to secrecy.

Deng Divine progenitor of the Dinka people in the Sudan. With his club he generates lightning, thus bringing rain and fertility. It is in Deng that the universal spirit has revealed himself to humankind.

Dercetius A mountain-god venerated in ancient Hispania.

Dev (pl. dev.k) In Armenian belief, spirit beings corresponding to the Iranian → daēvas. They were held to be immortal; they lived in ruins and appeared to man in various guises. The → ays formed a special category. With the coming of Christianity, the word *dev* came to mean the old pagan gods.

Deva (Sanskrit = heavenly, divine) The general Vedic appellation for what is divine. According to the Rigveda there are 33 devas. In Hinduism, the word is used for a certain category of traditional gods, whose significance falls far short of the national gods like → Śiva or → Viṣṇu. The Mahābhārata speaks of 3333 gods. Among the devas are the → Ādityas who rule the heavens, the → Rudra who control the atmosphere and the → Vasus who are of the earth. In the original Vedic scheme of things the devas were immortals; in the post-Rigveda period they are part of creation; and in Jainism and Buddhism the gods are subject to the law of Karman like other creatures. In Buddhist texts, the devas appear almost exclusively as disciples or servitors of → Gautama Buddha.

Devaputra ('son of the gods') In Buddhism, a designation for gods, otherwise unnamed, of lower rank. The term is also sometimes used pejoratively for the gods of Hinduism.

Devel (or Del) This is what the gipsies call their highest being. Contact with Christianity led to a distinction between *baro* (or *phuro*) *devel*, 'great' or 'old' god, and *tikno* (or *tarno*) *devel*, 'small' or 'young' god: the latter being Christ. The word *devel* is cognate with Sanskrit *deva* = god.

Devi In Indian religions, the designation of female deities, which may be incarnations of natural phenomena (e.g. → Uṣas) or hypostatizations (e.g. → Vāc). The spouse of → Śiva is designated Devi, though she is usually called → Durgā or Mahādevī, i.e. 'great goddess'.

Dharana → Pārśva

Dharma (Dharman in the Rigveda) Originally, the appellation for the inner 'law' (dharma) which determines conduct; subsequently, the personification of this law. Dharma then becomes a kind of → Prajāpati or world creator. As Dharmarāja, blue-skinned and armed with a club, he takes the place of → Yama.

Dharmadhatuvāgīśvara A form of the bodhisattva → Mañjuśrī. He is white-skinned, with four faces and six arms, and he sits in a posture of blessed grace on the moon above a double lotus. In his specific mandala he is called → Mañjughoṣa.

Dharmapāla ('protector of the teaching'; Chinese, Hu Fa) In Buddhism, especially in Tibetan Buddhism, divine beings who are supposed to protect the faithful from evil demons. The → Caturmahārājas can also appear in this capacity.

Dhritarāṣtra (in Pali, Dhatarattha; in Chinese, Chi Guo) One of the four Buddhist guardians of the world (→ Caturmahārājas). He is specifically entrusted with the East. His allotted colour is white; he holds a mandoline, and is lord of the divine musicians (→ Gandharvas).

Dhruva ('the constant one', 'the fixed one') In Indian mythology the Pole Star, belonging to the group of gods known as the → Vasus. In Vedic times, the Pole Star was invoked in the marriage ceremony as a symbol of constancy.

Dhyāni-Bodhisattvas The five meditative and world-creating powers, the spiritual sons of the five → Dhyāni-Buddhas: → Sāmantabhadra ('rich in blessings on all sides'), → Vajrapāni ('bearer of the thunderbolt'), → Ratnapāni ('bearer of the jewel'), → Avalokiteśvara, and → Viśvapāni ('in whose hand all things are').

Dhyāni-Buddhas The five 'meditating' Buddhas who arose from the primeval Buddha (→ Adibuddha), and who are classified in terms of heavenly quarters, colours, seasons, magic formulae and phonological divisions of the Devanagari script. Individually, they are named as → Vairocana, → Akṣobhya, → Ratnasambhava, → Amitābha and → Amoghasiddhi. These heavenly Buddhas are, in a certain sense, the ineffable body of the dharma, while the five 'human' Buddhas who appear on earth during our age form its manifest and material emanation. The term Dhyāni-Buddha is being gradually replaced by 'tathāgata' ('the perfected one', '(having) thus fared').

Diana Ancient Italian goddess of woods and forests; in Rome and Latium, she was also held to be the protectress of virginity, and she was worshipped as the moon-goddess. Her name is derived from Diviana = the shining one (female). As goddess of the federal cult of the Latins she had a temple on the Aventine Hill. Tales from Greek myth about the divine huntress → Artemis were taken over by the Romans and applied to Diana.

Dian-Cecht In ancient Ireland, a god of healing who could heal wounds miraculously. When the god → Nuadu lost his hand in battle, Dian-Cecht was able to fit him with a silver one.

Dieva dēli ('sons of god')   In Latvian myth, two, sometimes three heavenly beings, sons of the sky-god → Dievs. They mow the heavenly meadows on which the daughters of the sun (→ Saules meitas) then rake up the hay. In the heavenly bath-house they pour water on the heated stones.

Dievini   In Latvian belief, a body of minor gods who are entrusted with looking after houses.

Dievs   Latvian sky-god, who appears in mythology as a sort of well-to-do farmer. He wears a cap, and has a sword at his side. Sometimes he is mounted on a fine horse, at other times he is shown riding in a wagon. There is a detailed description of how he and his sons (→ Dieva dēli) set free the sun and her daughters (→ Saule).

Dii Mauri   The 'Moorish gods' mentioned in Latin inscriptions in North Africa, who are almost never named; they were supposed to be 'salutares' (redemptory), 'immortales' (immortal) and 'augusti' (exalted).

Díke (Greek = usage, manner)   Personification of righteousness, belonging to the → Horae. Aeschylos shows us the prosperous sinner coming to grief on the rock of Díke.

Dimme   Sumerian female demon of puerperal fever and diseases of infants, often known as 'daughter of → An'. She corresponds to the Akkadian → Lamaštu.

Diomédes   One of the most celebrated Greek heroes in the Trojan Wars: probably in origin an ancient war-god in Argos. This would explain why he is presented in the Iliad as an opponent equal in birth, if not superior to → Ares and → Aphrodíte. He is regarded as the founder of several towns in southern Italy, where he was subsequently revered as a god.

Diónysos   Greek god of fertility, of wine and drunkenness. His name is taken to mean 'son of Zeus'. His original homeland seems to have been Thrace and/or Asia Minor; his alternative name, Bakchos (Latin → Bacchus) may be of Lydian origin. According to the myth, his mother → Semele died when her lover → Zeus revealed himself to her in all his divine majesty as a bolt of lightning. Diónysos has several epithets; thus, Bromios ('thunderer') and Lyaios ('the deliverer' of men from their cares). First and foremost, however, he is the god who created the vine and caused milk and honey to flow from nature. His cult was tumultuous, ecstatic and orgiastic. Women (maenads or Bacchae) distracted by his influence ran and danced through the woods waving torches and thyrsus staves. The thyrsus staff entwined with ivy and vine and with a pine cone at the tip was the main attribute of the god; theriomorphically he was visualized as a goat or a bull, both of them symbols of animal fertility. In dionysiac processions a phallus was borne along. Dionysos was seen as a god who dies and is resurrected; and his entry into Athens on a ship on wheels was construed as a return from the underworld. In the later cult of Orphism he was equated with → Zagreus.

Dioskúroi   (Greek = 'sons of Zeus')   The twin brothers Kastor and Polydeukes, a pair with many parallels in the mythology of other Indo-Germanic peoples: e.g. in India, the Aśvins, and among the German tribes the → Alcis. They came to live with men and helped them in battle and when they were in peril on the sea. In their cosmic function as sons of heaven they were thought of as theriomorphic; the Greeks called them *leukippoi* = having white steeds. Their cult has also an astral aspect, and they figure in the Zodiac as Gemini, the Twins.

Dīpamkara ('Lighter of lamps') A Buddha who preceded → Gautama. In East Asia, the concept of a triad of Buddhas took root and became very popular: Dīpamkara for the past age, Sakyamuni (= Gautama) for the present, and → Maitreya for the future. The Chinese name for Dīpamkara is Ran Deng Fo.

Discordia → Eris

Disir (Old Norse; Old High German *idisi*) Collective appellation for certain goddesses of fertility and destiny in Germanic mythology. The *disir* sacrifice (*disablot*) performed in autumn, recalls the cults of vegetation gods and goddesses. These goddesses were also supposed to be helpful as midwives, and in this function → Freyja bears the name '*dis* of the Vanir' (Vanadis). Among the West Germans, the *disir* took over the role of goddesses of destiny and fate, as well as that of goddesses of battle (cf. the first Merseburg Zauberspruch). In the Edda, → Valkyries and → Norns are described as *disir*.

Dis Páter Roman god of the underworld, and giver of riches. In Rome, he was venerated along with Proserpina (→ Persephóne). It was in his honour that the *ludi Tarentini* were celebrated every hundred years. Dis Pater corresponds to the Greek → Hades.

Diti Ancient Indian goddess: she who gives us what we wish for. In order to avenge her sons (→ Daityas), killed or banished by Indra, she was to bear a son who would slay him: but Indra split the embryo into seven pieces which became the → Maruts.

Diwe Gigantic anthropophagous monsters in Iranian folklore; they have animals' faces and horns but they can assume many other forms. The name is connected with the → Daēvas.

Di-ya and Tian-long A pair of Chinese gods. On the one hand, they appear as servants of the god of literature, Wen Chang; on the other hand, all creatures are said to have risen from their union. Tian-long's name contains the word for 'heaven', *tian* while Di-ya is also referred to as Di-mu = Earth-mother.

Di-zang Chinese → Bodhisattva and ruler over hell, from which he seeks to rescue men. He is thus a kind of guide of souls, who leads anyone who trusts in him to the shore of wisdom. In origin, he may well have been an earth divinity.

Djall The Albanian name for the devil, cognate with Latin *diabolus*. Another name for the devil in Albanian is *dreqi*, from the Latin *draco* = dragon, snake.

Djata (also called Putir = earth) . A goddess of the Ngadju-Dayak in Borneo. Her original name was Tambon = water-snake, and it is in this form that she appears to men. She lives in the underworld, and crocodiles are her subjects. Djata is the female counterpart to → Mahatala; in ceremonial chants they both appear in tandem as 'the water-snake which is also rhinoceros-bird'.

Djebauti (Zebauti) Egyptian local god in the form of a heron perched on a pole. He was later absorbed into the falcon-god → Horus.

Dolichénus Syrian god of weather and of war (like → Baal); thereafter, an epithet of → Zeus who was worshipped in the north Syrian town of Doliche. His own cult was transferred to Jupiter, and Roman troops spread it across Asia Minor into the Danube area. He was represented as a bearded man standing on the back of a bull; his attributes were a double-headed axe and a cluster of lightning flashes.

Donbittir The Ossetian god of waters and of fish: accordingly he is invoked by fishermen.

Dong-yo Da-di ('Great Emperor of the Eastern Peak')´ In Chinese mythology, the helper of the sky-god → Yu-di. He is a kind of cabinet minister in divine government, and within his competence falls supervision of all areas of human life. It is also in his department that the times for birth and death of all creatures are laid down.

Doris → Okeaninai

Druden (Truden; Gothic *trudan*, Old Norse *trotha* = tread, push) Drude (pl. Druden) is a term, particularly widespread in south Germany and Austria, for a female demon which harries you in sleep (in this, similar to the → Alp) or casts evil spells. The word means 'ghost' in Middle High German, and it has become synonymous with *Hexe* = witch. In folklore the pentagram (*Drudenfusz* in German) is regarded as a protective charm against evil spirits.

Drug In the form *druh* a designation for a class of demons, dating back to Vedic times. In Iranian religion, interpreted as 'falsehood' and assigned to → Ahriman, whose hypostases they become. They dwell in a dark cave. Drug may also simply mean 'demon of falsehood'.

Dryads (Greek *drys* = oak-tree) Female spirits of nature who live in trees (→ Nymphs) in Greek mythology. The fate of such a tree-nymph is closely connected with that of the tree she inhabits.

Dua Egyptian god, whose name is interpreted as meaning 'the morning one', 'the matutinal'. He is the god of toiletry, who washes the king's face and gives him a shave. According to the Pyramid texts, he also plays a part in the so-called magical 'mouth-opening' ceremony, by means of which the dead regain the use of their organs.

Duamutef ('who praises his mother') One of the four sons of → Horus, who were entrusted with the protection of a corpse. The corpse's stomach fell within the jurisdiction of the jackal-headed Duamutef. The east was the heavenly quarter allotted to him.

bDud In the ancient Tibetan Bon religion, an appellation for heavenly spirits who were later degraded by Lamaism to the status of devils. The bDud were black and lived in a black castle.

Duillae Ancient Hispanic goddesses, occurring in pairs. They were nature goddesses who protected vegetation. They have been compared with the Gallic → Matres, whose role seems to be very similar.

Dumuzi (Sumerian = true son) Usually given the Hebrew/Aramaic form of his name – Tammuz. Old Mesopotamian god of vegetation, representative of the male principle (as → Ištar was of the female). One of his epithets is Ama'ušumgal ('whose mother is a heavenly dragon'). Dumuzi was supposed to be the lover and the spouse of → Inanna, who handed him over to the demons of the underworld, where he then ruled as king. His descent to the underworld and his return therefrom symbolize the natural cycle of decay and reawakening in the vegetable world. The cult of Tammuz spread beyond the confines of Mesopotamia (cf. Ezekiel 8: 14).

Dumuziabzu (Sumerian 'true child of Abzu' → Apsu) Old Mesopotamian goddess who formed part of → Enki's group in Old Babylonian mythology. Her main function was that of tutelary goddess of the town of Kinirša.

Dur Kassite god corresponding to the Babylonian god of the underworld → Nergal.

Durgā (Sanskrit = 'she who is difficult of access') Hindu goddess of the Great Mother type, particularly revered by the broad masses in Bengal, Assam and the Deccan. She is the spouse of → Śiva. In her friendly aspect she is → Gauri; and as Annapūrṇā – represented with rice-bowl and spoon – she is a giver of food. In her fearsome aspect she appears as Caṇḍi ('the cruel one') or as → Kālī ('she who is black'). Finally she is also Tārā ('she who sets free') and merges into the figure of → Pārvatī. These names indicate that Durgā is a composite figure incorporating various goddesses, once independent, who gradually merged with her cult. Her main feast (Durgapūjā) is celebrated in the autumn.

Dusares (Duš-Šara) The chief god of the Nabataeans. The name means 'he (the god) of eš-Šara', this being the area between the Red Sea and the Dead Sea. In the Hellenistic period the god was equated with the Greek → Dionysos, and represented with a vine. The sacred image of Dusares was originally a black stone in Petra. The panther and the eagle were sacred to him.

Dvārapāla ('gate-keeper') Buddhist deities: in Mandalas they guard the 'gates' or keep watch at the entrances to temples and monasteries. They are represented as → Yakṣa-demons, or as mighty warriors in splendid armour. In China they are known as *er jiang* ('the two commanders'), named respectively Hong and Ha, though they form only one single being representing the two halves of the absolute: Ha represents the matrix world of the elements, while Hong represents the diamond world of the spirit.

Dyaus (Dyaus pitar) Ancient Indian sky-god and father of the gods, usually mentioned in association with the earth goddess → Prithivī. Together, Dyaus and Prithivī are thought of as bull and cow. The sun-god → Sūrya is regarded as the son of Dyaus.

E

Ea Babylonian god corresponding to the Sumerian → Enki. It has been suggested that the name means 'water-house', but this is not generally accepted by scholars. Ea's realm was the sweet-water ocean under the earth, and his temple was in the house of → Apsu. He was the god of wisdom and of the magician's art, the great artist whose hands formed man. He was taken over by the Hittites under the name of A'as, and was regarded by them as the keeper of the tablets of destiny and as 'king of good counsel'.

Eacus Old Hispanic god venerated in the area of present-day Castile. He was equated with → Jupiter Solutorius, a Roman god by whom Eacus was finally completely absorbed.

Eate (also known as Egata) Basque god of fire and storms, whose voice may be heard in advance of a hail-storm or a destructive fire.

Ebech A Canaanite mountain god who was overcome by → Inanna.

Ebisu → Shichi-Fukujin

Echidna (Greek = snake) Demonic monster in Greek mythology, half-woman, half-snake. From her coupling with Typhon there arose → Kérberos and the → Chimaira.

Egeria Nymph associated with springs and wells in Roman mythology, who gradually assumed the functions of a goddess of birth.

Legend has it that she was the counsellor of King Numa Pompilius to whom she came by night to reveal the will of the gods.

Egres (Äkräs) God of vegetation and fertility venerated by the ancient Finns, especially in Karelia. He was first and foremost the protector and the donator of turnips. The twin fruit of the turnip was his symbol and was known as 'holy äkräs'.

Eileithyia (Latin Ilithyia) Greek goddess of birth, whose cult was particularly widespread on Crete and in Lakonia. Her name probably means 'she who comes to help'. She was supposed to be the daughter of → Zeus and of → Hera. Later, → Artemis took over the functions of Eileithyia.

Eirene (Latin Irene) Greek goddess of peace, one of the three → Horae, the daughter of Zeus and of → Themis. In Athens she was worshipped from the end of the fifth century BC onwards. At the feast of Synoikia bloodless sacrifice was made to her.

Ek → Bacab

Ekajaṭā ('she who has but one shock of hair') One of the terrible deities in Buddhism, whose appearance strikes fear into men. She is usually represented as having one head and three eyes; she is blue in colour, her face is distorted with rage, and she wears a tiger's skin round her loins. If she has two arms, her attributes are a serrated knife and skulls; if she is shown with four arms, she is holding in her right hands sword and arrow, in her left hands bow and skulls. She is also known as Ugra-Tārā ('the terrible → Tārā'). Those who worship her can look forward to being suitably rewarded. A specific form of the goddess is → Vidyujjvālākarāli. In Tibetan, Ekajaṭā is called Ral-gCig-ma.

Ekchuah The Maya god of travelling merchants. In specialist literature he is known as god M. He is represented as black in colour with a dangling lower lip and a long scorpion's tail.

Ekhi (Eguzki) A Basque designation for the sun and for its personification, who is said to be a daughter of Mother Earth (→ Lur). Sorcerers and evil spirits lose their potency when a ray of sunshine falls upon them.

El An appellation among the ancient Syrians and Canaanites for a deity, known in south Arabia as *Il*. The name was also used to designate the supreme god. There is some disagreement among scholars as to what the name means precisely: some opt for 'the mighty one', 'the powerful one', others prefer 'the first one'. In the mythology of Ugarit, El appears as father of the gods and 'creator of creatures'. He also has the epithets 'creator of the earth' (Qone'ars) and 'bull', a reference to his significance as a fertility symbol. The god has his throne 'at the source of the rivers'. In Palmyra he was known by the name of Elqonera; and as 'he who causes the springs to flow' he was equated with → Poseidon.

Elagabal (Greek Heliogabalos or Elaiagabalos) The local god of the Syrian town of Emesa (the modern Homs). His cult centred round a black stone shaped like a bee-hive. The god's name seems to be derived from Elah-gabal ('lord of the mountain'). In the Hellenistic period he was also connected with the sun-god → Hélios. The fact that his symbolic creature is the eagle is further proof of a solar connection.

Elben (German plural form: also as Alben; Old Saxon *alf* (sing.); Old Norse *álf, álfar*) Nature spirits in Germanic mythology. In Snorri's Edda, a distinction is made between *álfar* who are light and beautiful in colour, and *álfar* who are dark. The *álfar* were the objects of a cult, and this distinguishes them from the dwarfs. They were seen as spirits of fertility and as protective spirits; often again their behaviour suggests souls of the dead. They may suffer a transition into a demonic aspect, and then they are bringers of sickness and ill-fortune (→ Alp). The semantic field is widened through contamination with the word 'Elfen' (= English 'elves') which makes its appearance in the eighteenth century in German literature.

Elel Malevolent demonic being in the beliefs of the Puelche Indians in Argentina. He causes storms, illnesses and death; he also plays a part in initiation ceremonies.

Eljon Old Syrian deity. The name is derived from the root *alaj* ('to go up, be up'). Philon of Byblos calls him Eliun; in Greek form Hypsistos ('the most lofty'). In the Old Testament, the name Eljon can be taken as identical with → Jahwe, as the latter is called *el eljon* ('most high God') in Genesis 14:22.

Elkunirša The name of this Hittite god probably means 'El (god) creator of the earth'. In one myth, → Ašertu is presented as his spouse. There is good evidence for the thesis that this god was taken over from a Canaanite cult.

Ellel (also Ellilus) A Hittite god, taken over from the Babylonians (→ Enlil) and very largely equated with the Hurrian father of the gods (→ Kumarbi).

Elohim (Semitic → *el*) Common expression for 'God' in the Old Testament. The word is plural in form, but is also used in the singular: 'god' or 'gods'. Pagan gods are thus designated, as well as the God of Israel (→ Jahwe). Elohim is the omnipotent God, the creator of heaven and earth.

Elves (cf. German *Elben*) The word was taken over from English and used in German literature in the form *Elben*, to denote certain friendly female spirits. They are fond of music and dancing, and are in general well-disposed towards human beings. By analogy with the king of the dwarfs, Alberich, their ruler is called king of the elves. The Danish form is *elverkonge*, which went into celebrated poems by Herder and Goethe as 'Erlkönig'.

Emeli-hin A name for God used by the Tuareg in West-Central Sudan. The word means 'my lord', and the 1st person singular marker *hin* may be replaced by the 1st person plural *neneg*; thus *emeli-neneg* = our lord; similarly *emeli n terna* = lord of power.

Emma-o (or Emma-ten) In Japanese Buddhism, → Yama in his capacity as King of Hell. He rides on a water-buffalo, and bears aloft a standard with a human head. He may also be depicted as a stern judge holding a tablet or a book in which he enters the sins of those who have been condemned to be reborn in purgatory (the eschatological state of purification) and determines the extent of their punishment.

Empung Luminuut Female deity of the Minahasa tribe in North Celebes (Sulawesi). She arose from the earth or was sweated out of a stone. Impregnated by the west wind, she gave life to the sun-god Toar. Mother and son separate; and when they meet they fail to recognize each other and marry. From their union are born the race of gods and the human race.

Empusa A female monster in ancient Greek popular belief. She could appear as a beautiful maiden, but then again as a hideous ghost with the feet of an ass. Usually, she forms part of → Hekáte's retinue.

En An Old Illyrian god whose name lives on in the Albanian word for Thursday. With the coming of Christianity, En was demoted to demonic status.

Enbilulu Sumerian god of irrigation and agriculture. In Babylon he was regarded as the son of → Ea, and finally figured as one of the fifty names of → Marduk.

Endouellicus (Endouolicus) A god venerated in Lusitania (present-day Portugal), for the sick a source of oracles which could lead to their recovery. At some of his shrines pigs are depicted, and it is possible that these animals were sacrificed to him: equally, however, they may have purely chthonic significance, serving to emphasize the god's function as a god of the underworld. On some of his altars a palm tree is represented.

Enki (Sumerian = 'lord of the earth' or 'lord of the nether-regions')   In Sumeria, the ruler of the sweet-water ocean which was believed to lie under the earth, and of the life-giving springs and wells. In addition, he is god of wisdom and of magic. In myth he appears as the creator of vegetation and of human beings. On cylinder seals he is shown sitting enthroned in his temple surrounded by flowing waters; jets of water come from his shoulders. The number specific to him is forty. In Akkadian, → Ea corresponds to Enki.

Enlil (Sumerian = 'lord (of the) wind') In Akkadian as Ellil, in Greek as Illinos. The supreme god in the Sumerian pantheon. He is 'King of lands'; because of his strength he is called Rimu ('wild ox'), and another of his epithets is *kur-gal* ('great mountain'). His weapon is the storm-flood. Enlil's father is the sky-god → An, his spouse is → Ninlil. As lord of the tablets of destiny he can determine the course of the world. He is not always well-disposed towards human beings; and to their misfortune he sends them the Deluge and the monster → Labbu. As a symbol of his power Enlil bears a head-dress decorated with horns (the so-called horned crown). His specific number is fifty.

Enmešarra   The name of this Sumerian god means 'lord of all the *me*'. The word *me* seems to denote the divine rules and regulations. In one very old list of gods, Enmešarra actually takes precedence over the sky-god → An. His function makes him a god of the underworld.

Eos   Greek goddess of the dawn, sometimes also known as Hemeras (= day). She is the 'rosy-fingered', youthful and beautiful, sister of the sun (→ Hélios) and the moon (→ Seléne). Every morning she drives the team of horses which pull her chariot up from the depths of the ocean. When she weeps for her son Memnon who fell at Troy, her tears fall on the earth as dew. Her Roman counterpart is → Auróra.

Epaphos Son of → Zeus in hs taurine metamorphosis, and → Io (in the form of a cow). A later Greek tradition makes Epaphos the progenitor of the Egyptians.

Ephialtes → Aloádes

Epona (Celtic = the big mare) A goddess worshipped in Gaul, usually shown riding a horse. Her attribute is a cornucopia, sometimes also a dog. It is uncertain whether the horse and the dog are to be interpreted as dead animals, and Epona herself as a goddess of the underworld. The cornucopia also suggests a fertility cult.

Eranoranhan The protector or tutelary god of men on the island of Hierro in the Canaries; the goddess Moneiba played the same part for women. The god lived on one rock, the goddess on another.

Erato One of the nine → Muses. She is the muse of lyric poetry, especially of love poetry, and she is usually portrayed holding a stringed instrument in her hands.

Ereškigal A Sumerian goddess of the underworld; one of her epithets is 'great earth'. She is the sister and underworld counterpart of → Inanna/Ištar, who dwells in the lofty regions of heaven. Her spouse is → Nergal.

Erge In Basque folklore – and attested in myth – a spirit which takes men's lives.

Erinyes (Greek pl.; sing. Erinys) Avenging goddesses of the underworld in Greek mythology. They arose from the drops of blood soaked up by the earth (→ Gaia) when Kronos mutilated his father. The Greek tragedians call them 'the daughters of the night'. They are three in number, and bear the names Allekto ('she who is unremitting'), Teisiphone ('she who avenges murder') and Megaira ('she who is envious'). With snake-bedecked heads and waving threatening torches they come from the underworld to pursue all sinners, especially those who have killed members of their own family or close relatives. They were later presented in more favourable guise as the *Semnai* ('the venerable ones') or the *Eumenides* ('the well-disposed'). In Rome, they were known as the Furiae ('the mad ones'), furies.

Eris Greek goddess of dissension and strife, sister of the war-god → Ares. Hesiod makes a distinction between the fearsome Eris, the instigator of enmity and affliction, and the benevolent Eris who stimulates men to engage in competition. One of the best-known scenes in Greek mythology shows us Eris throwing an apple (the apple of contention) on which is written 'for the fairest', among the wedding guests, and thus provoking a quarrel among the goddesses present. Roman writers took Eris over under the name of Discordia (= dissension, discord).

Eriu (Eire) Name for Ireland; personified as the goddess of the island. Her husband is → Mac Gréine.

Erlik Among the Altaic peoples of southern Siberia, the adversary of God, he who led the first men to commit sin. His heaven is destroyed, and he himself is banished to the underworld.

Éros Greek god of love, the son of → Aphrodíte and → Arés. Hesiod hymns his praises as the most beautiful of the gods. In popular belief and in classical art he is shown as the winged youth with his bow and arrows which he fires into the hearts of gods and men, thus awakening them to love. He also fosters friendship between men and boys, and this is why the Spartans paid homage to him before battle. His cult in Thespiai in Boeotia, was of very ancient standing: here he was worshipped in the form of a stone. His power to arouse and move the world led the Orphic cults to recognize him as creator of the world. → Ámor is the corresponding figure among the Romans.

Erótes Boy-like gods of love in late Classical art; known in Latin as *amoretti*. They were taken over in the Renaissance and remained popular through the Baroque and Rococo periods in the guise of *putti* or genii.

Erra (Irra) Babylonian god of plague. Stung by the demonic → Sebettu, he brings plague and other misfortunes to mankind. His adviser, who succeeds in pacifying him, is → Išum. It is not certain whether there is any connection between the Akkadian word Erra and the Hittite → Jarri.

Es Sky-god of the Ket people who live on the Yenisei in Siberia. He is invisible, but is portrayed as an old man with a long black beard. He is the creator of the world and he kneaded the first humans out of clay: whatever he threw with his right hand towards the left became a man, and what he threw with his left hand towards the right became a woman.

Esenchebis The Greek name really means 'Isis in Chembis'; and refers to the goddess → Isis, who was worshipped on the island of Chembis, as well as elsewhere (e.g. at Bubastis).

Ešmun Phoenician god of healing, whose cult was widespread in Cyprus, Sardinia and North Africa (Carthage). He was thought of as a

handsome youth, and, as such, connected with →
Melqart.

Estanatlehi A goddess of the Navajos. She
used maize meal and the dust from her breasts to
create the progenitors of the Navajo people. Then
she became ruler in the land of the setting sun
(the land of the dead) whence she dispenses
whatever is good to mankind. War and illness
come from the east.

Esus Gallic god, whose name remains un-
explained (though not for want of suggestions).
The classical writer, Lukianos, reports the god's
desire for human blood. Two altars have been
found which show him using an axe against a
tree: it is not known exactly why. Equally
mysterious is the bull accompanied by three birds
(cranes?) which seems to be associated with him.

Etemmu ('dead man's ghost') The Babylonians believed that the soul of a dead person
who remained uninterred, wandered about as a
ghost: it could turn nasty and harm people.

Eunomía ('heavenly order') One of the →
Horae, who were entrusted with the job of
looking after the gates of heaven and of Olympus.

Euphrosine → Charites

Euros Greek god of the wind which blows
from the south-east. His epithet is Argestes, i.e.
'he who clears up'. Like the other wind-gods
associated with different quarters of the heavens
he is a son of → Eos.

Eutérpe ('she who brings joy') One of the
nine → Muses. She is portrayed playing a double

flute, thus representing lyrical poetry accompanied by flutes.

Evan A being belonging to the → Las in Etruscan religion. Usually thought of as female, it is sometimes portrayed as masculine. It has been suggested that it may be a mythic personification of personal immortality.

F

Fafnir ('gripper', 'clasper') In Germanic mythology, a demonic being who killed his father and then, in dragon form, guarded the great golden treasure of the Nibelungs, until slain by Sigurd (Siegfried).

Fagus Pyrenean tree-god venerated in Roman times. As the name suggests, the tree in question was the beech, worshipped as divine.

Fairy Fairies were thought of as nature spirits of a lower order – to some extent, of demonic character – who dwelt in springs, forests and caves. They were, in general, well disposed towards human beings, though they were not slow to punish those who failed to show gratitude. Such beings were called elves among the Germanic tribes, while the Baltic peoples knew them as → Laume. The word 'fairy' comes via Old French *feie*, *fée* from Latin *fatua* = (female) seer, and *fatum* = fate, destiny. In association with the Greek → Moirai and the Roman → Parcae, three fairies were thought to be the goddesses of fate.

Fama Roman personification of rumour. She plays no part at all in Roman religion, and is purely a product of Latin literary allegory. Vergil pictures her as a horrible creature with several tongues and babbling mouths. The Greek author Hesiod, on the other hand, makes her a goddess under the name of Pheme.

Faro Sky and water god of the Bambara (in West Africa). Faro is an androgynous being who is made pregnant by the oscillations of the universe and thereupon gives birth to twins who are the progenitors of the human race. Faro also gives mankind language and tools for fishing and agriculture. Faro's sacred colour is white.

Fatit (Albanian pl.; sing. *fati*) Female beings associated with individual destiny, in south Albanian popular belief. On the third day after a birth, three of them approach the cradle and determine the child's fate. They are also known as *miren* (from Greek → Moirai). They are visualized as riding on butterflies.

Fauna Old Italic goddess of fields and woods; she appears as either sister or wife of Faunus. As she promotes fertility in the fields and among livestock, thereby blessing the farmer, she was revered as Bona Dea ('good goddess').

Faunus Old Italic god of nature, protector of shepherds and peasants. As Innus ('he who makes fruitful') he increases the herds. He was supposed to be the son of → Picus, and grandson of → Satúrnus. If he was valued as an oracular source, he was rather more feared because of his goblin-like propensities. It was only after his blending in the popular mind with the Greek figure of → Pan, that he was furnished with horns and goat-legs. His temple was situated on the Tiber island. At a very early date Faunus was identified with the wolf-god → Lupercus.

Favonius → Zéphyros

Fe'e → Aitu

Fei Lian (also found as Feng Bo) Chinese god of the wind; he lets the winds escape from a large sack. In mythical times he figures as an agitator and trouble-maker, but he is restrained by the 'heavenly archer' (→ Shen Yi). In various myths, Fei Lian is described as a winged dragon with a deer's head and a snake's tail.

Fene Hungarian demon, whose name still crops up in such expressions as 'Fene eat you!' (egye meg a fene). The word also means a place where demonic beings hang out.

Fenrir (Fenrisulfr = the wolf Fenrir) Lupine demon in Nordic mythology, the son of the god → Loki and the female giant Angrboda. His siblings are the → Midgard-snake and the Queen of the underworld → Hel. When the Aesir (→ As) began to fear Fenrir they fettered him with the unbreakable cord Gleipnir; in the process, the god → Tyr lost a hand which he had put into the monster's jaws in order to deceive it. When the world is being destroyed (Ragnarök) the wolf breaks free and kills → Odin.

Fidi Mukullu God of creation among the Bena Lulua (Zaire). The sun is said to have come forth from his right cheek, the moon from his left. He taught men to use bow and arrow, and gave them iron and foodstuffs.

Finn The hero of a very extensive cycle of tales in Ireland (Leinster). The saga centres round the red deer. Finn's progeny are called the Oisin, i.e. deer-calves; one of his wives, Saar, is a hind, and he himself can appear as man, dog or stag, according to how he turns his hood. He can also appear as a manifestation of King Mongan, who is a son of the sea-god → Manannan.

Fjörgyn A north Germanic goddess. In the Völuspa she appears as the mother of → Thor. Nothing is known of any cult that may have surrounded her. The etymology of her name would suggest that she is a mountain or forest goddess, and she was probably revered as a goddess of fertility.

Fjörgynn A god mentioned in Snorri's Edda as being the father of → Frigg. Nothing further is known about him, but it has been suggested that he may be a god of thunderstorms whose origins go back to pre-Germanic times.

Flóra Roman goddess of growing corn and blossoming flowers, originally worshipped by the Oscans and the Sabines. In Rome, her feast (Floralia) was celebrated from 28 April to the beginning of May. It was an uninhibited and somewhat immoral popular revel; Flora herself was known as *meretrix* = whore, but the lasciviousness was probably intended to promote fecundity, and has also been interpreted as a vernal counter-thrust against the world of the dead.

Fo The Chinese name for → Buddha. Specially revered is Shi-jia-mu-ni, i.e. Šakyamuni (→ Gautama Buddha), the 'great hero' (da xiong). Iconographically he is shown seated, without any kind of decoration, in the diamond posture: the right foot on the left knee, the left foot on the right knee. He wears the ancient Indian monk's robe and in his left hand there is usually a begging-bowl. His particular characteristics are the *uṣṇiṣa* (turban), the *ūrṇā* (a kind of divine eye) and extended ear-lobes. In art, a trinity of Buddhas is often represented – Shi-jia-mu-ni, Ran Deng Fo (→ Dīpamkara) and → Mi-lo Fo.

Fomore (Fomore) In Irish tradition, the demons who are the adversaries of the gods (→ Tuatha De Danann). Though the Fomore can count on having the upper hand for a time, they are to be finally defeated in the battle of Mag Tured, and will have to give his harp back to → Dagda.

Forneus It is possible that the name is a parodic version of → Fornjotr. Forneus appears in late medieval literature of magic and necromancy as a demonic being, a spirit from hell or as a sea-monster.

Fornjotr A primeval giant in Germanic mythology, progenitor of the frost-giants. One tradition makes him father of the giants Hler, Logi and Kari, who rule the sea, fire and the wind.

Forseti A Germanic god. It has been suggested that his name means 'he who presides', but the exact meaning is a matter of dispute. According to the Edda he is a son of → Balder, he lives in the shining hall called Glitnir, and he administers justice to men and gods. It is likely that this Nordic Forseti corresponds to the Friesian god Fosite.

Fortúna (also Fors Fortuna) To begin with, the old Roman goddess of women, whose cult

was, in part at least, oracular. First and foremost, however, Fortúna turned into the goddess of good fortune; indeed, she herself, as her name indicates, personifies fortune, luck, which proves effective in a given situation. In Cicero's time she was already being identified with the Greek → Tyché. In art she is portrayed with rudder, cornucopia and globe as attributes. In the Renaissance, Fortuna came back into popular favour as a motif in art – now, however, equipped with a wheel to remind the viewer that luck may not last.

Fravaši (usually translated as 'she who confesses' or 'she who is chosen') In Old Iranian religion, the *fravaši* denoted the spiritual pre-existence of the believer, which watched over him as a protective spirit. As a collective, the *fravaši*s helped → Ahura Mazda to create the world; they foster plants and, as riders armed with spears, they defend heaven. In their capacity as warriors they resemble the Indian → Maruts.

Freyja (Old Norse = mistress, lady) North German goddess of love and fertility; one of her functions is to assist women in childbirth. Her attributes are the necklace called Brisingamen (*brisa* = to shine, glitter; possibly a solar symbol), a falcon cloak, and a chariot drawn by cats. She rides on the boar with golden bristles, Hildeswin. As a daughter of → Njörd she belongs to the race of the → Vanir; in due course, however, she joins the Aesir (→ As) and becomes the wife of Od (variant of → Odin). When she loses him she weeps golden tears for him. On occasion, she becomes indistinguishable from → Frigg. Cf. also → Gefjon.

Freyr (Old Norse, = Lord, master) North Germanic god of thriving crops and peaceful prosperity: the son of → Njörd, brother of → Freyja, and one of the → Vanir. In a temple in Old Uppsala there was a statue of the god in his phallic aspect as god of fecundity. The Swedish royal dynasty of the Ynglinge regarded him as their progenitor. In myth he figures as the owner of the miraculous ship Skidbladnir and golden-bristled boar Gullinborsti. The esteem in which Freyr was held is evident from his epithets such as 'patron of the gods' and 'world-god'.

Frigg (south German Frija, Lombard Frea) Germanic goddess, incorporating on the one hand gross sensuality (she is accused of adultery) and, on the other hand, the maternal principle. Her name is translated both as 'she who is loved' and also as 'spouse'. She protects life and partakes in the wisdom of her husband → Odin. If she had a specific cult nothing is known of it. The Latin *dies veneris* ('day of Venus') was taken over by the Germans as 'Frija's day' (Friday). The historian Paulus Diaconus mentions the goddess as patroness of the Lombards.

Fudo Myoo Japanese god who wields the sword of knowledge in his fight against the hate and the greed which are characteristic of ignorance.

Fufluns Etruscan god corresponding to the Greek → Dionysos. The name may derive from an Indo-Germanic root meaning 'to beget' or 'to swell, overflow'. On an altar in Tarquinia we find the cult name Pacha given to the god.

Fujin God of the wind in Shintoism. He is shown carrying a sack full of winds on his shoulders.

Fukuro kuju (Japanese = luck, riches, long life) Japanese god of good luck, portrayed with an exaggeratedly high cranium. He is often accompanied by a crane and a tortoise as symbols of longevity.

Fulla ('fullness') Germanic goddess, attendant in retinue of → Frigg. The second Merseburg charm makes her Frigg's sister.

Furies → Erinyes

Fu Shen Chinese god of luck. He is usually portrayed in the blue robes of an official, with his son on his arm. Often he forms a triad along with → Shou Lao and → Cai Shen.

Fu-xi The first of the three Chinese cultural heroes; he instituted marriage, and we also have to thank him for teaching us how to fish. He married his sister → Nü-gua, thereby ensuring due balance in the forces of *yin* and *yang*. Nü-gua's attribute is the compass while Fu-xi's is the protractor: together the two symbolize the construction of the world – the round heaven and the square earth.

Fylgir (or Fylgjur; Old Norse = female attendants) In Germanic belief, protective spirits attached to individuals. If they choose to appear, it is in the form of a woman or an animal. They were not the object of any sort of cult.

G

God G Maya god, so designated in specialist literature, who represents → Kukulcan in his solar aspect: possibly the nocturnal stage of that aspect.

Gabija (Gabieta, Gabeta) A spirit of fire in Lithuanian mythology, which sometimes appears as a goddess. She was the mistress of the 'holy fire' to whom homage was paid by throwing salt on the fire and saying, 'Holy Gabija, be thou satisfied!'

Gabjauja Lithuanian goddess of corn, to whom prayers were said for general prosperity and riches. Demoted with the coming of Christianity to the status of an evil spirit.

Gabriel (Hebrew = 'the strong one of God') In the Bible, an angel who appears as a messenger from God: first, in Daniel 8: 16-27. In the New Testament, it is he who brings Mary the tidings that God has chosen her to be the mother of his son (Luke 1: 26-28). In Jewish apocalyptic literature he figures as an angel of retribution and death; in Christianity as an archangel together with → Michael, → Raphael and → Uriel. In Islamic tradition he is called Gabra'il, and is at the apex of the angelic host.

Gad A designation for various beneficent divinities in ancient north Arabia. Gad is really a personification of (good) luck, and corresponds to the Greek → Tyché. The name was also used by the Nabataeans for a specific god.

Gaia (Ge = earth) Greek goddess; together with Chaos and → Éros she belongs to the first principles of the cosmos. From her are born heaven (→ Uranós) and sea (→ Pontos). Made pregnant by Uranós, she gives birth to the → Titans and the → Cyclops. Her union with the underworld (Tartaros) results in the birth of the monster → Typhón. It was in Attica alone that Gaia was of religious significance. In Homer, she is invoked in oaths along with the sun (→ Hélios). In art, her beneficent fecundity is often symbolized by attributes such as a cornucopia and the fruits of the earth.

Galla (Akkadian Gallu) Sumerian demon of the underworld. It was by Galla-demons that the god of vegetation → Dumuzi was taken to the underworld.

Gandarewa In the Avesta, a demon living in the water who is constantly trying to swallow the good works of creation; finally he is slain by the hero Keresāspa.

Gandharvas A class of Indian demigods, spirits of nature who inhabit the heaven of → Indra, along with the → Apsaras. According to the Rigveda there was in the very beginnings a Gandharva who united with an Apsara to give birth to the first pair of humans (→ Yama and → Yima). At a later date, unspecified Gandharvas appear at Indra's court as musicians and singers.

Ganeśa (or Ganapati = lord of the host) Indian god of the art of writing and of wisdom: the son of → Pārvatī and → Śiva, whose retinue he leads. He is portrayed as having the head of an elephant, one tusk and a pot belly. He rides on a rat, and in his four hands he holds a thorn, a garland of roses, the broken-off second tusk and a bowl with a rice-cake. On south Indian monuments he wears a crown. In Nepal a form of

Gaṇeśa called Heramba appears, which has five elephant heads; while in Thailand the god is often depicted with four heads and two arms. Gaṇapati was also taken over by Buddhism.

Gaṅgā
The masculine form – Ganges – derives from Greek. Indian river-goddess; she is depicted with two or four arms. In her right hand she holds a water-pot, in her left a lotus. The Gaṅgā is supposed to emerge from one of → Viṣṇu's feet and to flow into the moon and the starry firmament.

Ganymédes
Originally perhaps a demonic guardian of the well of life. In Greek saga he appears as a beautiful youth. → Zeus falls in love with him, and sends his eagle to abduct the youth and bring him to Olympus. There, he becomes the cup-bearer of the gods, who gives them their daily life-giving draught. In the late Hellenistic and Roman periods Ganymede was transferred to the heavens in the shape of Aquarius the Water-bearer.

Gao Yao
(Also known as Ting-jian) Proto-Chinese god of judgment; his familiar animal was the ram which assisted him in the detection of injustice.

Gapn
Old Syrian god who appears as a messenger of → Baal. His name means 'vine'. He is not mentioned in ritual texts.

Garm
(Old Icelandic *Garmr*) Mythical dog which howls and barks before its cave at the onset of Ragnarök, the destruction of the world, and which fights with the god → Tyr in the apocalyptic final battle.

Garmangabi(s) Beneficent goddess of the Sueves (Suebi), a Germanic tribe who lived in the Neckar area. The second component of the name – gabi – is probably cognate with 'give, gift' (German, 'geben, Gabe'), and it figures also in the name of a group of matronly goddesses whose cult was once practised in the Rhineland: Alagabiae, i.e. those who give richly. Cf. also → Gefjon.

Garuḍa (Sanskrit *garut* = wing) The prince of birds in Indian mythology, the enemy of snakes and the most fervent devotee of Viṣṇu, who rides on his back. His anthropomorphic body is golden in colour and has the head, the wings and the claws of an eagle. Garuḍa has been interpreted as a sun symbol. In Buddhism, the Garuḍas are divine bird-like creatures, and → Gautama is said to have been a Garuḍa-king in a former existence.

Gatumdu(g) Sumerian goddess, daughter of the sky-god → An. She was the local mother goddess of Lagaš.

Gaueko In Basque popular belief and mythology the lord of darkness, a spirit of the night. He may on occasion prove friendly and helpful; but he can also appear as a devil. He often manifests himself in the shape of a cow or as a gust of wind.

Gaurī In Indian religion, a good-hearted and sympathetic variant of the Great Mother. She is, as her name suggests, the 'white one', contrasting thereby with the black → Kālī.

Gautama Buddha His real name was Siddharta of the Gautama family (Pali form Gotama); poetically he is also called Šakyamuni – 'the wise man of Šakya race'. He was able to withstand all the temptations put in his way by his adversary → Māra. Gautama became the Buddha ('the enlightened one') who upon entry into Nirvana severs all connection between him and the world and who is then inaccessible even to prayer. In the course of time, however, he was deified and became the → Buddha prototype, the exemplar for all Buddhas, both past and future. The → Bodhisattvas and the → Dhyāni-Buddhas are hypostases of him. His most important symbols are closely connected with his life on earth: the footprints (his presence on earth), the Bodhi-tree (enlightenment), the wheel (the teaching of the way), and the stupa (entry into Nirvana). Images of Buddha are characterized by the *uṣṇīṣa*, the raised portion of the cranium, and the *ūrṇā*, a radiant point (originally a lock of hair) between the eyebrows, signifying enlightment.

Gayomard (Gayō Marta) The first human being in Iranian mythology; his name means 'mortal life'. According to one tradition, it was from his body that the parts of the cosmos were fashioned. According to another version, his seed impregnated the earth from which there then emerged the first man and the first woman. From Gayomard's decomposing body there arose the seven metals. As the first mortal being, this primeval human will be resurrected.

Geb (earlier incorrect reading: Seb) Egyptian earth-god. The name is probably an old word for 'earth', which later fell into disuse; in the Pyramid texts we are told that the dead enter 'geb'. One myth relates how the earth-god copulated with the sky-goddess (→ Nut) to beget the sun, thus becoming 'father of the gods'. The kings of Egypt designated themselves as 'heirs of Geb'. When the god is represented anthropomorphically he is usually wearing the crown of Lower Egypt on his head. Exceptionally he may also be shown with a goose decorating his head (in the script, the goose is his determinative sign).

Gebeleizis Herodotus mentions this god of thunderstorms venerated by the Thracians who lived in the Balkans; he has been identified with → Zalmoxis, but this is a moot point.

Gefjon Germanic goddess belonging to the Aesir (→ As). Her name seems to be connected with the root meaning 'to give' (German *geben*), and she herself lives up to her name by functioning as a goddess of good fortune and prosperity. In Denmark, she herself handles the plough. Among the south Germanic tribes her counterpart may well have been → Garmangabis. And behind both of these goddesses we may well discern the figure of the goddess of fertility → Freyja, who indeed bears the epithet 'Gefjon'.

Genii (pl. of *genius*) Protective spirits who guide human beings. In Etruscan and Roman art they were represented as naked winged youths.

Since the seventeenth century the term has been applied to male and female winged figures; and, in the art of the ancient east, to hybrid beings with the heads of birds who appear in a posture of greeting or who are fertilizing the sacred tree, e.g. on Assyrian relief tablets and, similarly, on Cretan cameos (see illustration). Today, the term denotes ghostly beings endowed with supernatural powers.

Genius Roman deity, a personification of the creative powers invested in man: the female counterpart of Genius is → Júno. Every man was accredited with his own *genius*, representing his male vigour and strength; and under Greek influence this came later to correspond to → Daimon. In the domestic chapels belonging to distinguished Roman families in Pompeii, the *genius* of the *pater familias* is depicted as a snake. The belief that every place has its tutelary spirit, its *genius loci*, is a product of the Roman Empire. → Genii.

Geštinanna (Sumerian = vine of heaven) Old Mesopotamian goddess, sister of the vegetation-god → Dumuzi, and wife of → Ningišzida. The fact that she was equated with the 'book-keeper' of the Babylonian underworld → Bēletsēri, suggests that she too was connected in some way with the nether regions.

Geuš Tašan ('fashioner of cattle') In old Iranian religion the divine creator of cattle, often equated with → Ahura Mazda.

Geuš Urvan (also as Gošurvan, Gošurun) In Old Iranian religion, the heavenly guardian of cattle. In poetry, he himself appears as a cow. The name means 'soul of the cow'.

Ghul → Jinn

Gibil Sumerian god of fire; in Akkadian (Babylonian) he is called Girra or Girru. He was regarded as the bringer of light – but also as a fire-raiser. In incantations he was invoked to combat spells. Even → Marduk once visited the fire-god in order to get his insignia of office cleaned when they had been soiled.

Giants (Gigantes) In Greek mythology, a savage race of giants born from the earth (*ge genis*), implacable adversaries of the Olympian gods. They arose from the drops of blood spilt on the earth (→ Gaia) by the emasculated → Uranós. It is possible that the gigantes were originally embodiments of natural earth forces, such as volcanic eruptions and earthquakes. In their struggle with the gigantes (gigantomachia) the gods can only win with the help of a mortal (→ Heraklés).

Gilgameš Early historical king of the Sumerian town of Uruk. In his mythological aspect he is shown fighting the heavenly bull and → Ḫuwawa, the demonic ruler of the cedar forest. He engages in a fruitless search for eternal life. After his deification he was counted among the gods of the underworld. The Hittites knew the hero under the names of Giš.gim.maš, the Hurrians as Galgamiš. In texts from Asia Minor the name is always written with the determinative sign for a god.

Giltine Lithuanian goddess of death. Her name derives from the verb *gelti* = to sting, harm. Clad in white, she approaches the house in which the sick person lies; then she strangles or suffocates him.

Glaúkos (Greek = bluish-green) A sea-god known for his gift of prophecy who was very popular among sailors and fishermen in the ancient world. The legend is that he was once a fisherman himself who became a god when he ate of a magic herb and jumped into the sea. On occasion, he shares with other sea-gods the name *halios geron* ('the old man of the sea').

Gluskap (Kluskave) Cultural hero among the north-east Algonquin of Canada. Born of a virgin, he fights his evil twin brother, and, after the great flood, he creates a new earth out of a piece of mud. Occasionally he is conceived in the form of a hare. After his withdrawal from the world, he lives in the northland and continues to work for the welfare of the world.

Glykon Gnostic-Mithraic demon with a human head and the body of a snake. The snake Glykon was often regarded as a reincarnation of → Asklepiós.

Gnomes In popular belief a group of demonic figures who inhabit woods, mountains and water. The word may be derived from Greek *genomoi* = earth-dwellers, or from Greek *gnome* = understanding.

Goibniu In ancient Ireland the god of the blacksmith's craft, whose magic powers enabled him to turn out weapons which could not fail. The name is derived from *goban* = smith. Grievously wounded in a battle with the → Fomore, he was restored to health in a fountain of youth. Goibniu possessed the mead that gave eternal life. In the Welsh tradition the god is called Govannon; farmers need his help to clean the ploughshare.

Gong Gong Chinese devil who lets loose the great flood and who is the adversary of the ruling god. He is embodied in a black dragon and he is attended by the nine-headed, snake-bodied Xiang Yao, whose excretions generate evil-smelling springs and swamps.

Gorgons In Greek mythology, the three daughters of the sea-god → Phorkys, named Stheno, Euryale and Medusa. They were winged creatures, with snakes for hair and prominent tongues. The *gorgonaion*, a representation of the horrifying head of the *gorgo*, was used in temples and at graves to ward off evil powers. Alone among the three sisters Medusa was mortal, and when → Perseus struck off her head, the goddess → Athéne fixed it to her shield. Reference to 'the gorgon' in the singular is always to Medusa.

Gou Mang and Ru Shou The messengers of the Chinese sky-god: the former promises good luck and long life, while the second augurs punishment and disaster. They share the attribute of the double dragon. Gou Mang is associated with the spring and the east; Ru Shou with autumn and the west.

Govannon Celtic god of the Welsh, corresponding to the Irish → Goibniu.

Graii (Greek = old women) The daughters of the sea-god → Phorkys, who guard the way to the Gorgons. They have one eye and one tooth among the three of them.

Grāma-devatā ('village deity') A local tutelary god in India. Such gods look after the fields and the village boundaries, guard the villagers against epidemics and try to meet their personal wishes. A rock or stone, unadorned save for red colouring, marks the seat of the grāma-devatā.

Grannus Gallic god of healing. The city of Aquae Granni (Aachen) was a centre of his cult. The name may come from a Celtic root *ghrena*, meaning 'hot, warm', which would connect the god with hot springs. Grannus is one of the gods whom Caesar designated as → Apollo(n).

Gratiae, Graces (Latin *gratia* = grace, charm) In Roman belief, divine figures incorporating youthful grace and *joie de vivre*; they correspond to the Greek → Charites. They symbolize the arts of sculpture and poetry. They are mostly portrayed as naked, often garlanded and with flowers.

Guan Di Chinese god of war, patron of literature and protector of trade and merchants. In the Manchu dynasty he was particularly venerated because of his warlike functions; but in other periods of Chinese history he was regarded as the guardian of righteousness which protects men from strife and evil. In origin, Guan Di was an ordinary man called Guan Zhong done to death by his adversary, but later deified on account of his many and signal virtues.

Guan Yin A female → Bodhisattva venerated in China, who developed from → Avalokiteśvara. She is enthroned on a mountain or an island in the Eastern Sea. Guan Yin bestows the blessing of children, helps all beings to attain to the enlightenment which brings deliverance, and is in general the 'goddess of compassion'. She is often depicted meditating by the seashore; sometimes she has a child in her arms. In Japan she is known as Kwannon.

Guhyasamāja ('secret union') Buddhist protective deity (→ Iṣṭadevatā). In Tantrism, a mystical god of initiation ceremonies, with three heads and six arms.

Gui Xian (Gui) In China, a designation for certain demonic beings. The *gui* component means 'devil'. The *gui xian* were the souls of people who had been drowned or who had committed suicide, and who could therefore not be reincarnated. They are doomed to wander about as evil spirits. One of the *gui xian* was deified (→ Zhong-Kui).

Gula (Sumerian 'the great one') Old Mesopotamian goddess of healing, wife of → Ninurta.
In the old Babylonian period she was equated
with → Nin'insina, and the dog was the symbolical animal of both.

Gullveig A sorceress belonging to the →
Vanir race of gods in Old Norse mythology,
though with pronounced demonic traits. It was
through Gullveig that the lust for gold entered
the world: a lust, to which even the Aesir (→ As)
succumbed. The latter made three unsuccessful
attempts to burn Gullveig.

Gul-šeš (also as Gul-ašeš) Hittite goddesses
who always appear in the plural. A possible but
not universally accepted translation of their name
is 'scribes' or 'determiners (female) of fate'. In
the Hurrian pantheon they were called Ḥutena.
They are the goddesses of fate who dispense good
and evil, life and death. In this function, they are
comparable with the Greek → *moirai*.

Gurzil A god in the shape of a bull,
venerated in ancient Tripolitania. One tradition
relates that he was begot by → Ammon on a cow.

Guta In Hungarian folklore a demonic being,
a representative of the seamy side of things. He
strikes down his victims.

Gwydyon A god venerated in ancient Wales
who was born in a mysterious way. He was
concerned with war and with poetry. He also
shows characteristics of an underworld god: thus,
in later folklore the Milky Way – seen as the way
taken by the dead – was named Caer Gwydyon.

H

Ha The old Egyptian god of the western desert: hence his epithet 'Lord of the Libyans'. As god of the west, he plays a part in the cult of the dead; and on sarcophagi of the Herakleopolites period he is shown seated at the right hand of the defunct person, i.e. at the west side. He is depicted in purely human form, and in the script he bears the determinative of the desert on his head.

Hachiman In origin, a Japanese emperor (named Ojin) who was subsequently venerated as a god of war. His sacred creature is the dove.

Hades (Aidoneus, from Greek *aides* = the invisible one) Greek god of the underworld, son of → Kronos and of → Rheia, husband of → Persephóne. His name is no doubt connected with the magic cap conferring invisibility which Hades possessed. As Pylartes ('closer of gates') the god watches over the entrance to his realm, to ensure that no one who enters can turn and go back. His cult seems to have been confined to Pylos. As the interior of the earth has treasure hidden in it, he was also called Plutos (*plutos* = riches) and coupled with → Plutos. His Roman counterpart is → Orcus.

Hadúr (Hungarian *had* = army, *úr* = master) In the first half of the nineteenth century, this designation was used in Hungary for the War Lord of the spreading light, in contrast to → Ármány. This is a poetic recapitulation of older traditions, according to which the supreme god of the Hungarians was comparable with the Roman god of war → Mars.

Hah Egyptian god, personification of infinity and eternity. He was regarded as the bearer of heaven, and is accordingly depicted with arms outstretched, often supporting the sky. His image provides the hieroglyph of the word for 'million'. As an ornamental symbol the figure of Hah carries a palm-frond (a year-sign) on his head or in his hands. He is often associated with the god of the atmosphere → Šu.

Hainuwele A → *dema*-deity in the mythology of the Wemale people on the island of Ceram in the Moluccas. She is a divine maiden who arose from a coconut and who was slain by men in the primeval period. From her dismembered and buried body there arose the first fruits of the earth. With the death of Hainuwele man too became mortal.

Hala A Kassite goddess of healing, corresponding to the Babylonian → Gula.

du-l Halasa A pre-Islamic god in southwest Arabia, subsequently demoted to the rank of idol. His cult symbol seems to have been a white stone.

Haldi Tutelary god of the kingdom of Urartu (ninth – seventh century BC in Armenia).

Halki Hittite god of corn; his name means 'barley'. On occasion, he appears also as the tutelary deity of wine.

Hammon The god of the setting sun worshipped by the ancient Lybians. He was depicted with the horns of a ram and may coincide conceptually with the oasis god Ammon. There is no connection with the Punic god → Baal-Hammon.

Hananim Old Korean god of the sky, and supreme god: he moves the stars, rewards good and punishes evil.

Ḥannahanna Hittite goddess of birth, and mother goddess. The word *hanna* means 'grandmother'. In the cuneiform script, taken over by the Babylonians, she is called Dingirmah (= exalted deity) or Nintu (= mistress of birth). The bee serves her. In myth she plays a part in the search for a vanished god.

Hanuman (also Hanumat = he who has strong jaws)   In India, an ape venerated as a god. Indra hurled a thunderbolt at him and smashed his left jaw, because he tried to grab the sun (believing it was something to eat). Hanuman was regarded as the patron saint of learning. In the Rāmāyana he figures as the minister of the ape-king Sugriva, and the loyal companion of → Rāma in the war against the island of Lanka; pictures of Hanuman show him trampling the overthrown goddess of Lanka under his left foot.

Ḫanwašuit   Tutelary goddess of the Hittite throne. It is probable that her original locus was the royal city of Zalpa on the Black Sea. From her the king received his mandate.

Han Xiang-zi   One of the 'eight immortals' in Chinese popular belief (→ Ba Xian). He can make flowers grow and bloom at will. His attribute is a flute or a basket of flowers.

Haoma   In Old Iranian religion, a deified plant from whose sap an intoxicating drink was extracted, which was used in sacrificial ceremonies (cf. → Soma in India). Haoma is lord of all curative plants, and confers immortality.

Hapi (1)   One of the four sons of → Horus; corpses – especially the entrails – were placed under their protection, and Hapi, who was portrayed as an ape, was in charge of the lungs. The north is the heavenly quarter allotted to him.

Hapi (2)   Egyptian god, a personification of the Nile, represented as a well-nourished man. Although he was described as 'father of the gods', no specific centres were devoted to his cult. He is usually depicted as one making sacrifice (i.e. bringing gifts) to gods and kings.

Harachte   Egyptian god of the morning sun. The name means 'Horus of the horizon', i.e. of the place where the sun (→ Horus) rises. Harachte was represented as a falcon, and he tended to coalesce with the sun-god → Re in the figure of Re-Harachte (occurs also in the form Re-Hor-achti) who was especially venerated at Heliopolis. In one temple founded by Ramses III he is invoked as 'mighty god, lord of heaven'.

Harendotes ('Horus, who protects his father') in Egyptian texts, a special form of → Horus who ensures the continued survival of his father → Osiris in the underworld. Thus Harendotes became one of the protective gods who surround the dead person on the walls of the sarcophagus.

Harihara A designation for → Viṣṇu (Hari) and → Śiva (Hara) as a twin divinity: in Campuchea his image has two heads. When the two gods are represented in one single figure, the right side, with right hand holding a trident, is Śiva, the left side, with a wheel in the hand, is Viṣṇu.

Hāriti (Japanese Karitei-mo; Chinese He-li Di) This female demon used to eat children but through the influence of the Buddha she turned into a protector of children and a goddess who blessed couples with the gift of children. Her attribute is the pomegranate – a symbol of fertility.

Harmachis The Greek form of an Egyptian name which means 'Horus on the horizon'. It was applied to the Sphinx of Gizeh (originally the image of King Khafre) which was later taken to represent the matutinal appearance of the sun-god → Horus.

Harmerti ('Horus of the two eyes') Egyptian tutelary god of Seden (in the delta) who denotes → Horus as the falcon of heaven. The two eyes are sun and moon. A triumphant hero, he does battle with → Apophis.

Haroeris (in Plutarch Harueris) The Egyptian form of the name, Her-ur, means 'the elder Horus'. The designation serves to distinguish the old falcon-god → Horus from the Horus of the Osiris myth: that is to say, the god is a theological device. Haroeris is a sky-god, and in the tradition of Kom Ombo he is the son of the sun-god → Re. In the sequel, he becomes indistinguishable from → Šu. Because he fights to regain the lost eye of the sun, he became the tutelary god of oculists.

Harpies (Greek *harpyiai* = the snatchers) Female malevolent demons in Greek mythology. They are variously named – Aello, Aellopus, Podarge, Okypete, Kelaino – but all the names suggest the stormy wind. They are described as hideous hybrids, part woman, part bird.

Harpokrates (Egyptian Hor-pe-chrod = Horus the child) Veneration of → Horus as a child was very widespread, especially in the late period, and in the Graeco-Roman era he was one of the most popular deities. A favourite method of representation shows him as a solar child sitting in the lotus flower. The formations Hor-Amun and Harpokranum (or Harkpokrammon) point to a coalescence with → Amun. In the late Egyptian period the god was regarded as a giver of fertility, especially of pulses, and was accordingly depicted with a bowl, which became a cornucopia in the Greek period.

Harpre ('Horus the sun') Egyptian god, the child of → Month and of → Rat-taui, worshipped in Hermonthis. His function was to protect the king from illness and misfortune.

Harsaphes ('he who is upon his lake') Greek form of the Egyptian Herisef, the ram-god of Herakleopolis. Originally, the primeval creator, who emerges from the primeval deluge (lake); according to the myth, the lake arises from the blood of the god. In the Middle Kingdom, Harsaphes is often taken as a manifestation of Osiris. Later, he is equated with the sun-god → Re.

Harsiesis (Harsiese = Horus, son of Isis) Egyptian god, a specific form of → Horus, received by → Isis from the dead → Osiris, whom she protects from all dangers during his childhood. In necromantic texts Harsiesis appears as a sort of protective god.

Harun and Haruna Water-spirits in Morocco; they can assume the form of snakes. To placate them, people throw pieces of bread or cous-cous into the river.

Hašam(m)eli The Hittite god of blacksmiths and the art of wrought iron. A certain tree was sacred to him, but exactly which tree is not known.

Hathor Egyptian sky-goddess. Her name means 'house of Horus', where 'house' may be taken to denote both the cosmic house (heaven) and the womb. At an early period, Hathor was regarded as the mother of the sun-god → Horus, until replaced in this function by → Isis. Thanks to the conception, prevalent in the Nile delta, of the sky as an enormous cow, the goddess herself was portrayed in the form of a cow. Mostly, however, she is depicted anthropomorphically, in which case she bears the cow's horns on her head with the solar disc between them. She is also the goddess of dancing, of music and love; and in this capacity her main attribute is the sistrum, a kind of rattle. An ancient tree cult is also connected with Hathor – she is 'queen of the date-palm' and 'queen of the sycamore' – and she dispenses food and drink to the dead.

Hatmehit ('first of the fishes') Egyptian goddess, the centre of whose cult was at Mendes. She is portrayed in anthropomorphic form, and she bears a fish (dolphin?) on her head.

Hatuibwari Hybrid being, half divine, half demonic snake, on the island of San Cristoval in Melanesia. She has a human torso, four eyes and four breasts, in order to suckle all created creatures. On her back she has two wings. It is widely believed that the winged snake fertilizes the mothers of priests. This snake-like being can also appear under the name of Agunua, and it is from him that the human race derives.

Haubas (Hobas) A pre-Islamic god frequently mentioned in Sabaean (south Arabian) inscriptions. It has been suggested that he may represent a particular form of → 'Attar.

Haukim Old South Arabian deity. The name comes from the root HKM = 'to be wise' or 'to pronounce judicially'.

Haurvatāt ('health') A personification belonging to the → Ameša Spentas. Haurvatāt is also associated with life after death.

Hayagrīva ('Horse's neck') One of the Buddhist → Krodhadevatās. He is of dwarfish stature, with a pot belly and a horse's head. In Indian literature he is regarded as an avatar of → Visṇu, in Buddhism as an emanation of → Amitābha or of → Akṣobhya. In Tibet, he belongs to the protective deities who see to it that demons are kept at bay.

Ḥazzi Mountain god of the Hittites and the Hurrians. He forms part of the retinue of the god of weather, and he was invoked in Hittite state treaties as god of oaths. As a mountain – geographically, Mount Sapon near Ugarit – Ḥazzi is the seat of the gods.

Ḥebat (Hepat, Hapatu) The chief goddess of the Hurrians, 'Queen of heaven' and wife of the weather-god → Tešub. She was also taken into the Hittite pantheon and then frequently equated with the sun-goddess → Arinna. She is portrayed as standing on a lion or a panther; sometimes she is shown sitting on a throne, wearing the pointed regal cap.

Hébe (Greek = 'freshness of youth') Daughter of → Zeus and of → Hera, Greek goddess of youth. She is active as the cup-bearer of the gods, and she is the wife of the deified → Heraklés. Her Roman counterpart was → Juvéntas.

He Bo (also known as Bing-yi) In China, the divine ruler over all rivers; also called 'River Duke'. It is said that he weighed himself down with stones and threw himself into the river, thus achieving immortality. Until the end of the Zhou

Dynasty (256 BC) a maiden was sacrificed to him every year by being thrown into the river as his bride.

Ḥedammu Snake demon of the Hurrians. He lives in the sea and is insatiably voracious.

Hedetet The scorpion-goddess in the Egyptian Book of the Dead. As 'daughter of Re' she merges into the figure of → Isis.

Heimdall (Old Icelandic Heimdallr) Germanic god who acts as watchman of heaven. His dwelling is called Himinbjörg ('heavenly mountain'). He is the son of nine giant maidens (held to be daughters of the Aesir (→ As)). The etymological derivation of the name is uncertain; at one time the meaning 'the brightly shining one' was proposed which would make Heimdall a god of light or a sun-god. Another proposal was based on comparison with a poetical word for 'ram' – *heimdali*: Heimdall would then figure as the focal point for a primitive agrarian cult. Yet another suggestion – that he was the progenitor of the human race – is based on a passage in the Völuspa. As 'watchman of the gods', Heimdall stands at the bridge Bifröst (the Milky Way?) whence he announces the onset of Ragnarök by blowing the *gjallarhorn*. This juxtaposition of horn and world-tree has led to yet another interpretation of Heimdall – as a personification of the *axis mundi*.

Heitsi-Eibib National hero of the Hottentot people in South Africa. He is invoked as 'grandfather' and he grants the hunter luck in the chase. More than one place is cited as the scene of his death, and at all of these sites – each of them seen as his grave – a heap of stones is erected in his honour. In terms of comparative religion he is probably best classified as a kind of bush-spirit.

Hekáte A goddess in Greek mythology who originally hailed from Asia Minor (Caria). She does not appear in Homer. She is a chthonic deity, the mistress of all sorts of nocturnal nastiness, including necromancy. Her ghostly aspect is indicated in her epithet Antaia ('she who encounters you'): on her nocturnal hunt she could spell disaster for those who met her. She has snakes in her hair, she carries a torch, and is attended by howling dogs. In spite of all this, she was a popular goddess, and in Athens there was a small altar to her in front of every house. Hekáte was also seen as the goddess of cross-roads. In this capacity she was called Enodia or Trioditis, and was then depicted as three-headed or with three bodies.

Heket Egyptian goddess in the form of a frog (a symbol of life and fertility). She ranked as a primeval goddess and tutelary goddess of childbirth. In the town of Kus she was revered as the mother of → Haroeris.

Hel (Old Norse = hell) In Old Germanic mythology, the name of the realm of the dead and of its queen. Hel is the daughter of → Loki and the giantess Angrboda; and as the sister of → Fenrir and of the → Midgard-snake, she has demonic character. Hel is entitled to claim dominion over all those who die in the land except those who fall in battle. Even the gods must tread the 'way of Hel' – like → Balder after his early death.

Heléne Daughter of → Zeus and of → Leda, sister of the → Dioskuroi. In origin, a goddess of vegetation, and honoured in some places as a tree divinity (Dendritis): in Sparta, the plane tree was sacred to her. The myth tells how she was abducted by the Trojan prince Paris, an act which led to the outbreak of the Trojan war.

Heliades → Phaéton

Hélios
Greek sun-god, the son of the → Titan → Hyperion and the female Titan Theia; brother of the moon-god → Seléne. Hélios is he who sees all and hears all, and who is invoked as witness to an oath sworn. As god of light he can make the blind see – but equally he can strike sinners blind. He played little part in Greek religious observance, though he was worshipped on Rhodes and, to some extent, in the Peloponnese. In art, Hélios was often represented driving a chariot drawn by four (often winged) horses, his head surrounded by a halo of rays. In late classical times he was equated with → Apóllon. His Roman counterpart was → Sol.

Hemen
A falcon-god venerated in the Egyptian city of Hesfun (Asphynis). Thought to be identical with → Haroeris.

Hemera → Nyx

Hemsut
(Hemuset) Egyptian goddesses of fate, female counterparts of → Ka, who were also seen as protective spirits. They were supposed to take a new-born child into their arms. Their head-dress comprises a shield with two arrows transfixing it; the arrows represent the force which is transmitted by the Hemsut.

Ḥendursanga
A Sumerian god, concerned *inter aiia* with the proper functioning of the judicial system and the nation's laws. King Gudea named him 'herald of the land of Sumer'. He corresponds to the Akkadian god → Išum.

Heng E
(Change-e) Chinese goddess of the moon, a younger sister of the river god → He Bo. After stealing the pill of immortality from her

husband, the sun-god → Shen Yi, she fled to the moon, where she has lived ever since as a toad. She is represented in art wearing regal garments; in her right hand she carries the disc of the moon. Heng E is a symbolical figure for the cold, dark female principle (*yin*).

Hephaistos (Latin Hephaestus) Greek god of fire, of smiths and craftsmen. The son of → Zeus and of → Hera. As he was lame when he came into the world, his mother threw him out of Olympus. In his underworld smithy he fashions precious weapons and implements, e.g. the sceptre of Zeus, the chariot of → Hélios and the aegis of → Athená. In his work, he is helped by the → Cyclops. In origin, Hephaistos was a god of Asia Minor; and on the island of Lemnos he was revered as the embodiment of the fire which breaks out of the earth. At the end of the sixth century BC his cult reached Athens. The Romans identified him with → Vulcanus.

Hera (Here) Greek goddess, daughter of → Kronos and of → Rheia, sister and wife of → Zeus, the king of the gods. She is the mother of → Arés, ↛ Hephaistos, → Eileithyia and of → Hébe. She keeps a jealous eye on her divine husband, whose amorous liaisons infuriate her. Hera was invoked as the guardian of wedlock and she also figured as goddess of childbirth. In Athens and on the island of Samos her union with Zeus was celebrated as 'holy wedlock' (*hieros gamos*). She was a particular object of veneration for women, and her epithet was *teleia*, i.e. 'she who brings fulfilment'. The main centre of her cult was in Argos, and hence she was also known as Argeia. Her sacred animal was the cow, and among her attributes were the peacock and the insignia of her status as queen of the gods, the diadem and sceptre. Her Roman counterpart was → Juno.

Heraklés (Greek = 'made famous by (the land of) Hera') Son of → Zeus, the father of the gods, and the mortal Alkmene. Jealous as usual, the god's wife → Hera dispatched two snakes to finish the infant Herakles off, but he strangled them in his cradle. The twelve labours (*dodekathlos*) in the service of King Eurystheus, ending with his conquest of → Kérberos, the hound of hell, and his voluntary death on the pyre on Mount Oite, mark his progress from hero to immortal; finally he is received into Olympus and → Hébe is given to him as his wife. In his aspect as *kallinikos*, the radiant victor in all forms of contest, he became the national hero of the Greeks. Among the ordinary people he was very popular as someone one could turn to in need, and a protector against all sorts of unpleasantness (*alexikalos*). Young people especially saw in him their protector, and they called him Herakles Enágonios. The cult of this demi-god was also widespread in Italy (→ Hércules). Among his attributes is the skin of the Nemean lion.

Hércules The Latin name of the Greek → Heraklés. The demi-god had himself travelled far and wide, and it was fitting that he should become god of trade and traffic in goods and patron of traders. In Rome's imperial age, as the invincible conqueror of all difficulties (Hércules *invictus*) and the benefactor of mankind, he was magnified into the epitome of all the imperious and imperial virtues.

Herensugue Among the Basques, a devil-ish spirit who appears in the shape of a snake, though one tradition gives him seven heads and the ability to fly.

Hermanubis In the cult of Isis, the Egyptian god of the dead → Anubis was united in one figure with the Greek god who guided the souls of the dead → Hérmes. The priests of Hermanubis, the resultant amalgam, wore the dog's head of Anubis, and carried the herald's staff (the *kerykeion*) of Hérmes.

Hermaphróditos

Son of Hérmes and of → Aphrodíte. He was passionately loved by the spring-nymph Salmakis, so much so that their bodies merged and united forever, thus giving rise to an androgynous being. The cult of this twin divinity (which may have ancient oriental antecedents) reached Athens by way of Cyprus.

Hérmes

One of the most popular of all Greek gods; the son of → Zeus and the mountain nymph → Maía. Sacred to him were the piles of stones erected in ancient Greece to guide travellers – hence, presumably, his name (Greek *hermaion* = pile of stones). In front of Greek houses stone pillars used to stand (*hermen*) in which Hérmes was supposed to reside in order to protect the dwelling from harm. In this capacity, the god was known as Pylaios or Propylaios. Hérmes is the messenger of the gods, equipped with herald's staff (*kerykeion*), winged shoes and hat; he is protector of tradesmen and travellers – but also of thieves. The myth relates how Hérmes while still a small boy, stole a herd of cattle belonging to his brother → Apóllon. In his aspect of *psychopompos* he leads the souls of the dead into the beyond. He is also 'the good shepherd' and is often portrayed carrying a ram under his arm or over his shoulder (*kriophoros* = ram-bearer). As god of herds and flocks he has the epithet Nomios. He has in addition a happy relationship with music, and is said to have invented the lyre. His Roman counterpart was → Mercurius.

Hermes Trismegistos

(Greek = Hermes the thrice great) The Greek name for → Thot, the Egyptian god of writing and learning. As the putative founder of philosophy and mysticism he was also known as Hermes Logios. In late antiquity he was regarded as the harbinger of the one true God and creator of the world. His role in hermetic literature is that of a sage and legislator.

Hermod(u)r A deified hero in the north Germanic myth of → Balder. After the murder of Balder, he rides to → Hel as a messenger of the gods, to ascertain whether there is any possibility of Balder's return from the underworld. Hermod and the Danish king Heremod in the Beowulf saga are probably one and the same.

Heron A god who appears on Egyptian monuments of the Ptolemaic and Roman periods; he is shown as a rider who is bringing a libation to a rampant snake. This is very probably the horseman god → Heros, who was worshipped in Thrace and Asia Minor and who was brought by the troops of Alexander the Great and the Diadochoi to Egypt.

Heros A Thracian god represented as a horseman who makes his appearance as the conqueror of a monster. He was also a god of the dead, and as such his image was used on funerary steles. His name is cognate with the Greek word *heros* = hero.

Heruka Buddhist god, an emanation of → Akṣobhya. In Tibet, he is reckoned as one of the protective deities (→ Iṣṭadevatās). As normally represented, he is three-eyed, shows his teeth and has tousled hair; he has a severed human head and he is smeared with ashes, and he sits or dances on a corpse. In some representations he appears with his female partner (→ Prajñā) in the Yab-yum posture: in this case he bears the name Hevajra (= Oh Vajra!). A particular form he may adopt is that of Saptākṣara. *Inter alia*, Heruka confers Buddhahood and protects the world from the forces of evil.

Hesat ('the grim one', 'the wrathful one') Divine white cow: she was supposed to be 'the first of the cows' and was later associated with → Isis. In the Egyptian texts she appears as the mother of → Anubis and of → Imiut, and she provides the new-born king with his lactic nourishment.

Hesperides Greek nymphs who guard the tree with the golden apples in the garden of the gods, along with the dragon → Ladon. They were supposed to be daughters of the night (→ Nyx) or of the giant → Atlas.

Hestia (Greek = hearth) Greek goddess of the heart and its fire: daughter of → Kronos and of → Rheia. The hearth was the sacred focus of the household, the central point which vouch-safed protection: and here a small sacrifice was made to the goddess before meals. The corres-ponding figure in the Roman pantheon was → Vésta.

Hetepet An Egyptian cult centre in the north of Heliopolis. In the theology of Heliopolis the goddess 'Queen of Hetepet' is identified with the 'divine hand' of Iuesae. From the eighteenth dynasty onwards, she merges into the figure of → Hathor.

He Xian-gu The only female in the group of the 'eight immortals' (→ Ba Xian). She is usually shown holding a lotus blossom; often also with a peach (symbol of immortality) or a ladle – this last in token of her function as patron goddess of housewives.

Hez-ur Egyptian baboon-god; 'the great white one'. Even in the Old Kingdom, he was taken to be a particular form of → Thot.

Hiisi Karelian (east Finnish) forest-god, later demoted to the status of forest-spirit or troll. The word 'hiisi' is now used to mean 'devil' in a diluted sense.

Hike (another reading is Heka) In ancient Egypt, the personification of the magical properties which are inherent in the gods. Theological speculation made Hike the eldest son of the primeval god → Atum, with whose creative organs (heart and tongue) Hike was further identified. Hike even had his own shrines in On and near Memphis. It is noteworthy that doctors liked to call themselves 'priests of Hike': in other words they wanted to invoke his magic powers in the treatment of their patients.

Hilal (Hillaliy) The name means 'new moon', and denoted the moon-god, especially in his aspect as new moon, in ancient Arabia.

Himavat (Sanskrit *himavan* = bearing snow) Personification of the Himalaya mountains. This mountain god is the father of → Pārvatī and of the → Ganga.

Hina In Polynesia, a woman of semi-divine status who appears in the moon; sometimes she is elevated to the rank of moon-goddess. She appears as the mother or the wife of the culture-hero → Maui.

Hine-nui-te-po The Maori goddess of the underworld who rules the spirits and sees to it that the dread → Whiro does not harm them. When → Tane forced his way into her body, she squashed him with her sexual organ – and thus death entered the world.

Hinkon God of hunting and lord of the animals among the Tungus tribes who live on the Yenisei river in Siberia.

Hinokagutsuchi The Japanese fire-god. When he was born from the goddess → Izanami, she went up in flames – a metamorphosis which is linked with the death of the old year and the birth of the new.

Hintubuhet (Hin, Hina = woman) The supreme being venerated on the island of New Ireland in Melanesia. In spite of her name she is an androgynous being, as both parties to a marriage invoke her as progenitor in terms of their own sex: in one aspect she is equated with the male sun and the male butterfly Talmago, in the other aspect she is equated with the female moon and the female butterfly Heba.

Hiraṇyagarbha (Sanskrit = womb of gold) In the Rigveda, the unnamed god of creation, who subsequently appears as → Prajāpati. In later Sanskrit literature the name is used to denote → Brahman.

Hiraṇyakasipu → Narasimha

Hirguan → Orahan

Hittavainen (Hittauanin) The god of the hare-hunters of the Karelian (east Finnish) people, mentioned in an ancient list of gods. The etymology of the word is uncertain; it may be connected with Finnish *hitto* = devil, or it may be derived from the name of the patron saint of hunters, Hubertus, who was introduced into these parts along with Christianity.

Hlodyn (Hlödin) Old Icelandic goddess of the earth and of fertility: one tradition makes her the mother of → Thor, a role allotted in other traditions to → Fjörgyn. There is probably a connection here, both etymological and semantic, with the name of the west German goddess Hludana; and the latter has been seen as the matrix for the figure of Frau → Holle.

Hludana → Hlodyn

Höd(u)r North Germanic god, son of → Odin. His name means 'battle, struggle' but nothing about him suggests a war-like character. In the myth, Hödur is blind; and he judges people not by their outward appearance but by their inner worth. Incited by the malicious → Loki, he unwittingly slays his brother → Balder.

Holle Like → Bercht, originally the leader of a more or less demonic band of spirits (named as Hollen or Hulden), who are popularly believed to be sometimes friendly but at other times punitive. Holle lets the newly born emerge from her underworld realm, where she also receives the souls of the dead. When she shakes her cushions, it snows. Bishop Burchard of Worms (c. 1000) knew about Frau Holle, and translated her name as → Diana, after the Roman goddess. It is possible that Frau Holle is connected with the old Germanic goddess Hludana (→ Hlodyn).

Hong and Ha → Dvārapāla

Hönir North Germanic god who had a hand in the origin of the human race, along with → Odin and → Lodur (Loki ?): Odin gave the first men life, Lodur gave them language, sight and hearing, while Hönir gave them understanding and feelings. Hönir was reputed to be the fastest runner and the best of hunters.

Honos (Latin = honour)   A Roman god, the personification of military renown. He is shown as a young man with a lance and a cornucopia.

Horae (Greek *horai*)   The Greek goddesses of the three seasons: Spring, Summer and Winter. Originally they represented the seasonal forces of growth. The Athenians called them Thallo (goddess of blossom), Auxo (goddess of growth) and Karpo (goddess of ripened fruit). According to Hesiod they are the daughters of → Themis, and have ethical significance: their names in this version are → Eunomía (law and order), → Díke (justice) and → Eirene (peace).

Horagalles   A god venerated by the Lapps: 'the old man', usually portrayed carrying two hammers. Reindeer used to be sacrificed to him. He is actually Thor, the god of thunder, borrowed from the Old Norse religion.

Hor-Hekenu ('Horus of ointments')   A specific form of → Horus worshipped in Bubastis; the burning heat surrounding him drives the powers of evil away. As 'lord of protection' he personifies the protective ointment and the supernatural powers attributed to it. He is usually portrayed in human form with the head of a falcon.

Horus   Egyptian god, whose name – meaning 'he who is above', 'he who is afar' – would seem to indicate a sky-god. He was depicted as a falcon, with the sun and the moon as his eyes. At the very beginning of the historical period, the king was equated with this divine falcon; and every Pharaoh's name had the 'Horus name' as one of its elements. In line with the dualism characteristic of Egyptian thought, the mythological clash with → Seth (who deprives Horus of one of his eyes) leads to a division of their sphere of power: Horus is lord of Lower Egypt, Seth of

Upper Egypt. As the bearer of the solar eye, Horus is closely connected with the sun-god → Re (cf. also → Harachte). A special significance attached to Horus as a child (→ Harpokrates, → Harsiesis). In Edfu, the god of light was conceived in the form of the winged sun (→ Behedti). Horus is the adversary of the Typhonic powers, incorporated for the Egyptians in the hippopotamus and the crocodile; and he exercises the specific function of a protective deity in the form of → Hor-Hekenu. The offspring of Horus included → Duamutef, → Hapi, → Imset and → Kebechsenef.

Hotei One of the Japanese gods of good fortune (→ Shichi-Fukujin). He is seen as the friend of the weak and of children. Typically, his fat paunch is bare – a symbol of friendly good cheer.

Hu and Sia The constant companions of the Egyptian sun-god → Re. Hu is the personification of the word or 'utterance' which the creator spoke to bring all things to life. Sia is the personification of the knowledge and understanding which make the work of creation possible.

Huang-di ('the Yellow Emperor') Mythological Chinese Emperor and culture-hero. Among many other achievements he invented the wheel, thus enabling men to build carts. In his fight against the rebel Chi-yu he was assisted by the winged dragon. The goddess → Ba sometimes figures as his daughter.

Huang Fei-hu ('yellow flying tiger') Known also, in abbreviated form, as Fei. A Chinese god, lord of the sacred mountain of Tai Shan, in eastern China. Originally a chthonic deity in the form of a one-eyed bull with a snake's tail, he subsequently became the judge of the dead, whose souls call at the sacred mountain.

Hubal Pre-Islamic god venerated in central Arabia. His anthropomorphic image in red carnelian still stands in the Ka'aba in Mecca; and it is possible that the black stone of the Ka'aba is connected with him in some way. The god was famous for his oracle (performed with seven arrows).

Huh and Hauhet → Ogdoad

Huiracocha (Viracocha)   The supreme god of the Inca empire. Traditionally he was connected with Tiáhuanaco, whose importance as a cult site extends back into pre-Inca times. According to the myth he was born of a virgin, and he often displays solar characteristics. His epithet Pachamac designates him as 'creator of the world'. Those who fail to do fitting homage to the god are destroyed by fire or flood.

Huitzilopochtli ('humming-bird of the south')   Tribal god of the Aztecs; also a solar god. His animal manifestation (*nahualli*) is the

humming-bird, which is also a symbol of the sun; his weapon is the 'turquoise snake', the symbol of earthly and heavenly fires. The myth tells how he arose from the body of the earth-goddess → Coatlicue. He is the adversary of the moon and the stars. Huitzilopochtli embodies the morning sun, the day-time sky, the summer and the south, all of which makes him the luminous adversary of the dark → Tezcatlipoca.

Ḥumban (Ḥuban) A god venerated in Elam. He can be equated with the Mesopotamian → Enlil.

Hunab Ku Supreme god and creator in the Maya pantheon: he is 'the god set over the gods', invisible and incomprehensible, corresponding to the Aztec → Omoteotl. He had to yield in significance to his son → Itzamna.

Hunapu (Hunahpu) A god of the Quiché Indians in Guatemala: the son of → Hun-Hunapu and a virgin. Together with his twin brother Ixbalanque he overcomes the evil adversary → Vucub-Caquix. Like his father, Hunapu too lost his head – this time in the 'house of the bats'. After their victory over the forces of death and the underworld (Xibalba), the twins are promoted to the heavens as the sun and the moon; and they then proceed to create the first human beings.

Hunhau (also known as Ahpuch) The Maya god of death; he rules over Mitlan, the underworld, and corresponds to the Aztec → Mictlantecutli. Sometimes he is depicted as a man with the head of an owl, and then again he is associated with the dog, the symbol of death and entry into the beyond. Specialists in Central American studies refer to him as 'god A'.

Hun-Hunapu Among the Quiché Indians, the father of the divine twins → Hunapu and Ixbalanque. In the book of Popol Vuh it is related how the god lost his head (here, a solar symbol) while playing with a ball in the underworld: the head was hung up in a calabash tree which had previously never borne fruit, and as a result the tree became fruitful.

Huracan High god and creator god of the Quiché Indians who live in Central America. He is the 'heart of heaven'. He created the first land by calling out the word 'earth'; and he formed the human race from maize-dough. He dwells at one and the same time in heaven, on earth and in the underworld.

Ḫurri → Šeri

Ḫuwawa (Mod. Assyrian Humbaba) Demonic guardian of the 'land of the cedar mountain' (Lebanon), appointed to the role by → Enlil, but destroyed by → Gilgameš.

Hvar This Iranian word denotes not only the sun but also the sun-god, though the role the latter plays is inferior to that of → Mithra. One of his epithets is 'he who possesses swift horses'. Through his worship one can withstand the powers of darkness and the demonic → Daēvas.

Hyákinthos (Latin Hyacínthus) Pre-Hellenic god of vegetation whose death symbolizes the decay and rebirth of nature. In Greek myth he was a favourite of → Apóllon. He was killed by an unlucky throw of the discus, and from the blood of the beautiful youth there grew the flower known after him as the hyacinth. In Amyklai in Sparta he was accounted a hero, whose grave was supposed to be under the throne of Apóllon.

Hygíeia Greek goddess of good health, daughter of the god of healing → Asklepiós. The creature sacred to her is the snake, and she is depicted giving it water in a bowl or a drinking vessel.

Hymén (also as Hyménaios) Greek god of weddings, who was solemnly invoked as part of every marriage celebration. He was supposed to be the son of → Dionysius and of → Aphrodíte, though sometimes → Apóllon and a muse are said to be his parents. He was represented as a winged youth carrying a wedding torch and a garland.

Hymir A Nordic giant living at the edge of heaven; he possesses a large beer vat. His female companion is the mother of the god → Tyr. Tyr and → Thor visit him to borrow the vat.

Hyperion Old Greek god of light, → Titan and husband of → Theia; their children were the sun-god → Hélios and the moon-goddess → Seléne.

Hýpnos Greek god of sleep, the son of night (→ Nyx), and brother of death (→ Thanatos). In art, he is usually depicted as a winged youth with a poppy-stalk and a small horn in his hands. The Romans called him Somnus.

I

Iakchos A youthful demon, perhaps a god, in the Eleusinian mysteries. He is in fact the personification of the shout of 'Iakche!' – a triumphant cry in honour of the Eleusinian goddesses, uttered by the faithful during the ceremonial procession. In Greek myth, Iakchos is the son of → Demeter or of → Persephóne, and he is seen as the reborn → Zagreus.

Iapetós In Greek myth, a → Titan opposed to the gods; the father of → Atlas and → Prometheus.

Iblis (Arabic form of the Greek *diabolos*) The Islamic designation for the devil. As he refused to fall down before Adam and worship him, he was expelled from heaven.

Idā ('libation') In Hinduism, the ceremonial sacrifice of milk and butter; mythologically the daughter of → Manu, and the wife of the planet-god → Budha. She is the goddess of prayer and devotion. Idā was originally a man who was turned into a woman when he inadvertently entered the enclosure where → Śiva was sojourning in female form.

Idun (Old Icelandic *idunn*; (*id*) 'she who renews, makes young') Germanic goddess, she who holds the life-giving fruit and the gift of everlasting youth. When the giant Thiassi abducts the goddess, the Aesir (→ As) begin to age in the absence of the golden apples. The gods send → Loki to retrieve the goddess, and are rejuvenated when she is safely returned.

Ifa A demi-god of the Yoruba people in Nigeria; he is connected with the art of soothsaying. He set up an oracular shrine in the holy city of Ife, and taught mankind the art of healing. Ifa is often equated with → Orunmila.

Igigi Akkadian designation for the great gods of heaven in contrast to the underworldly Anunnaka (→ Anunna).

Ihi (Ehi) Young son of the Egyptian goddess → Hathor; he is the lord of the sistrum, the musical instrument which drives away evil powers. Accordingly, the sistrum is his attribute.

Ikenga The function of this god, worshipped by the Ibo in Nigeria, was to guide men's hands or arms correctly – hence his name which means 'right upper-arm'. He is represented wearing two enormous horns (symbolizing his power) with a sword and a severed human head in his hands. The two horns may be doubled; that is, there may be four of them. The images of Ikenga set up in households are supposed to ensure prosperity and good fortune, and their advice is often sought by the inmates.

Ilazki (also occurs as Illargui or Iretargui) The moon is regarded as female by the Basques and this is one of the names given to it; it is also known as 'grandmother' or 'holy grandmother'. In some places in the Basque regions, they tell children that the moon is the face of God. The name Illargui means 'light of the dead', the nocturnal light that shines for the souls of the dead.

Illapa (Ilyapa, also as Katoylla) The god of lightning, thunder and rainstorms in the pre-Columbian Inca empire.

Illujanka Hittite snake demon, which was slain by the weather-god. The myth was taken up by the Canaanites in the form of the mythical struggle of → Baal Sapon against → Leviathan, and reached the Greeks as the story of → Typhón. The tale of the weather-god's battle against Illujanka was recited at the feast of the New Year (*purulli*); a new era begins with the destruction of the monstrous snake.

Ilmarinen (ilma = air, weather) In Finnish myth, the ruler over wind and weather; he is also the protective deity of travellers. He is also the divine smith who studs the sky with stars, and who has created not only the vault of heaven but also the Sampo (probably the *axis mundi*). It is he, as a culture-hero, who first educates mankind in the use of iron.

Imdugud Half-demonic, half-divine being in old Mesopotamian mythology; it appears as an eagle with a lion's head. As a sinister power it threatens domestic animals; in its other aspect it figures as an emblem of the god → Ningirsu.

Imhotep Celebrated Egyptian architect and doctor at the time of King Djoser (*c.* 2600 BC). Later, he was revered as god of healing and was said to be the son of → Ptah.

Imiut ('he who is in the mummy-cloth') Egyptian god who was venerated in the form of a headless skin hung up on a pole. In the earliest period, Imiut was set up as a protective emblem at the royal throne. As a protective deity he is associated with the god of the necropolis → Anubis.

Imra The supreme god in Kafiristan in the Hindu-Kush. He is the creator who breathed life into the other gods. Among the Kati, he is said to have created mankind by means of a sort of butter-making process in a golden goat's udder; among the Prasun, he is known as Mara.

Imset (Amset) One of the four sons of → Horus, who watch over the viscera in the canopic jars. Imset, who is represented in anthropomorphic form, is specifically charged with the care of the liver, and the south is his allotted heavenly quarter.

Inanna (Inini) Sumerian goddess of love and war. As Ninanna, she is the 'Queen of heaven' and as Ninsianna she is the goddess of Venus. Her symbol is the reed-bundle, and this is also her determinant in the cuneiform script. She is described as the daughter of the sky-god → An, or of the moon-god → Nanna. Iconographically, Inanna belongs to the class of naked goddesses, though often she is shown with bright rays streaming out from her back. Her Akkadian counterpart is → Ištar.

Inar (Inara) This goddess was worshipped in Asia Minor; she was supposed to be the daughter of the Hattic weather-god → Taru. In the → Illujanka myth she helps the weather-god to overcome the snake demon.

Inari The god of foodstuffs in Shintoism, represented as a bearded man carrying two bundles of rice. His messenger is the fox, and this is why there are always stone or wooden foxes sitting in front of Inari shrines. In popular belief, the god and the fox could merge together to form one being. In Japanese myth there was also a goddess of rice called Inara, who could assume the form of a fox.

Incubus (Latin = he who lies on top) Among the ancient Romans, and even today in

Italy, the name of an → Alp. Since the Middle Ages, a designation for male demons who force sleeping women to have sexual intercourse. In the literature of witchcraft, incubus is also a designation for the devil as paramour.

Indra (the original meaning is 'strong', 'mighty') The supreme god in the Vedic pantheon. He brings rain, and is the heavenly representative of warriors; his weapon is the thunderbolt, which may have four or a hundred edges (*vajra*). He is red or gold in colour, and he is mounted on horseback or sits in a chariot drawn by horses. As Vṛtrahan, Indra is the great dragon-slayer, who frees the streams obstructed by → Vritra. In Hinduism, Indra is white in colour, clad in red, and he rides on the elephant Airavata which was generated by churning the ocean of milk. He is ruler of the easterly quarter. Indrāṇī or Śací (= power) are named as his wives, and he is constantly accompanied by the → Maruts. In Jainism, the word denotes the highest rank in divine hierarchies: that is to say, each class of gods has its specific Indra.

Ing Divine progenitor of the Germanic Ingwaeones who lived on the Baltic coast. The meaning of the word is not clear: 'lance', 'yew' or even 'man' have all been suggested. According to an Anglo-Saxon runic poem, the god Ing seems to be connected with the eastern Danes, and corresponds to the Yngoi of the Scandinavian tradition. It is possible that the Vandals brought the cult of Ing from their homeland in Sweden.

Inguma A Basque spirit, something like an → Alp. He creeps into people's houses by night and throttles them.

Inmar Sky-god of the Finno-Ugric Votyak (Udmurt) people. The *in* part of the name means 'sky'. The name is applied to other divine beings in their mythology, and after the coming of Christianity it was transferred to the Mother of God ('Inmar-mother').

Inmutef (Iunmutef) Egyptian god; the name means 'pillar of his mother'. Accordingly, he was the bearer of the heavens (conceived as female) and figured in a joint cult with → Hathor. Later, he was associated with the king and his sacrificial service.

Inó In Greek myth, the daughter of King Kadmos of Phoenicia. Fleeing from her husband Athamas, she throws herself into the sea, where she is sympathetically received by the → Nereids, and elevated to the rank of a sea-goddess, under the name of Leukothea.

Inti (Quechua = sun) The Inca sun-god, the object of particular veneration along with the creator-god → Huiracocha. Inti was seen by the Inca rulers as their progenitor. He was represented by a gold disc with a human face.

Inuus Old Latin god, invoked to protect herds; later, equated with → Faunus.

Io (1) In Greek mythology, the daughter of Inachos, the King of Argos. She was a priestess serving the morally strict → Hera, who was outraged to find → Zeus making love to her. There are differing versions of what happened next: one tradition says that Zeus turned Io into a cow to hide her identity; another agrees about the cow but asserts that Hera did this to punish her. In any case, Io was handed over to the hundred-eyed watchman → Árgos for safe-keeping. Zeus organized her escape, and she wandered restlessly over the earth until she reached Egypt where her human form was restored to her, and she gave birth to → Epaphos. The Greeks resident in the

Nile delta equated her with → Isis, who was usually represented with cow's horns.

Io (2) (or Kiho) The chief god of the Maori people in New Zealand. Some of the statements made about him suggest Christian influence: thus, Kiho is 'the eternal one', 'the omniscient', 'the god of love' and he who has created all things through 'the word'. Only the priests and the high nobility knew anything about him, and his name might only be whispered in lonely places. On the Polynesian island of Mangaia, the word Io means something like 'marrow', 'kernel', and can also denote 'god'.

Ipet (Ipi in the Pyramid texts) Egyptian hippopotamus goddess who soon merged with a similarly named local goddess of Luxor to form a goddess of the Great Mother type. As the consort of the tutelary god Amun she figures as the 'Queen of the two lands' – that is, of Upper and Lower Egypt.

Iris (Greek = rainbow) A sister of the → Harpies, a virgin goddess who hastens down from Olympus as messenger of the gods bearing the commandments of → Zeus and → Hera. She is usually shown as winged and bearing the herald's staff.

Irmin Old Germanic god, whom we can probably equate with the war-god Tiwaz (→ Tyr). Originally, the name seems to have meant 'divine', 'holy', but it came to mean 'strong', or 'mighty'. The name of the Irmin-pillar in Saxony probably refers to this god. The Irmingot ('great god') found in the Hildebrandslied is perhaps a late echo of this old Germanic god, though the poem itself shows Christian influence.

Išara (older form: Ešara) Ancient Mesopotamian goddess: 'Queen of the judgment seat and of the sacrificial display', and guarantor of oaths. Her emblem is the scorpion. In Ugarit, her epithet was Hulmittu = snake, lizard. She was deeply venerated by the Hittites as 'Queen of the mountains'. In Syria, it was her sexual potency that was emphasized.

Isdes This god makes his appearance in Egypt from the Middle Kingdom onwards. He was regarded as 'lord of the west' and as a judge of the dead. Later, he merged into the figure of → Thot, or of → Anubis.

Išduštaya and Papaya Proto-Hattic goddesses of fate worshipped in ancient Asia Minor. They use spindle and mirror to determine human destiny. It is a moot point whether they belonged to the → Gul-šeš.

Isinu Janus-headed god in ancient Mesopotamia; his Akkadian name was Usmu or Usumu. He was regarded as messenger of → Enki (or of → Ea).

Isis (Ese, in cuneiform Ešu) Egyptian goddess. In origin she was perhaps the personification of the throne, conceived as a (female) deity; and she bears on her head the determinant of the seat of authority. The myth tells how she sought out her dead brother and husband → Osiris from whom she received the child → Horus; she buried him and mourned him together with her sister → Nephthys. When, later, every dead person came to be identified with Osiris, she became protector of the dead. As 'she who is rich in spells' (Urthekau) she was accepted into the world of magic and necromancy. From the Middle Kingdom onwards, her solar aspect is displayed in her epithet 'eye of → Re'. In addition, she was Queen of Sirius, and Greek

authors (e.g. Plutarch) interpreted her as a moon-goddess. In the Hellenistic period, Isis became patron of sea-farers, and was given a rudder as attribute. She was, with very few exceptions, portrayed in human form; the cow's horns and the sun disc she bears on her head she owes to her coalescence with the figure of → Hathor.

Iškur Hittite weather-god, comparable with the Hurrian → Tešub. His sacred number is 10 and his sacred animal the bull; his attributes are a club and shafts of lightning. He sits on two mountain-gods or rides in a chariot drawn by bulls. Iškur manifests himself in thunderstorms and rain; he is 'king of heaven' and helps the earthly king in time of war.

Isrāfil In Islam, the angel who sounds the trump of doom at the Last Judgment.

Iṣṭadevatā ('desired deities') Buddhist protective deities (especially in Tibet) which are chosen by the neophyte himself as he prepares to undergo Tantric initiation: as a rule, after being blindfolded, he throws a flower on to a mandala.

Ištanu Hittite sun-god; the Hattic form is Eštan (= 'sun', 'day'). For the written form of his name the Sumerian cuneiform determinant for → Utu was used. In iconography, one of his main attributes is a winged sun as part of his head-dress; in his right hand he bears the *lituus*, i.e. a staff whose lower tip is crooked. As the sun-god sees all things, he is judge over men and animals.

Ištar (original form: Eštar) Babylonian (Akkadian) goddess of love and sexuality. One myth tells of her descent to the underworld, where her sister → Ereškigal ruled. In Ištar's absence, all procreation ceases on earth. Although she is hailed as 'virgin' she has many

lovers, notably Tammuz (→ Dumuzi). Like →
Inanna, her Sumerian counterpart, she has,
alongside her erotic aspect, both war-like and
astral functions. She is the goddess of Venus as
morning star, and on Middle and late Babylonian
border markers she is represented as an eight-
pointed star. Her brother is → Šamaš. Her
importance was such that her name could be used
as a general appellation for 'goddess'; and *ištarāta*
are 'the goddesses'.

Isten (1) (Isden) Egyptian god, attested from
the Middle Kingdom onwards; he is related to →
Thot, in the latter's aspect as *cynocephalus
hamadryas*. It is doubtful whether there is any
connection with → Isdes.

Isten (2) Supreme god of the ancient Hungarians, sometimes conceived in monotheistic
terms. He was seen as the creator of all things.
Among his attributes were the arrow, the tree, the
horse and the phallus. He sent his eagles to guide
his people – the Hungarians – into their new
homeland. His epithets include *úr* (= lord,
master) and *elő* (= the living one). With the
coming of Christianity, Isten merged into the
figure of God the Father.

Išum Akkadian god, brother of the sun-god
→ Šamaš, and herald of the gods. It is true that
he serves the god of plague → Erra, but he is
well-disposed towards humanity. It is not certain
that the name is connected with *išātum* = fire.

Īśvara ('lord', 'ruler') Sanskrit designation for
the supreme world ruler, especially for → Śiva. In
certain sects, the name is used to denote the
supreme divinity. In Hinduism, Īśvara becomes
synonymous with a supreme personal god who is
capable of releasing those who believe in him for
the cycle of reincarnation. It happens also that
other major gods are increasingly identified with
various manifestations of Īśvara.

Itzamna Son of the Maya god → Hunab Ku. He it was who introduced such foods as maize and cocoa to mankind, and who instructed them in the art of writing. As the bringer of culture to his people, Itzamna became the national god of the Maya. When identified with the sun-god, he is also lord of the east and the west. He is also called Yaxkokahmut, 'lord of knowledge'.

Itzpapalotl ('obsidian butterfly') A local fire-goddess of the Aztecs, in the form of a butterfly. As an astral being, she could also take the shape of a deer.

Iwaldi In Germanic mythology, a dwarf skilled in forging and casting; father of the goddess → Idun. He and his sons built Freyr's ship Skidbladnir and forged Odin's spear Gungnir.

Ixbalanque → Hunapu

Ixchel Moon-goddess of the Maya, who was also regarded as the protective patron of women in childbirth and of weavers. → Itzamna is often mentioned as her spouse.

Ixtab A Maya goddess, the guardian of suicides, who enter her paradise.

Iya Among the Sioux Indians, the embodiment of evil, a demonic monster which swallows men and animals, or harms them in other ways. His foul breath spreads sickness, and he manifests himself sometimes in the shape of the hurricane.

Izanagi (Isanagi; Japanese = 'the lord who invites you to enter') Forms, together with → Izanami, the primeval pair of divinities of Shintoism. As the two of them were crossing the bridge of heaven, Izanagi hurled a spear into the water which thereupon gave birth to an island. Izanagi is the embodiment of all that is bright and heavenly; his children are the sun-goddess → Amaterasu, and the moon-god → Tsukiyomi.

Izanami (Isanami; Japanese = 'she who invites you to enter') Primeval goddess in Shintoism, the embodiment of the earthly and the gloomy. She is the Earth Mother. When giving birth to her youngest son, the god of fire, she died, and went then to rule over the underworld. Her husband was the sky-god → Izanagi.

J

Jabru An Elamite god, who was equated with the old Mesopotamian god of the sky → An.

Jagannātha ('Lord of the world') In some parts of India, especially in Puri, this is the usual name for Viṣṇu in his manifestation as → Kṛṣṇa. It is in his honour that the feast of *rathayatra* is held, when the image of the god is wheeled along in a chariot and differences of caste are ignored.

Jagaubis Lithuanian fire-god, who was gradually ousted in popular belief and tradition by Gabija.

Jahwe (Jahve) The name of the god of Israel. The Third Commandment states, 'Thou shalt not take the name of the Lord thy God in vain,' and this was taken to heart so seriously that while the four consonants of the name could be written – J H W H – the name itself was pronounced with the vowels of 'Adonai' (= Lord). Exactly what the name means is a disputed point: 'he who exists', 'the breather', 'he who summons to existence' are some of the suggestions, all of them questionable. Exodus 3: 14 glosses the word as 'I am that I am'. Cf. also the spurious form → Jehovah. In origin, Jahwe was very probably a mountain-god (Sinai). For the Israelites he was *jahwe zebaoth*, 'the lord of hosts'. In I Samuel 17: 45, the word *zebaoth* refers to earthly hosts, but elsewhere the hosts may be of angels (I Kings 22: 19) or of stars (Deuteronomy 4: 19). In Old Testament times, the Ark of the Covenant was the visible token of the divine presence. The god himself could not be represented in any form. In Christian art, the tetragrammaton – the four Hebrew letters – symbolizes the almighty God.

Jambhala Buddhist god of riches, in origin a → Yakṣa. He has a pot-belly; in his right hand he holds a lemon, and in his left a mongoose, which is spitting jewels (the mongoose pelt as purse). It is said that several Buddhist teachers received gold or food from Jambhala.

Jamm Phoenician-Canaanite god of water, especially of the sea; one of his epithets makes him 'Ruler river'. He presumed to claim a ruling position *vis-à-vis* the other gods, but was overcome by → Baal. According to one tradition, his consolation prize was the goddess Attart (→ Astarte) who became his bride.

Jāṅgulī ('the poisonous one') Also known as Mahavidya; the Buddhist goddess who offers protection against snakebite and poison. She may be portrayed as single-headed with four arms, bearing a musical instrument (a *vina*) and a white snake, but she also appears with three faces and six arms, and yellow in colour.

Janus (Ianus) Roman god of gateways, of entrances and exits. Metaphorically the double-headed god also stands for beginning and end, the threshold point at which the old year becomes the new, and accordingly January is named after him. Among his attributes are keys and a janitor's staff. His temple was a double door which was kept locked in peacetime and opened in times of war. Important matters of any kind were commended to his care, thus, for example, sowing and harvest. In Roman mythology, it is Janus mankind has to thank for agriculture and law.

Jariḥ (Erah) Canaanite moon-god.

Jarovit (Latinized as Gerovitus) West Slavonic god, venerated in Pomerania. The *jar* component in his name means 'violent', 'fiery'. At the time of the conversion of the West Slavs, Jarovit was compared by one writer to → Mars; that is to say, he was accredited with the functions of a war-god.

Jarri Hittite god of plague and pestilence, who had to be placated when there was an outbreak. He had the epithet 'lord of the bow', and he could also figure as a god who helped the monarch in battle.

Jehovah From the thirteenth century onwards, this form is used as an appellation for → Jahwe. It results from adding the vowels of the Hebrew word *adonai* = lord, master, to the consonants of the tetragrammaton J H W H. This demonstrably spurious form was adopted by the Jehovah's Witnesses.

Jetaita An earth-spirit much feared by the Yamana, a tribe living in Tierra del Fuego. He is supposed to be present at initiation ceremonies in the cult-house, where he is represented by a man painted red and white.

Jian Lao (Chinese = the stable one) A Buddhist goddess of the earth and of permanence, revered in China. She is represented with her hands placed together, or with an ear of grain (a symbol of fertility).

Jinn This appellation for a class of demonic beings goes back to pre-Islamic times. The jinn were originally nature-spirits, who were also believed to cause madness. A specific sub-class of jinn were the ghouls, female spirits of the wilderness who appeared in animal form.

Jizo In Japan the → Buddha of great compassion. The protector of pregnant women, of children and of travellers, he is also invoked as a god of healing. In art, he is shown bald-headed like a monk, with a pilgrim's staff in his right hand.

Joh (Jah) The Egyptian word for the moon and for the moon-god. Originally much venerated especially in Thebes, he was gradually absorbed by → Thot.

Jörd (Old Icelandic = earth) North Germanic goddess. In the Edda, Snorri describes her as at once the daughter and the wife of → Odin. Like → Fjörgyn, she is supposed to be the mother of → Thor.

Jötun (Jöten) Germanic appellation for gigantic demonic beings possessed of enormous strength. According to the Völuspa, they are the 'early-born', those who were already present when the world came into being. As primeval beings they are wise – but they are also hostile to the gods. The giants live in Jötunheimr or 'giant-land'. One of the best-known of them is → Mimir. The dividing line between the Jötun and the → Thursen is not clear.

Juesaes (Jusas, Iusas) Egyptian goddess: a theological fiction, a personification of the 'hand of god' with which → Atum masturbated to create the world from his own seed. According to another tradition, Juescaea was born from the skull of the earth-god → Geb.

Julunggul The creator god, venerated by Australian aboriginals in Arnhem Land as the bringer of culture. He is identified with the rainbow-snake. In initiation rites boys are supposed to swallow him and then bring him up again, in symbolic token of the transition from child to man.

Juma (Finno-Ugrian root *juma(la)* = god, the heavenly one) The sky-god of the Mari people (Cheremis) who live between the middle Volga and the Vjatka. His customary epithet is 'the great one'. The word *juma* is, however, also applied to the spirits of the earth, the water, the wind and the household.

Jumala The Finnish appellation for 'god', 'holy one'; originally the name of a sky-divinity, transferred subsequently to the Christian God the Father.

Jumis Latvian god of fertility, symbolized by two fruits joined in growth – ears of rye, nuts or flax stalks. In order to feed the strength of Jumi back into the ground, ripened ears are bent over to the earth and held there by stones.

Junit An Egyptian goddess of local significance in Tuphium (the modern El Tod), and therefore connected with → Month. It seems likely that in origin she was the personification of a sacred pillar.

Júno (Iuno) The Roman goddess after whom the month of June is named. To begin with, she symbolized the youthful powers of women, forming thereby a counterpart to male → Genius. First and foremost, she is the goddess of marriage and protector of married women; under the name of Pronuba she gives away the bride, and as Lucina she is goddess of birth, i.e. she helps the newly-born into the world. As Juno Regina, she protects the whole Roman Empire. Yet another epithet of hers was Moneta, signifying 'recollection'; this epithet came to mean 'coin' because a mint was set up close to the temple of Moneta. Juno was originally an Etruscan goddess who was especially venerated in Vei. In Rome she was honoured by women in the feast of the Matronalia, held on 1 March. The Latin poets made her out to be both sister and spouse of → Jupiter, and she came to acquire the significance of the Greek → Hera, whose peacock she also took over as attribute.

Júno Caeléstis (Iuno Caelestis)

Tutelary goddess of Roman Carthage, who took over the functions of the Punic → Tinnit. In Libya she was called simply Caelestis. The Phoenicians called her Astroarche and regarded her as the moon-goddess.

Júpiter

Latin name (more correctly, Iuppiter) of the Indo-Germanic sky-god and god of light. The name comes from an original *diu-pater* meaning something like 'father of light' (*dies* = day, from a root *deieu* = shining). The Ides, the days when there was a full moon, were sacred to him. His shrines were to be found on mountain tops. On the Capitol, Jupiter was revered as best and greatest of gods: Iuppiter Optimus Maximus was the supreme tutelary god of Rome, forming a trinity with → Júno and → Minerva. As Fulgur he loosed lightning, as Tonans he made the thunder boom. As the Roman Empire expanded, his warlike functions were more and more extolled: as Iuppiter Stator he helped the legions to hold their ground, and as Iuppiter Victor he gave them victory. The Roman god merged to a large extent with provincial gods in far-flung parts of the Roman Empire, thus, for example with the Syrian → Dolichénus. In myth, → Zeus and Júpiter are equated.

Júras máte

'Sea-mother', a goddess of water in Latvian folklore. She plays some part in spells and charms designed to heal or cure.

Jurojin

Japanese god of longevity. He rides on a deer, and is often accompanied by cranes and tortoises as symbols of long life and a happy old age.

Jutúrna (Iuturna) Roman goddess of springs and wells who was often invoked in time of need especially when there was a shortage of water.

Juvéntas (Iuventas) Roman goddess of youth, corresponding to the Greek → Hébe. Sacrifice was made to her when boys first donned the toga worn by men.

Jw (Ja'u, Jawi) The existence of the ancient Syrian god has been deduced from a study of personal names. Nothing certain is known about him; but he may be identical with the harvest-god Ao mentioned by the Latin writer Macrobius. There is no evidence to support an equation with → Jahve, the god of the Israelites.

Jyotiṣka Stellar gods in Jainism. Five classes are distinguished: suns, moons (both in the plural), planets, stations of the moon (*nakṣatra*) and fixed stars.

K

God K Identification tag adopted by specialists in pre-Columbian American studies to designate a god who sometimes appears as a form of → Kukulcan, and who at other times seems similar to → Itzamna. But cf. information given under → Ah Bolom Tzacab.

Ka The ancient Egyptian designation for the generating and sustaining vital forces, especially of men: then extended to denote the spiritual life-force in general. The Ka-sign, made by raising the open hands with palms facing outwards, served to protect one, and the hieroglyph for Ka had the same effect. Like the female → Hemsut, the Ka are a class of protective spirits, who are still active and effective even after the death of the person associated with them.

Kabandha ('Barrel') The chief demon in the Indian epic, the Ramayana; he looks like a barrel because → Indra squashed his head and his lower limbs into his body, making him into an enormous torso with an all-devouring mouth in its breast.

Kabiroi (Greek *kabiroi*) In origin, oriental vegetation-deities in Asia Minor, whose cult reached Greece via the Aegean, especially the islands of Samothrace and Lemnos, where it was transformed under the influence of Orphic ideas. The Kabiroi were now seen as the sons of → Hephaistos; they were invoked as 'great gods' and had their own mysteries. They were usually conceived of as twins, and often equated with the → Dioskúroi as protectors of sea farers.

Kabrakan → Zipakna

Kadeš Canaanite goddess of love and sexuality. She is shown standing naked on a lion, holding a snake in her hands. At the time of the New Kingdom, she was taken over by the Egyptians.

Kāhil(ān) A god often invoked in pre-Islamic inscriptions in Arabic. The name probably means 'the mighty one'.

Kaia Demonic figures believed in by tribes on the Gazelle Peninsula of New Britain (Melanesia). In their underground realm (especially below volcanoes) they prefer to take on human form, but they appear to the natives above as snakes, possibly as eels or wild pigs, or in some other form. In the beginning, the Kaia were the creators of all things, but now they are evil and bent on doing harm.

Kaiamunu (Kaiemunu) A demon in the folk belief of the Papuans in the Purari Delta of New Guinea. He plays a big part in the initiation ceremonies for boys, whom he is supposed to swallow and then regurgitate to new life. The Kaiamunu is represented as a kind of wickerwork image, and the long houses belonging to the men of the tribe seem to reflect his shape.

Kāla In Indian thought, the personification of time as a cosmogonic force; first mentioned in the Atharvaveda. Kāla was his own father, and hence his own son. From the fifth century BC onwards, we find the god of death → Yama occasionally referred to as Kāla.

Kalevanpojat ('sons of Kalevala') In Finnish folk tradition, gigantic demonic beings who turn fertile land into heaps of stones and wasteland, and forests into marshy meadows.

Kālī ('she who is black') An Indian goddess of the Great Mother type. She is the menacing and fearful aspect of → Durgā. She is usually shown standing on her husband → Śiva, or placing her left foot on him. She has black hair, her tongue hangs out, and she wears a string of human skulls round her neck. As Kālaratri ('black night') she is the mythic embodiment of a natural force which veils everything at the time of the creation (or of the destruction) of the world.

Kalki (Kalkin) The tenth and final avatāra of → Viṣṇu. When our present age (Kaliyuga) draws to a close, and our social and spiritual life has reached its nadir, Viṣṇu will appear on earth to initiate the end of the world. He will appear in human form with a horse's head, or he will ride on a white horse, holding a shining sword in his raised hand.

Kalliópe ('she of the beautiful voice') One of the → Muses, specifically the one concerned with heroic epic and elegy.

Kallistó ('she who is most beautiful') In origin perhaps an old Arcadian (south Greek) bear goddess, later ousted by → Artemis. The myth tells how she was loved by → Zeus, turned into a bear and, finally, raised to the constellations (the Great Bear).

Kalteš A goddess venerated by the Ugric peoples in west Siberia. She is supposed to be the sister, wife or daughter of the sky-god (→ Num). She has various functions including supervision of childbirth, and determining people's destinies. At certain festivals she is represented by the birch-tree. Her sacred creatures are the goose and the hare, and she may manifest herself in their shapes.

Kalunga The supreme being of the Ndonga in Angola. Kalunga, it is believed, gave himself this name; and he looks like a man, though it is true that he never allows himself to be seen as a whole. He is characterized by wisdom and compassion, he sees and hears all, and he is a just and righteous judge. His son is → Musisi.

Kalypso A Greek nymph who rescues the castaway Odysseus and keeps him with her for seven years. Her name comes from the Greek verb *kalypto* = to cover, conceal; and this has prompted the suggestion that she is really a goddess of death.

Kāma ('desire') Indian god of love; his consort is Rati (= voluptuousness). To begin with, he was the demonic spirit which animated → Prajāpati. When → Brahmā began to be seen as the creator god, Kāma was said to have sprung from his heart. Kāma is represented as an ageless and unageing youth, riding on a parrot. Both the bow and the arrows he bears as his attributes are tipped and strung with flowers. He is symbolized by a piscine monster (Makara), often shown in a red banner. His epithet *ananga* (= bodiless) is connected with a myth according to which he was burned to ashes by Śiva who had lost his temper with him.

Kāmākṣī ('she who ogles') A benign goddess who is particularly venerated in south India. She ranks as *paraśakti*, 'the highest → Śakti' and is represented as four-armed and seated on a lotus. She is also worshipped in the image of the Śri Cakra (Diskus).

Kaménae (Camenae) Italic goddesses of springs and wells; at their shrine in Rome, the vestal virgins drew water every day. Later, as the goddesses of Italic poetic creation, they were equated with the Greek → Muses.

Kami Divinities of Shintoism. The word *kami* means, basically, 'above': the gods are those who are above. Apart from the gods, spirits are also known as *kami*; indeed, the word can be applied to single trees, animals and mountains (e.g. Fujiyama) which are feared and revered because of their unusual or supernatural properties. At a later period, the designation *arami-kami* = visible god was officially applied to the Emperor.

Kamoš Chief god of Moab (in present-day Jordan), equated in a list of gods with the Old Mesopotamian god → Nergal. Kamoš had his devotees even among the Israelites, and Solomon built 'an high place' for him (I Kings 11: 7, 33). When the Greeks took Kamoš over, they stressed his warlike functions and equated him with → Arés.

Kamrušepa Hittite goddess of healing, the mother of the sea-god Aruna. In the myth of → Telipinu she proves unable to placate the angry god of vegetation.

Kamui Sky-god of the Ainu people on the Japanese island of Hokkaido; he is also called Tuntu, i.e. 'support, pillar' of the world.

Kamulla A Kassite god in the sense of the Babylonian → Ea.

Kan → Bacab

Kappa Japanese water-spirits who feed on cucumbers and blood and get up to all sorts of mischief but who are very knowing and can therefore prove helpful to people.

Karei (or Kari) The supreme being of the Semang people in Malaya. The name of the good is synonymous with the word for 'thunder'. It is believed that when it thunders, Karei is angry and is letting his voice be heard. To placate the god a few drops of blood are offered to him in sacrifice.

Karpo → Horae

Karta A goddess of fate and destiny mentioned in Latvian folksong and reminiscent of → Laima.

Karuileš šiuneš ('the earlier gods') In origin, old Syrian divinities who were subsequently taken over by the Hittites as gods of oaths. In groups of seven or nine they figure as gods of judgment, and are hence connected thereafter with the underworld.

Kašku Proto-Hattic name of the moon-god, who was accepted into the Hittite pantheon, and who corresponds to the Hurrian → Kušuh.

Kastor and Polydeukes The names of the → Dioskúroi, who distinguished themselves by many heroic deeds, especially as tamers of wild horses; Polydeukes was also outstanding as a boxer. When the mortal Kastor fell in battle, the immortal Polydeukes persuaded Zeus to let them spend ever afterwards one day together in the world and one in the underworld. There was an ancient shrine to both in Sparta, and Kastor had a temple on the Forum in Rome.

Kaśyapa ('tortoise') In India, Kaśyapa belongs to the divine minstrels (→ Riṣis) and is venerated as a creative force. With his wife → Aditi he begot the sun-gods (→ Ādityas), but he is also seen as the father of the demonic → Daityas.

Kataragama One of the four great gods in the island of Ceylon (Sri Lanka). He is equated with the Hindu god → Skanda and has developed into a national god in modern times. In Old Tamil, Kataragama was called Cēyōn = 'the god with the red-coloured body.'

Katavi A demonic being in the popular belief of the Nyamwezi (in Tanzania); he is said to be chief of the water-spirits, but he also haunts barren lands and deserts.

Katavul (Kadavul) The Tamil name for the supreme personal being who is constantly present and who is the source of all that exists. The name means 'He, who is'. Katavul is the final and absolute arbiter, who rewards or punishes people according to their deeds.

Ka Tyeleo Supreme god of the Senufo in the Ivory Coast in West Africa. On the fifth day of creation he created the animals, and on the seventh the fruit-bearing trees.

Kaukas A spirit-like being in Lithuanian popular belief: usually taken to be a sort of goblin who brings good luck, though it is also bound up with the notion of a dragon guarding a treasure. In both Finnish and Estonian, *kauko*, *kauki* means 'spirit' and 'devil'.

Kauket → Kuk

K'daai A fire-demon of the Yakuts in Siberia. He is supposed to be the originator of work in wrought iron.

Kebechet An Egyptian goddess, a personification of the purifying libation of water, deeply significant in the cult of the dead as a means of revitalization. She was supposed to be the daughter of → Anubis, the god of the dead, and was depicted in snake form.

Kebechsenef (Kebehsenuf = 'he who refreshes his brothers and sisters') Falcon-headed son of → Horus. He watches over the lower part of the body of a dead person, and to him is allotted the westerly quarter.

Kekri An ancient Finnish feast of fertility connected with the sacrifice of a sheep. This was misunderstood by various writers – for example, we find the mistake in a sixteenth-century list of gods – and as a result Kekri came to be regarded as a god concerned with the rearing of cattle.

Kékrops In Greek tradition, the primeval autochthonous man born from the earth, with legs like snakes; also, the first king of the Athenians. In a dispute between → Poseidon and → Athená, he acted as arbiter. His three daughters, known as the Argaulides ('field-girls') had divine status, and were so revered.

Ke'lets A demon of death in the popular belief of the Chukchi people in north-east Siberia. He hunts men down, accompanied by dogs.

Kematef In the late Egyptian period, the name given to the primeval god → Amun who emerged from → Nun in the shape of a snake.

The name means 'he who has fulfilled his time'. Kneph was the name given to this divine primeval snake by Greek writers.

Kemwer (Kemur)   The black bull venerated in the Egyptian city of Athribis. It was variously identified with → Chentechtai, also worshipped in Athribis, and with → Osiris. It was also interpreted as referring to the left eye (of the moon).

Kentaures → Centaurs

Kephissos → Narkissos

Kérberos (Latin form Cerberus)   The Greek hound of hell, with three heads covered with snakes. The son of → Typhón and → Echidna. It greets new arrivals in hell by wagging its tail obsequiously, but woe betide those who try to get out. Only → Heraklés was able to overcome it.

Kéres   Malevolent demons in Greek popular belief. The root *ker-* means 'bane, evil, death'.

Keto → Phorkys

Kettu → Šamaš

Keyeme   Lord of animals among the Taulipang in the north of South America. He is a man who can change himself into a water-snake by donning a multi-coloured skin.

Khasarpana ('he who glides through the air')   Also known as Khasarpana-Lokeśvara, a form of the Bodhisattva → Avalokiteśvara, known in India. White in colour, he sits on the moon above a double lotus. There is a smile on his face, his right hand forms the 'wish granted' gesture, and in his left hand he holds a lotus.

Kholomodumo A mythical monster which, say the Sotho in south-east Africa, lived at the beginning of time and ate up the whole of humanity save for one old woman. She bore twins who went forth as forest hunters along with a mangy dog: they tracked down the demonic being and killed it – and all the people it had swallowed came out of its inside.

Khyung-gai mGo-can Old Tibetan god with the head of the mythical Khyung bird (corresponding to the Indian → Garuḍa). Like the bird, the god too may have been connected with the sun.

Ki → An

Kingu A demon mentioned in the Akkadian creation epic Enuma Eliš; the son of → Tiamat, who wanted to promote him to be chief of the gods. But → Marduk overcame the forces of the underworld, and → Ea created men from the blood of Kingu.

Kinich Kakmó (Kinich Ahau) The sun-god of the Maya, the fire-bird corresponding to the solar aspect of the Aztec → Quetzalcoatl.

Kinnara A group of spirit-beings belonging to the → Gandharvas in Indian mythology. They are supposed to look like birds with human heads. They bear a red lotus and belong to the retinue of → Kubera. In Burma they are called Keinnara, and they also figure in the art of Thailand and Java.

Kinyras A god revered in Cyprus though he originally hails from Syria (→ Kotar). He was supposed to be a master in the art of iron-smelting, and also the originator of magic and music. His name is probably of Canaanite origin, and may be derived from *kinnor* = lyre, harp.

Kirišša → Pinikir

Kirke (Latin form Circe) The daughter of the Greek sun-god → Hélios; a highly skilled magician, who turned the companions of Odysseus into pigs.

Kis An Egyptian god venerated in the town of Kusae. He is represented as a man who is gripping two creatures (giraffes or snakes) by their long necks and quelling them: hence, probably, his name which means 'the tamer'.

Kišar → Anšar

Kiskil-lilla A Sumerian night-demon (female) dwelling in the Ḫaluppu-tree of → Inanna, which is later felled by → Gilgameš. The *lil* component in the name was construed as *lilu* = night by a process of folk etymology.

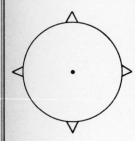

Kitanitowit Supreme god of the Algonkin Indians living in eastern Canada and the north-eastern United States. He was the first existent being, eternal and omnipresent; his name means 'good creator'. Since he is invisible and embraces the whole world, he is represented as a circle or oval: in the middle is a point marking the cosmic centre, and round the periphery are four pointers indicating the heavenly quarters.

Klio (Greek *kleió* = 'she who praises'; in Latin Clio) The muse usually associated with the study of history; her attribute is a parchment scroll.

Klotho → Moires

Kobold A domestic spirit in Central European popular belief; he teases, and he enjoys his victim's discomfiture – but he may also bring prosperity. The name is a compound of an old word for 'house', 'building' (cf. English 'cove') and the root *old* = to rule: so the kobold is 'he who rules in the house'. They are also imagined as mountain dwarfs, who take silver and give the (once worthless) cobalt in exchange. There is no clear dividing line between them and nature-demons.

Kolanthes A youthful god venerated during the Graeco-Roman period in the Egyptian city of Panoplis and called 'son of Isis and Osiris'.

Köndös Finnish god of sowing and young crops; possibly, a personification of wheat. With the coming of Christianity the figure of Köndös merged with that of St Urban, the patron saint of wine in southern lands and of wheat in the Baltic area.

K'op'ala A protective god of the heathen mountaineers in eastern Georgia. His weapon is a club into which he sometimes transforms himself.

Kore-Arethusa A Greek goddess portrayed on coins from Syracuse and Carthage; interpreted by the Carthaginians as a form of → Astarte-Tinnit. Her characteristic symbol is a woman's head adorned with ears of corn – a reference to Kore (→ Persephóne) who took over the life-giving aspect of Arethusa, the ancient Greek goddess of wells and springs.

Korrawi The Tamil goddess of battle and victory. Her temples were scattered about in the forests and were guarded by corpse-demons and spirits. As Kātukilal she is a goddess of the woods, 'the lady of the jungle'. Her son is → Murukān.

Korybantes Demonic companions of the ancient Phrygian mother of the gods (→ Kybéle) in Asia Minor, and then of the Greek → Rheia. They indulge in orgiastic dances accompanied by raucous music on percussion and wind instruments. According to the myth, they are the progeny of → Zeus, who impregnated the earth by falling on it as rain.

Kotar (Kautar, later pronounced as Kušor) Old Syrian god of the blacksmith's craft, and lord of magic spells and incantations. In the Ugaritic myths he appears as master of all arts: he erects a palace for the god → Baal, and forges the

weapons for the fight against the sea-god →
Jamm. Other names for this god are Chusor, and,
on the island of Cyprus, → Kinyras.

Kótys (also as Kotytto) A Thracian goddess,
whose cult spread over Greece and Italy.

Koyote (Coyote)   Among the Apache and the
Navajo tribes in North America, the name of the
culture-hero who had to get rid of the children of
the water-monster Tieholtsodi, in order that the
flood should recede and the fifth – i.e. the
present – world should emerge. The name means
'prairie wolf'. Koyote taught man how to use
seeds. Among the Miwok people in California he
is creator and supreme being; while the Maidu
tribe in central California sees him as the divine
antagonist.

Krişṇa (Sanskrit, dark, the dark one)   Deified
hero of Indian legend, the eighth avatāra of →
Vişṇu, son of Vasudeva (of the lunar lineage) and
of Devaki. The Purānas tell how he grew up
among herdsmen in order to escape the persecu-
tion of his uncle. He is the charioteer of the
Prince Arjuna, and the spokesman of the
Bhagavadgītā, in which he designates himself as
supreme god. In Indian art, scenes from the
childhood and early life of Krişṇa are very
popular – for example, his victorious battle
against the snake-king Kaliya, his flute-playing
and his amorous dalliance with the cow-girls (→
Rādhā). Krişṇa died when a hunter inadvertently
shot an arrow into his only vulnerable spot – his
right heel.

Krodhadevatās ('angry deities')   Terror-
inspiring gods in Buddhism. They are bluish-
black or red in colour, they have a third eye and
they are adorned with skulls and eight snakes.
They serve to ward off enemies of Buddhist
teaching. → Acala and → Sumbharāja are
examples of Krodha (= anger) gods.

Krónos In origin, a pre-Greek fertility god who underlies the harvest feast of the *kronia* (cf. the Roman Saturnalia). In Greek mythology, Kronos is a Titan, the son of the sky-god → Uranós and the earth-goddess → Gaia. He attacked his father, castrated him and took over world dominion. To protect himself from a similar fate, he swallowed all his children except → Zeus, in place of whom his wife → Rheia handed him a stone wrapped in napkins. Zeus grew up in hiding and was finally able to dethrone his father and hurl him into Tartaros.

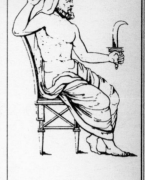

Kṣitigarbha ('whose origin is the earth') One of the eight great → Bodhisattvas; in Central and East Asia he developed into a god of the dead and judge in the underworld (→ Di-zang). In Japan he is known as → Jizo: he protects travellers and leads people to paradise.

Kubaba (also Kupapa) An ancient goddess of Asia Minor, worshipped in Upper Mesopotamia under the name of Gubaba. The most important centre of her cult was Carchemish. Subsequently she acquired the traits of a mother goddess. A mirror and a pomegranate were among her attributes. In many ways she is equivalent to the Hurrian goddess of love → Šauška. Transition to the Phrygian-Lydian → Kybéle if not demonstrable is highly probable.

Kubera (Kuvera) Indian god of riches; in Vedic times, the leader of the spirits (→ Yakṣas) who dwell in the dark abyss. The demon-king → Rāvaṇa is his half-brother. According to one tradition he achieved immortality through severe mortification of the flesh. His dwarfish, pot-bellied torso has three legs. His earliest attributes were a sack and a drinking-bowl; later he acquired a cudgel and a purse. He lives in the Himalayas and is guardian of the northerly quarter of heaven.

Kucumatz (Kukumatz) Supreme god of the Quiché Indians as recorded in their sacred scriptures. He corresponds to the → Kukulcan of the Maya, and the → Quetzalcoatl of the Aztec. He was imagined as androgynous: both father and mother, begetter and matrix. He is the 'heart of heaven' who, together with his three hypostases (described as *cakulha* = lightning) 'excogitated' the earth, the plants and the animals.

Kud In Old Korean religion, the embodiment of the dark and evil principle in the world, the baneful adversary of → Palk.

Kujaku Myoo ('Peacock King of Wisdom') In Japanese esoteric Buddhism, he who protects mankind from evil powers; he eradicates the evil passions and thoughts which stain men's minds. His cult was wide-spread as part of the teaching of the Shingon sect in Japan. In art, he is shown surrounded by the large fan-shaped peacock wheel.

Kuk and Kauket A pair of Egyptian primeval gods belonging to the Ogdoad. They represent the darkness that reigned before the creation of the heavenly bodies.

Kukulcan Originally a god of the Toltecs, taken over by the Maya. Both in his name (which means 'feathered snake') and in his function he corresponds to → Quetzalcoatl of the Aztecs. Students in this field refer to him as God B. He can figure as god of earth, water or fire, and his symbols are correspondingly the sprouting maize, the fish and, for fire, the lizard or a torch. First and foremost, he is a god of resurrection and reincarnation.

Kukuth (Kukudhi) In Albanian popular belief a female demon of sickness who brings pestilence to the land. The unhappy soul of a miser which roams about uneasily and does nothing but ill, is also described as 'Kukudhi'.

Kulshedra (Kuçedrë) A demonic being in Albanian folklore which appears either as an enormous hag with pendulous breasts, or as a dragon-like monster spitting fire. It uses its own urine as a weapon. The kulshedra can cause a water shortage, and can only be placated by means of human sacrifice. The name comes from the Latin *chersydrus* which means something like 'the snake that lives in the water and on the earth'. The male form, known as Kulshedër, acts as a devil.

Kumarbi This was the name for the 'father of the gods' among the ancient Hurrians in Asia Minor. He had to abdicate in the face of pressure from younger gods. One myth – the Ullikummi poem – tells how Kumarbi begets a son (→ Ullikummi) by means of a rock, counting on his help in the fight to retrieve his heavenly kingdom.

Kunapipi A sort of Magna Mater among the Alawa people in Arnhem Land in Australia. She slew young men and dined off them until an eagle killed her. Her secret name can still be heard in the whirring of the ceremonial bull-roarer. Men enter her womb (a channel in the ritual initiation site) to be reborn anew.

Kun-tu-bzan-po The chief god in the Tibetan Bon pantheon; he is the 'all-bountiful god' who has created the world from a lump of mud and living beings from an egg. He corresponds to the Indian → Sāmantabhadra.

Kurdalaegon The god of blacksmiths among the Ossetian people (in the Caucasus). His epithet is 'the heavenly one'. He shoes the dead man's horse, thus helping him on his journey to the other side: the obsequies reflect this.

Kurétes

Cretan demons closely connected with vegetation, whose antecedents go back to pre-Greek times. They were often equated with the → Korybantes. In Greek myth they perform noisy and warlike dances to protect the infant → Zeus from → Krónos.

Kūrma

(Sanskrit = tortoise) In Vedism, the tortoise was associated with → Prajāpati as an embodiment of cosmic power; in the Rāmāyana and in the Purānas it was identified with → Visnu. Visnu himself came down to earth in the form of a tortoise (usually taken to be the second avatāra), thus providing a fundament for the churning of the milk ocean.

Kurukullā

One of the most popular Buddhist goddesses; she can cast spells on men and women to inveigle them into serving her. In Tibet she has become a goddess of riches. Her main attributes are a red lotus and a bow and arrow – this latter suggesting the role of a goddess of love. When she is shown in the lotus posture, the god of love → Kāma, together with his partner, may be shown thereunder.

Kušuh

The moon-god of the Hurrians in ancient Asia Minor, corresponding to the Hattic moon-god → Kašku. His sacred number is 30, corresponding to the lunar month of thirty days. In one myth, the moon-god is pursued by the weather-god, but the goddess of healing → Kamrušepa comes to his aid.

Kutkinnáku

Beneficent spirit revered by the Koryak people in eastern Siberia. He taught mankind to hunt and catch fish, and gave them the fire-stick and the shaman drum. In myth he appears as a raven.

Kvasir In Nordic mythology, a being possessed of divine wisdom, the personification of a fermented drink. Kvasir is said to have originated from the spittle of the Aesir (→ As) and the → Vanir, when they stopped fighting each other. After he was murdered, his blood was mixed with honey and became the mead of the skalds: whoever drinks of it becomes a poet.

Kwoth In Nuer (a Nilotic language) the word for 'god' really means 'spirit'. God is then *kwoth a nial* = spirit of heaven: and he is like the wind, creator and mover of all things. He can be approached through prayer and sacrifice. A poetic epithet for him is Tutgar, i.e. an ox with widespread horns, in token of his strength and majesty.

Kybéle (also Kybebe; Latin Cybele) The Phrygian Magna Mater; in origin, probably a mountain goddess with dwarfs as servants. From Mount Ida she received her epithet of Idaea Mater, and in myth she also appears as → Agdistis. Her cult spread far and wide across the Aegean, and she herself was aligned with the mother goddesses of the Greeks, → Demeter and → Rheia. In the year 205/204 BC the black stone sacred to her was brought from Pessinus in Phrygia to Rome. In art, she is shown in a chariot drawn by lions and panthers. Her attributes are a mirror and a pomegranate, often also a key. As protective deity of towns, she is also entitled to wear a castellated crown. She is accompanied by a demonic retinue of ecstatically dancing → Korybantes. Kybéle was venerated as queen of nature and of fertility; her priests were the castrated Galloi. Her own cult was bound up with that of her lover → Attis. The faithful believed that through her mysteries they would achieve rebirth to a new life.

L

Labbu A monster mentioned in an Akkadian (ancient Mesopotamian) myth, possibly in the form of a snake, and associated with the Milky Way. The god → Tišpak is given the job of slaying it.

Lachesis → Moirai

Lactans Roman god of agriculture, who caused the crops to 'yield milk', i.e. to do well.

Ladon In Greek mythology, a demonic reptilian dragon which guards over the tree with the golden apples in the garden of the → Hesperides.

Lahama In Sumerian mythology, the water-demons who belong to → Enki. In the Babylonian pantheon, Lahmu and Lahamu were the children of → Apsu and → Tiamat, and the parents of the primeval gods → Anšar and Kišar.

Lahar A Sumerian goddess representing the mother sheep; she taught mankind how to breed and rear cattle.

Lahurati An Elamite god corresponding to the Sumerian → Ninurta.

Laima Latvian goddess of fate and good fortune, who also takes a sympathetic interest in women in childbirth. She is the creator of men, and takes a hand in their birth, their marriages and their deaths. No household can hope for things to go well unless Laima is resident there. In Lithuania, we find, apart from Laima, a trinity of Laimos – three sisters who correspond to the Fates (conceived as women) of other Indo-Germanic peoples (→ Moirai, → Norns).

Laka The goddess of song and dance in Hawaii. Although she occupies a rather secondary rank in the Polynesian pantheon, she was the object of a very special cult among the islanders, devoted as they are to the pleasures of the flesh.

Lakṣmī Hindu goddess of good fortune and beauty, also known as Śrī. In the Vedas, she was the consort of → Varuṇa or → Sūrya, in Hinduism she is the → Śakti of → Viṣṇu. In all the incarnations of Viṣṇu she figures as his female counterpart. When he was incarnated as the dwarf Vamana, she sat on a lotus flower and was therefore called Padma. For Viṣṇu as Rāma she was the faithful → Sītā; for → Kṛiṣṇa, she was first the cow-girl → Rādhā, and then his bride Rukmiṇī. Lakṣmī is usually portrayed as a golden-hued goddess standing or sitting on a lotus flower. The goddess was taken over by Buddhism: in Japan she is known as Kichijo-ten, in China as Gong De Tian.

Lalita Tripurasundarī A Tantric goddess, the symbol of cosmic energy and secret ruler of the world. She is the → Śakti, the female and – in India – dynamic force, from whose union with the male-static principle of → Śiva, the transitory world of deception (*māyā*) is generated.

Lama (1) (Akkadian Lamassu) In Sumerian myth, a benevolent and protective demon, conceived as female. In the later Assyrian period, the female Lamassu and the male → Šedu were installed at the entrances to palaces to act as guardians; in this capacity they were realized as winged hybrid creatures, half-man, half-bull.

Lama (2) As a Hittite-Luvian protective god, also known under the name of Innara. His cult was already known in Kanis. One myth tells how Lama seized power in heaven but was ousted by → Ea on account of his arrogance.

Lamaria The goddess of the hearth and tutelary goddess of women and cows among the Svan people in the western Caucasus. Her name shows Christian influence (Maria).

Lamaštu Akkadian demon of puerperal fever and diseases of infants; corresponds to the Sumerian → Dimme. In art, she is portrayed with bare breasts with which she is suckling a dog and a pig; in her hands she holds a comb and a whorl.

Lamia ('she who swallows up') This vampire-like spirit which abducts little children and sucks people's blood figured in popular belief in ancient Greece and continues to do so in modern Greece. It is similar to the Roman → Lemures.

Lan Cai-he One of the 'eight immortals' (→ Ba Xian). He is depicted sometimes as a boy, sometimes as a girl, and one tradition makes him a hermaphrodite. He holds a basket of flowers or a flute as attribute.

Lao-zi ('old master') The founding father of Taoism, who rose to one of the highest positions in the Chinese pantheon. His mother is supposed to have borne him from her armpit under a plumtree; he was born with white hair and could already speak. According to the legend he rides to the west on a water-buffalo, and is reborn there as Buddha. In popular Taoism he is regarded as the tutelary patron of occult science and alchemy. In his deified form he bears the name Lao Jun.

Laran Etruscan war-god, usually portrayed as a naked youth with a cape (*chlamys*), a lance and a helmet. The basic meaning of the name may be something like 'strong', 'mighty'.

Lares Roman tutelary gods protecting the household and the family. The *Lar familiaris* was venerated at the hearth, and his image was set up in a small shrine (*lararium*). In the Empire period, the lares were imagined in the dual rather than the plural, as pairs of dancing youths, each of whom held up a wreath or a horn. The *lares compitales* were the tutelary gods of cross-roads, while the *lares viales* ensured a safe return for travellers.

Larunda A Sabine (old Italic) goddess, often imagined as the mother of the → Lares; more probably, she is a form of the earth-goddess. Her name is explained as a verbal form meaning 'may she cause (the earth) to turn green'.

Lasas God-like female beings in the Etruscan pantheon; they are depicted as winged or unwinged, they carry wreaths and mirrors as attributes, and are often richly adorned with jewellery. They are often to be found in the retinue of the goddess of love → Turan; this is particularly true in the case of the *lasa* known as Acaviser (or Achvistr). A few other lasas are known by name, e.g. → Alpan and → Evan. Like the → *genii* the lasas are to be approached as supernatural, personal beings, who are not invested with the powers given to the true (higher) gods.

Laskowice (Leschia, derived from Old Slavonic word for 'forest') Satyr-like forest spirits in the mythology of the east and south Slavonic peoples. They protect wild animals, and have a particularly close relationship with the wolf.

Lature Danö For the inhabitants of the Indonesian island of Nias, this is the divine counterpart of their supreme god → Lowalangi. Lature Danö causes sickness and death, not to speak of bad weather. He is the lord of the underworld, black and red in colour, and darkness, the snake and the moon are aspects of his allotted realm.

Lauka mate Latvian goddess of fields and fertility, known as 'mother of the plough-land'. The peasants prayed to her and made sacrifice so that the fields might bear plentifully.

Laumé A typical → fairy in Lithuanian popular belief. She usually appears naked, likes to bathe and is keen on spinning and weaving. She helps the poor and protects orphans. In the course of time she acquired demonic traits, and in folk tradition she sometimes merges into the form of → Laima, the goddess of fate. The

Latvians know Laumé under the name of Lauma, and they also call her 'the white lady'.

Laverna Old Italic goddess, who may have been queen of the underworld, as libations to her were poured out with the left hand as was customary in cults of the underworld.

Leda In Greek myth, the mother of → Kastor and Polydeukes; also of → Heléne, after Zeus had mated with her in the form of a swan. It is possible that Leda developed from an ancient earth and mother goddess in Asia Minor; there was a Lycian word *lada* meaning 'woman'.

Legba A celestial trickster in Dahomey (West Africa) to whom mankind owes the art of prognostication and the interpretation of oracles. His sacred animal is the dog, which he uses as a messenger.

Lei-zi Chinese goddess of thunder and originator of silk-worm breeding. She was the wife of → Huang-di.

Lelwani A Hittite deity of the underworld, originally thought of as male and designated as 'king'. Subsequently, however, under the influence of the old Mesopotamian Ereškigal, Lelwani became a female deity. She dwelt 'in the dark earth'. Those threatened by death had surrogate images sacrificed to the goddess. Her shrines were connected with charnel-houses and mausolea.

Lemures (Larvae)   In Roman belief, the evil spirits of the dead who wander about as nocturnal bogeymen. Their feast, the Lemuria, was held on 9 November and 13 May: on these occasions the householder went out of doors at midnight and threw black beans to them as a peace offering, making sure to keep his face turned away.

Leto (Latin Latona)   In Greek mythology, the daughter of the → Titan Kois and of Phoibe. Impregnated by → Zeus, she went to the island of Delos where she bore the heavenly twins → Apóllon and → Artemis. The name Leto is connected by philologists with the Lycian word *lada* = woman, wife; it may possibly reflect an earlier deity once worshipped in Asia Minor.

Leviathan (Livjatan)   A monster in Phoenician mythology, known in Ugarit by the name of Lotan(?). In the Old Testament, it is the monstrous dragon of chaos which is overcome by Jahwe (Psalm 74: 14). In Isaiah 27: 1 it is referred to as 'the crooked serpent'. In general, it is regarded as a denizen of the sea, and hence is equated with the crocodile and the whale. In apocalyptic literature and in Christianity, Leviathan figures as one of the forms in which the devil manifests himself.

Leza   Chief god of south-east African Bantu tribes in northern Zimbabwe. He is conceived as bodyless and sexless. He is creator of all things; one myth makes him 'mother of the animals'. All that Leza does is good: above all, he sends rain.

Lha   In the ancient Bon religion of Tibet, the designation for 'gods', translated in Sanskrit as '*deva*'.

Lhamo   The Tibetan word means simply 'goddess'; this particular one is portrayed with flowing locks, fiercely protruding eyes, ten arms and enveloped in flames. She is regarded as a protective deity (→ Dharmapāla) who lends her aid to those who earnestly and devoutly seek it.

Li In Chinese popular belief the divine lord of fire; under the name of Zhu Rong he is regent of the southerly quarter of heaven. The myth tells how Li helped to divide heaven and earth from each other. In art, the god is shown riding on a tiger.

Liber Old Italic god of animal and vegetable fertility; after equation with → Dionysos, he figured on his own as nothing more than a god of wine. On the day of his feast (17 March) youths donned the *toga virilis* for the first time, in token of their reaching man's estate.

Libera Old Italic goddess, daugther of → Ceres and sister of the fertility god → Liber. As a chthonic triad the three formed a counterpart to the divine trinity on the Capitol: → Júpiter, → Júno and → Minerva. Libera was equated with the Greek → Persephóne.

Libertas Roman goddess, personification of freedom. She had a temple of her own on the Aventine Hill. Her attributes were the 'freedom hat', the *pilleus* (the felt cap which slaves put on when they were freed), and a sceptre or lance.

Libitina Roman goddess of interment; her temple and sacred grove formed the centre of funerary arrangements in Rome. In poetic language Libitina is a metaphor for death.

Lilith This female demon in Jewish popular belief is already mentioned in the Old Testament (Isaiah 34: 14). She has her origins in the → Lilitu of Babylonian demonology, but popular etymology has taken her name to mean 'she of the night'. Lilith (the plural form is *lilin*) was imagined as a blood-sucking nocturnal ghost. In Talmudic lore she was regarded as a devilish being, and as Adam's first wife. The owl was sacred to her. From Palestine, the cult of Lilith spread to Greece where she merged with → Hekáte.

Lilitu (or Ardat-lili) A Babylonian nocturnal demon, corresponding to the Sumerian → Kiskil-lilla and continuing to lead a ghostly existence in the Jewish → Lilith.

Liluri Ancient Syrian mountain-goddess, forming a pair with the weather-god Manuzi. Bulls were sacrificed to both.

Lir (The name is connected with the Irish word for 'sea' – *ler*) Sea-god in the Irish tradition, the bravest man of the → Tuatha De Danann. In Irish poetry, 'the plain of *lir*' is a kenning for the waves of the sea. In Wales, the god was called Llyr.

Lisa The name given to the (male) sun worshipped by the Fong in Dahomey (West Africa); from its union with the (female) moon → Mawu, there arose seven divine pairs of twins. One of these pairs – 'the iron twins' – gave mankind the first tools and weapons.

Li Tie-guai ('Li with the iron crutch') One of the 'eight immortals' (→ Ba Xian), a species of genii. He was said to have been a pupil of → Lao-zi. He possessed magic powers, and his attributes were the iron crutch, the bat (a symbol of good luck) and the bottle-gourd, which supposedly contained an arcanum which could resurrect the dead.

Ljubi A female demon in Albanian folk belief. She dwells in a wonderful vegetable garden, and can cause the waters to dry up unless a virgin is sacrificed to her.

Loa Divine beings revered in Voodoo, the set of occult beliefs and practices found in Haiti. The antecedents of the Loa go back to roots in Africa, and they have acquired many traits of Catholic saints. Cf. → Damballa.

Locana ('eye') A Buddhist goddess, assigned as partner (*prajñā*) to → Vairocana or to → Akṣobhya. She is white in colour, thus expressing the spirit of peace. Her attribute is the wheel.

Lodur(r) A god mentioned in the Germanic creation myth. Together with → Hönir and → Odin, he played a part in the creation of man. Etymologically, the name has been explained as meaning 'the blazing one', and he has been coupled with → Loki ('Lohe').

Logos (Greek = word, reason) The 'world principle' in Stoicism, the most powerful philosophical movement in the Hellenistic age. As *logos spermatikos* it is the power that informs all things and brings all things about. It is the divine spirit, indeed God himself, from which the other, mythological gods have arisen. With Philo of Alexandria, the Logos takes on personal and anthropomorphic characteristics. In the New Testament, the Logos is used as a designation of the person of Jesus as the son of God.

Lokapālas ('world-guardians') This designation appears, from the time of the Upaniṣads on, with reference to the gods who guard the four heavenly quarters; they are also known as *dikpālas*, i.e., 'guardians of the heavenly quarters'. These are, individually: → Indra in the east, → Varuṇa in the west, → Yama in the south and → Kubera in the north. At a later date, the following gods were added: → Sūrya for the south-west, → Soma (north-east), → Agni (south-east) and → Vāyu (north-west). In Tantrism, → Brahman is added for the zenith, and → Viṣṇu for the nadir.

Loki The artful dodger in the Germanic pantheon, and the sire of several agencies hostile to the gods – the wolf → Fenrir, → Hel and the → Midgard-snake. In one of his manifestations, as a mare, Loki is said to have given birth to the stallion Sleipnir. He can, in fact, take on almost any shape he wishes. Popular etymology has connected his name with the word *log* (German *Lohe* = fierce flames). Wherever Loki appears along with Odin, he acts as the factotum of the gods, never at a loss for sharp practice. Otherwise, however, he is their adversary: he causes the death of → Balder, and brings about the destruction of the world (Ragnarök). His consort is → Sigyn.

Lowalangi (Lowalani) The inhabitants of the island of Nias in Indonesia believe in Lowalangi as the god of the world above, the source of all that is good; his elder brother and adversary is → Lature Danö. Lowalangi is lord of life and death; he is omnipresent and omnisicient, the creator of mankind. His name figures in prayers of supplication and in solemn oaths. His sacred creatures are the cock, the rhino-bird and the eagle. He partakes in the sun and in light. Men are the property (the pigs) of Lowalangi, and just as people take good care of their pigs, so does Lowalangi look after his people.

Lucifer (Latin = bringer of light) A name used in Christianity for the devil. It goes back to Isaiah 14: 12, where the casting into hell of the King of Babylon is likened to the fall of the resplendent morning star (Hebrew *helal*). The name was applied by the church fathers to → Satan, on the basis of Luke 10: 18, where Satan is said to fall as lightning from heaven. Certain Gnostic sects regarded Lucifer as a divine power in his own right, or as the 'first-born son of God'.

Lucina Old Italic goddess of birth, whose grove was on Cispius. She was absorbed by → Juno, in her capacity as goddess of women.

Lü Dong-bin (also known as Lü Yan) One of the 'Eight Immortals' (→ Ba Xian). Many tales are told of his wondrous deeds. He is the tutelary god of barbers; his attribute is a sword with which he slays demons.

Lug (Lugus) A Celtic god, after whom the ancient capital of Galliens Lugdunum (the modern Lyon) was named. His functions identify him as a god of war and of the magic arts, but poets benefit from him as well as warriors and magicians. The raven is particularly associated with him. In the Irish sagas, Lug is also called Lamfada = he of the long hand, and some students have seen in this a reference to the sun's rays, just as his spear has been interpreted as indicating lightning. His Irish epithet Samildanach ('he who can do everything') presents him as a master craftsman and artist. Lug had a particular relationship with the earth-goddess → Tailtu.

Lugalbanda Deified king of the Sumerian city of Uruk. In the Gilgameš epic, Lugalbanda and the goddess → Ninsun are mentioned as the parents of → Gilgameš.

Luna (Latin = moon) Roman goddess of the moon, whose chief temple was on the Aventine Hill. She was equated with the Greek → Seléne, and, like the latter, she took on traits of → Hekáte. Like → Sol, the sun-god, she was supposed to be the protector of charioteers in the circus ring.

Lupercus (Latin = 'wolf-repeller' or 'wolf-being') Roman god with whom the ancient Roman feast of the Lupercalia (on 15 February) was associated. Whether the equation with → Faunus, current already in antiquity, is justified is a moot point.

Lur Basque word meaning 'earth', and the name of the earth-goddess; she was supposed to be the mother of the sun (→ Ekhi) and the moon (→ Ilazki). In Roman times, there was a Pyrenean goddess called Lurgorr (Basque = red earth).

Lykurgos The Greek name of a god revered in north Arabia: possibly a Syrian god in origin, whose function was to promote the cultivation of fruit-bearing trees.

M

Ma A Cappadocian earth and mother goddess in ancient Asia Minor, a personification of fertile nature, intermittently blending into the figure of → Kybéle. She had a war-like function too, and was equated by Roman troops with their goddess → Bellona.

Maahiset ('earth-dwellers') In Finnish popular belief, dwarf-like beings dwelling under the earth. They are also called *maanalaiset* ('the subterranean ones'), and play the part of earth-spirits, widely respected and revered as they incorporate the beneficent – but also on occasion threatening – powers of the earth.

Maat Ancient Egyptian personification of the world-order, incorporating the concepts of justice, truth and legality. She was supposed to be the daughter of → Re, the creator of the world. The Pharaoh was the 'beloved of Maat, he who lives in her through his laws'. A favourite venue for judicial hearings was at the shrines of the goddess, and the judges were regarded as her priests. In art, Maat is shown with an ostrich feather on her head.

Mac Gréine (Ceathur mac Gréine) An Irish god who is invested with the kingly function, and who forms a triad with Mac Cuill the warrior, and Mac Cecht the 'son of the ploughshare'. The name Mac Gréine means 'son of the sun'; his wife is → Eriu.

Macha(s) In old Irish religion, a group of three goddesses who discharge various functions in the fields of motherliness, agriculture and war.

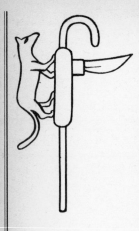

Mafdet Ancient Egyptian goddess in the form of a feline predator (a cheetah?); she is in charge of castigation, and is often shown together with apparatus for execution.

Māh In Persian, the word means both 'moon' and 'moon-god'. He is the source of the cow, the most important animal in Iranian religion and mythology. On Kushan coins we see the moon-god in cloak, doublet and trousers, with the tips of the sickle moon sticking out of his shoulders.

Mahadeo (Sanskrit *mahādeva* = great god) This word, taken over from Vedism/Hinduism, is used to designate the supreme god by certain primitive tribes in central India, e.g. the Gonds and the Baiga.

Mahākāla ('the great black one') A Buddhist god who reminds us, on the one hand, of → Śiva (e.g. in his possession of the trident and bowl made from a skull), and who on the other hand is a god of riches. In the main, he appears as two-armed and three-eyed, with a tiger-skin and the sacred noose or cord made from eight snakes. As a severe and wrathful god, his function is to destroy the enemies of the Buddhist teaching (the *dharma*).

Mahāprabhu (Sanskrit *mahāprabhu* = great master) The chief god of the Bondo people who live in Orissa.

Mahāsthamaprata ('he who has attained to great power') A → Bodhisattva, who has made no headway at all among the Indian population, but who has become very popular in China where he appears, in female form, under the name of → Da-shi-zhi.

Manasa An Indian snake goddess; her cult is, in some respects, that of a fertility goddess. She is particularly venerated in Bengal where she is invoked for protection against snakebite. Her Buddhist counterpart is → Jāṅgulī.

Manat Old Arabian goddess, one of the three so-called 'daughters of Allah'. Her chief image was set up in the area between Mecca and Medina. The name means 'fate', and in the areas where Hellenistic culture was in contact with Arabian, she was accordingly understood as → Tyché or → Nemesis.

Manda In India, the divine regent of the planet Saturn: he is also known as Śani. He is supposed to be old, ugly and lame, and he travels in a cart drawn by eight dappled horses or rides on a blackbird, a vulture or a raven.

Manda d-Hiia ('the knowledge of life') A god of the Mandaeans. As his name suggests, he personifies the Mandaean teaching – the teaching (*manda*) of life (*hiia*). He it is who has revealed this teaching; and as the teaching is mainly concerned with redemption, he also figures as the saviour or redeemer.

Mandah (Mundih) Designation of a pre-Islamic category of gods, who were primarily concerned with irrigation, but who also show the characteristics of protective deities. The collective designation *mandah* can be associated with the name of an individual god; thus, for example, in the case of → 'Attar.

Mandulis (Merulis) A Nubian god, an offshoot of whose cult was to be found in Philae in Egypt. He was still being venerated as a sky-god and sun-god in Roman times.

Manes (Latin *di manes* = the good gods)
The Romans believed that the souls of the dead
reigned in the underworld as *di manes*, 'good
gods', and it was in their honour that the feast of
the *parentalia* was celebrated. In the Empire
period, the name of the dead person on a grave-
stone was often preceded by the formula *Dis
manibus* (abbreviation DM); that is to say, he was
dedicated to the *manes*.

Māṅgala An Indian stellar deity, ruler and
representative of the planet Mars.

Mani In north Germanic tradition the moon
or the moon-god; the son of Mundilferi (in whom
we may perhaps recognize the old moon), and
brother of the sun (→ Sol). It is Mani who guides
the moon-vehicle through the heavens. When the
world is being destroyed (Ragnarök), the moon is
swallowed by a wolf.

Manitu (or Manito) A name given by the
Algonkin Indians of North America to an impersonal force which informs all things. In certain
tribes, e.g. the Lenape, it is also the designation
for the supreme being, the Great Spirit, the chief
of all the gods, who are his appointed representatives (*manitowuk*).

Mañjughoṣa ('beautiful voice') A form of
the → Bodhisattva → Mañjuśrī, particularly
revered in Nepal and Bengal. He has one head
and two arms, and is golden-yellow or saffron
in colour. He rides upon a lion or sits on a lion-
throne.

Mañjuśrī ('charming prince') One of the
most popular → Bodhisattvas, patron of wisdom,
who bestows knowledge and eloquence on his
disciples. His main attributes are the sword of
knowledge and the book of *prajñā pāramitā*.

Inconographically, he can be portrayed in fourteen different ways: see for example, Arapacana, Mañjughoṣa and Dharmadhatuvāgīśvara. Chinese Buddhists believed the Emperor to be an incarnation of Mañjuśrī (in Chinese, Wen Shu). In the Tibetan Books of the Dead, Mañjuśrī (in Tibetan, 'Jam-dpal-dbyangs') is saffron-yellow in colour, and in his hands he holds the blue Utpala blossom. In Japan he is given the name of Monju.

Manu In Indian, Iranian and Germanic tradition, the progenitor of the human race. In Old Indian thought, he is the son of → Vivasvat, or of → Sūrya, and was rescued by a fish during the flood. In gratitude he made a sacrifice of milk and melted butter: after a year, this offering turned into a beautiful woman, who confided to him that she was his daughter → Idā. Together, they begot the human race. Apart from Manu, another thirteen Manus will appear as demigods, creators and sustainers of the creatures belonging to a given period of time.

Manuzi → Liluri

Manzaširi The Kalmyks, a west Mongolian people, give this name to their primeval being from whose body the world was formed: the sun and the moon from his eyes, water from his blood and fire from the warmth of his internal organs. The name is very likely a corruption of → Mañjuśrī.

Māra (Sanskrit = death, destruction) In Buddhism, the evil principle, the insidious adversary of → Gautama Buddha. Overtly, he appears as a king and is so described. Subsequently, certain aspects of Māra are personified: thus, for example, Skandha-Māra represents spiritual 'defilement'.

Marama Moon-goddess of the Maori people in New Zealand. Periodically her body wastes away but it is restored to new splendour when she bathes it in the water of life.

Marchocias In medieval demonology, a prince of the hellish realm, with the wings of a griffin and the tail of a snake. Before the fall of his master → Satan, he belonged to the hierarchy of the angels.

Marduk (in Sumerian, Amar-utuk = calf of the sun-god: Hebrew, Merodach) Originally the tutelary deity of the city of Babylon; from the rise of King Hammurabi onwards, promoted to the office of tutelary god of the Babylonian Empire. His predominance was underpinned by the didactic poem Enuma Eliš, which relates the tale of Marduk's victory over → Tiamat. Thanks to his equation with → Asalluḥi, he became the god of exorcism, of the art of healing and of wisdom. In addition, Marduk displayed the characteristics of a god of judgment and of a bringer of light (god of the spring sunshine); he was indeed regarded as 'lord of the gods'. His wife was → Sarpanitu, and his son was the god of writing and literature → Nabu. Symbolically, Marduk is represented by the reptilian dragon (Mušussu); other attributes of his are the pick-axe (*marru*) or the sickle. His stellar body is the planet Jupiter.

Māri (1) A mother-goddess of the Dravidian peoples in southern India. On the one hand, she is the frightful goddess of smallpox; on the other hand, she is a goddess of rain. She is one of the most popular village deities.

Mari (2) The supreme deity in Basque mythology. The name means simply 'queen'. She appears as a richly bejewelled lady; often she flies through the air, exhaling fire, at other times she rides on a ram. She can also traverse the heavens in a chariot drawn by four horses. Finally, she can appear as a white cloud or as a rainbow. Her habitation is inside the earth; her husband is → Maju. Since the adoption of Christianity by the Basques, both Mari and Maju have sunk to the rank of spirits. But the belief that you can ward off lightning by placing a sickle (the symbol of Mari) in front of the house is still widespread.

Mārici ('beam of light'; in China, Mo li ji) A Buddhist goddess with solar traits. She is described in the Buddhist texts as surrounded by a garland of dazzling rays, and she travels in a vehicle drawn by seven boars. She is particularly invoked at sunrise. There are various iconographic representations of Mārici: as Aśokakānta she has two arms, is golden-yellow in colour, she rides on a pig and in her left hand she holds a branch of the Aśoka tree. Most frequent is the type known as Saṁksipta-Mārici, which has three faces (the left one being that of a pig) and eight arms.

Mars (Marspiter, Mamers, Marmar; often called Mavors by Latin poets) Roman god of war and protector of the fields and what grows in them. The third month is called after him. The Romans called themselves 'sons of Mars', as they regarded him as the father of Romulus and Remus. The holy shield of Mars (*ancile*) which was supposed to have fallen from heaven, was kept in the office of the *pontifex maximus* on the Forum, and was regarded as the pledge or guarantee for the continued existence of the Roman Empire. The lance was also a symbol of the god, and his sacred creatures were the woodpecker (→ Picus), the wolf and the bull. Every five years, the state performed a solemn sacrifice (*dei suovetaurilia*) in his honour. Because of the dance they performed during his rites, the priests of Mars were called *salii* – 'the jumpers'. Augustus consecrated a temple to Mars Ultor ('the avenger'). From the third century BC

onwards, Mars was equated with the Greek → Arés.

Mars, Gallic

The Romans gave this name to a god who was worshipped in Gaul under various names: as Camulos (also in Britain), as Segomo (especially in southern Gaul) and as Smertrios. The god whom the Romans called Hercules can also display Martian characteristics and, when the club became equated with the lightning-hammer, finally passed into the figure of → Taranis. The Gallic Mars is not merely a war-god: in many acts of consecration he appears as a god of healing and of fertility, thus similar to → Teutates.

Marsýas

The name of a demon venerated in Phrygia, regarded as a *silenus* after the Greek invasion. The story goes that he found a flute cast aside by → Athená, and mastered it to such an extent that he challenged → Apóllon to a musical competition. Apóllon won and, to punish Marsýas for his arrogance, had him bound to a tree and flayed alive.

Martanda → Ādityas

Martu

Old Mesopotamian god of the steppe or waste places, supposed to be the son of the sky-god → An; → Bēletsēri figures as his consort. On occasion Martu also appears as a storm-god who destroys settlements.

Marunogere

Mythical culture-hero of the Kiwai-Papua in New Guinea. He taught his people how to build their communal long-houses, and he created woman's sexual parts.

Maruts

A group of Indian storm-spirits, the sons of Rudra and the cow Priśni. They are the constant companions of → Indra. According to the description in the Rigveda they wore golden helmets and breastplates, and used their battle-axes to split the cloud-cliff so that the rain could fall to earth.

Mātaras (or, Ambikās = (little) mothers)   In India, a group of from seven to nine goddesses, who are usually shown in the company of → Śiva or of → Gaṇeśa, and whose functions are not very clearly defined. They are usually taken to play the part of → Śaktis.

Māte   This is the Latvian word for 'mother' and it forms part of the names of several deities. There are 'sea-mother' (→ Jūras māte) and 'fire-mother' (Uguns māte), 'berry-mother' (Ogu māte) and 'plague-mother' (Mera māte). There is even 'devil's-mother' (Joda māte).

Máter Matúta   Old Italic goddess of the dawn and the morning light. Gradually she developed into a goddess of women and child-birth, and later, in her equation with → Inó, into a patron goddess of seafarers.

Matres   In Roman Gaul, in Britain and in the Rhineland, a group of maternal deities, usually thought of as a trinity, though sometimes there seem to be only two of them. They are usually shown seated beside each other with baskets of fruit in their laps, or perhaps a cornucopia. Often, the woman in the middle has a babe-in-arms. It is likely that veneration of the *matres* was limited to members of the household.

Matsya   In Indian mythology the piscine *avatāra* in which → Viṣṇu rescued → Manu from the waters of the deluge.

Maui A sort of roguish demigod in Polynesian belief: on the one hand, he helped the gods to raise the vault of heaven and to order the course of the stars therein, on the other hand, he caught the sun in his net and stole fire in order to give it to man. Many inventions are due to Maui, for example the fish-trap and the cat's cradle. His epithet is Tikitiki, which suggests some connection with the first man (→ Tiki). Maui was never the object of any religious cult.

Mawu The sky-god of the Ewe people in Togo. He created the spirits (*mawuviwo* = children of god), in order to provide a link between himself and human beings. He is the giver of all things, and he loves the colour white – even the food he partakes of is white. Mawu is often equated with the deity known as Sodza (→ So). Among the Fong people in Dahomey, Mawu is female and identified with the moon; yet another version of the myth makes the god androgynous. Mawu is the sister of the sun (→ Lisa).

Māyā ('miraculous power'; later meaning 'deception') In Vedic times a designation for the power of the gods, a power created by → Viṣṇu as a female primeval principle, from which the world is generated. In the Upaniṣads, the world, engendered as it is by the forces of magic, appears as a kind of illusion which will be wiped away when the sole and universal reality of → Brahman is understood. Maya was finally personified and appears in Buddhism as the mother of → Gautama Buddha.

Mayahuel (Mayauel) Old Mexican goddess of pulque (an intoxicating drink). She is portrayed sitting on a tortoise in front of a blossoming agave plant. According to one version of the myth, she was abducted by → Quetzalcoatl from heaven, and when the goddess was torn to pieces by the demons of darkness he caused the first agave plants to arise from her bones.

opposite number in the Etruscan pantheon is →
Turms.

Mercurius, Gallic

Celtic names are extant for the god the Romans called Mercurius: thus, the Picts called him Adsmerius, while the Lingones and the Mediomatrici knew him as Clavariatis. He was especially venerated on mountain-tops: hence such names as Mont-Mercure in the Vendée, and Merkur near Baden-Baden. Like the Roman model, this god too has the caduceus as attribute, and in his hand he holds a purse. His sacred animals are the cock, the tortoise and the ram. In the area round the Mosel and the Rhine he was depicted along with → Rosmerta. Whether this Gallic god shares certain individual traits with → Teutates or is identical with him, is a moot point.

Meresger

(Meretseger = she who loves silence) Snake-goddess and protective deity of the Theban necropolis in ancient Egypt. Her epithet was 'queen of the west'.

Meret

(Mert) Ancient Egyptian goddess of song and rejoicing. As 'Queen of the treasury' she is often depicted standing on the hieroglyph for 'gold'. She appears also in double form as Meret of Upper and of Lower Egypt.

Mesaru → Šamaš

Mesenet

In ancient Egypt, the personification of the 'birth-tile' on which the mother giving birth crouched. The double spiral on the head of the goddess has been tentatively identified as a cow's uterus.

Meslamta'ea

A Sumerian god representing the war-like aspect of → Nergal, the god of the underworld.

Metatron A benevolent demon mentioned in the Kabbala, angel of the countenance and custodian of strength. He receives prayers from human beings and plaits them into crowns to be set on the head of God.

Metis The Greek goddess of wisdom, daughter of → Okeanos and of → Tethys. She was the first wife of → Zeus, who swallowed her because he feared she might give birth to a son mightier than he. Her child → Athená sprang from the head of Zeus.

Meža māte Among the Latvians, an inferior nature deity; the name means 'mother of the forest'. It is told in folksong how she protects all wild life – but she is also called the 'patron of hunters'.

Michael (Hebrew = Who is like God?) In the Bible, the prince of the angels who fights for Israel (Daniel 10: 13-21; 12: 1), and who hurls the apostate angels led by → Satan out of heaven (Revelation 12: 7-9). In Christianity, he is revered like → Gabriel as an archangel. His attributes, as God's champion, are the sword and the banner, and in pictures of the Last Judgment he is shown holding a pair of scales (the weighing of the souls). In Islam he is called Mikal and is regarded as lord of natural forces.

Mictlantecutli ('Lord of the realm of the dead') Aztec god of the underworld (Mictlan) where icy cold reigns and where poisonous snakes are the only food. The god of death is usually depicted with protruding teeth as in a skull.

Midgard-snake In Germanic mythology, an enormous demonic being, the progeny of → Loki. It lies in the world-ocean which surrounds the disc-shaped earth. Its arch-enemy is → Thor who tries in vain to fish it out of the water. At Ragnarök, the destruction of the world, Thor and the great snake kill each other.

Midir   An Irish god, lord of the wondrous land of Mag Mor, the tutor of the god → Oengus. Struck by a stake cut from a hazel-tree, he loses an eye which is replaced for him by the god of healing → Dian-Cecht.

Mihr (also as Mehr, Meher)   Armenian sun-god, semantically related to the Persian → Mithra. He was taken to be the son of → Aramazd. On earth, he manifested himself in the form of fire. He is accompanied by a black raven and he lives in a cave – symbols in sharp contradiction with his solar nature.

Mikal   A Phoenician god revered on Cyprus, in function perhaps a god of plague and pestilence.

Milkom   The chief god of the Ammonites who live in east Jordan. The name probably derives from the Semitic word for 'king' (*milk*, *melek*, cf. also → Malik). Milkom is mentioned several times in the Old Testament, and Solomon seems to have worshipped him for a time (1 Kings 11: 33).

Mi-lo Fo (also called Pu-Sa)   The Chinese name of the Bodhisattva → Maitreya, who is to make his appearance at the end of time. He is represented as a plump monk, with a happy laughing face, in a crouching posture; in his hands he holds a wreath of roses and a purse.

Mimir   In Norse mythology, the gigantic demon of a well, whose waters confer ultimate wisdom on those who drink of them. The god →

Odin pawned one of his eyes in order to be allowed to drink at the spring. A later version of the myth tells us that Mimir falls victim to the struggle between the Aesir (→ As) and the → Vanir; but Odin has the head of the decapitated monster preserved so that he can ask its advice from time to time.

Min Old Egyptian god of fertility: worshipped in prehistoric times in the form of a fetish, thereafter in human form with erect phallus. Among his attributes is a plot with lettuce plants (as an aphrodisiac!). As the local deity of Koptos he became tutelary god of the desert roads. One of his epithets was Kamutef, i.e. 'bull of his mother' in token of his auto-generation. His main feast was the so-called 'feast of the steps'; seated on his 'step' (threshing floor?) the god received the first sheaf of the harvest, cut by the king himself. The Greeks identified Min with → Pan or with → Priapos.

Mīnākṣī (Minaci) Hindu goddess, a manifestation of → Pārvatī. She arose from the sacrificial fire of a childless king, in the shape of a girl with three breasts. Her husband is → Śiva. She is venerated above all by fisher-folk, and she is portrayed riding on a fish.

Minerva An Italic goddess who may have reached the Roman pantheon via the Etruscan (→ Menrva). She is the protective deity of craftsmen and teachers, and her chief feast – the so-called Quinquatrus (19-23 March) – was solemnized mainly by artists and craftsmen. As Minerva Medica she was the tutelary goddess of doctors and had a shrine on the Esquiline. As tutelary goddess of Rome she had her main temple on the Aventine. She was later equated with the Greek goddess → Athená.

Minerva, Gallic Caesar mentions this goddess of handicrafts (*operum*) and arts (*artificiorum*). Her Celtic name is unknown. Many inscriptions have been found dedicated to her, and in these she is often given the epithet Belisama (Celtic *bel* = shining, resplendent). As a rule, she is portrayed as armed. She also appeared as *medica*, i.e. as a physician, and in this capacity her cult was connected with medicinal springs. Her counterpart among the ancient Irish was → Brigit.

Minos In Greek myth, the son of → Zeus and the Phoenician princess Europa. Because of his exemplary rule as king over Crete he was translated after death to the underworld, there to judge the dead (cf. → Aiakós). Minos displays traits of a bull revered as a god.

Minotauros In Greek myth a fabulous being with a human body and a bull's head. It was kept captive in the labyrinth by the Cretan king → Minos, and finally slain by the Athenian hero → Theseus.

Mirsa The celestial lord of light and fire in the popular belief of the Georgians and the Mingrelians in the Caucasus. It is possible that the name is a corruption of the Persian → Mithra. People turn to him for protection against diseases of the eye.

Mithra Iranian god of light and protector of pledges and contracts, similar to the Indian → Mitra. In the course of Zarathustra's reforms he was ousted by → Ahura Mazda from his hitherto predominant position; but in the fourth century BC he made a vigorous come-back as a cult figure, though Zoroastrian circles continued to ignore him. The Avesta tells us that Mithra has 10,000 ears and eyes; he rides in a chariot drawn by white horses. He causes the rain to fall and the plants to grow. In the post-Alexandrine period in Asia Minor Mithra took on traits of → Apóllon and of → Hélios, thereby tending more and more to the sun-god type. Cf. Mithras.

MVNIF·PII·SEXTI·P·M

Mithras The Graeco-Latin name of the Iranian → Mithra, whose cult and mysteries were spread by troops and seafarers over the whole of the Roman Empire in the first and second centuries AD. As the god of loyalty, truth and the fight against evil, Mithras became the favourite god of soldiers. The cult excluded women, and its rituals were held by night in underground rooms (*mithraea* sing. *mithraeum*). The central act was the slaughter of a bull – originally, it was believed, by the god himself – an act which engendered the world and/or its vegetation. Mithra's original identity as a god of light was gradually intensified until he appeared as the figure of *Sol invictus*, the 'invincible sun'. In late antiquity, the universal appeal of this god shows itself in a number of symbioses with other gods (Mercurius, Zeus, Serapis).

Mitra The Vedic god of friendship and of contracts. While → Varuṇa ruled the night and received dark sacrifices, Mitra ruled the day and received white sacrifices. He is one of the → Ādityas, and figures generally in the late Vedic period as a friendly god. In Iran, he is paralleled by → Mithra.

Mixcoatl ('cloud-snake') A manifestation of the Aztec god → Tezcatlipoca, the form he adopted when he made the first fire: as boring-stick he used the rotating firmament held in place by its two poles. Mixcoatl himself is the god of the pole-star.

Mnemosýne The Greek goddess of memory: the mother – by → Zeus – of the nine Muses.

Mnevis (Egyptian Mnewer) The sacred 'bull of Heliopolis', which was, like Apis, an agent of fertility. He was also described as the 'herald' of the sun-god → Re.

Mog Ruith An Irish god, who rides in a chariot of bright bronze, or flies through the air like a bird. The *ruith* component in the name may be connected with the word *roth* = wheel, thus indicating a solar trait in the god. One tradition makes him out to have lost an eye.

Moires (Moirai; Greek *moira* = portion, share) Originally, man's allotted 'portions' in life, his share of fate; thereafter, the three goddesses of fate, Klotho (the spinner) who spins the thread of life, Lachesis, who sustains it through all contingencies, and Atropos ('the inevitable') who cuts it through and thereby brings death. In Hesiod they are the daughters of → Zeus and of → Themis. In ancient art they are depicted with spindle, scroll or scales. The

Romans equated them with the Parcae. In popular belief in modern Greece they are called *mires*.

Mokoš
East Slav goddess of fertility, mentioned in the Nestor Chronicle. She figured as the protector of women in process of delivery. Her functions were later transferred, with the coming of Christianity, to the Virgin Mary.

Moloch
This is a Greek transcription of the Hebrew Molek – the name of a Canaanite god, to whom human sacrifice (of children) was originally made. Many Israelites consecrated their children to Moloch by throwing them into the flames (2 Kings 23: 10). Lately, the name Moloch has been compared with the Punic root MLK = offering, sacrifice; if a connection can be established, this would suggest that Moloch was not a god but rather a particular form of sacrifice.

Moma
The Uitoto Indians in South America believe in Moma as their creator and primeval father. When he was slain, death entered the world. Since then, Moma has ruled the underworld, which is in keeping with the lunar characteristics also ascribed to him.

Momos
In Greek religion the personification of blame, censure. Hesiod describes Momos as one of the sons of night (→ Nyx).

Mon
In the religious system of the Kafirs in eastern Afghanistan, the first divine creation of → Imra. He was represented as a man with a golden quiver, or as a zebu grazing in golden mountain grass. First and foremost, Mon is the victorious slayer of demons. Among the Prasun he is called Mandu.

Monimos → Azizos

Month (the Egyptian form of the name is Montu) Originally a falcon-headed god worshipped in Hermonthis. His function was warlike: he overthrows the adversaries of the sun-god, and gives the Pharaoh victory. In Thebes, he was first regarded as tutelary god of the monarch until he had to relinquish this office to → Amun. The sacred animal of Month was a white bull with a black face which came to be known in later days as → Buchis.

Mormo A ghost and bogeyman in Greek popular belief.

Morpheus (from Greek *morphe* = form, shape) The Greek god of dreams, the son of → Hýpnos. He plays no part whatever in Greek religion.

Morrigan (Morrigu) Irish goddess of war, whose name is interpreted as meaning 'queen of the ghosts'. She rages about as a sort of fury in battle, usually in the form of a bird, and also switches to the role of a goddess of the underworld.

Morta → Parcae

Mot (Semitic *mawt, mot* = death) Phoenician god of drought, of infertility and death. He is lord of the underworld, the 'charnel-house of earth'. Mot is adversary of → Baal, whom he slays. The goddess → Anat thereupon travels to the underworld, and cuts Mot to pieces with a sword, which leads to the resurrection of Baal. It is probable that Philon of Byblos had Mot in mind when he writes of a god 'Muth' whom the Phoenicians call 'death'.

dMu (also written as rMu)   In the Bon religion of ancient Tibet, equivalent to → Lha. The dMu are spirits which dwell in heaven; the sky-god is named dMu-bdud kam-po sa-zan.

Mugasa (or Mugu)   Mythical sky-god of the Bambuti (tribe of pygmies in central Africa). At first, it is related, he dwelt with the first men, who were his children, in a paradise-like land. He lived in a hut and did not wish to be seen by men, and when they disobeyed this command he took himself away. Since then, man is mortal. Apart from occasional invocation of Mugasa, no sort of cult attaches to his name.

Mu Gong   In Chinese Taoist literature, the god of the immortals, lord of the east and embodiment of the Yang principle. He is the husband of → Xi-Wang-mu who lives in the west.

Mula Djadi   The creator god of the Toba-Batak in Sumatra. He lives in the loftiest of the seven heavens, and two swallows serve him as messengers. Mula Djadi is the creator of all things.

Mulungu (often as Mungu)   The supreme god of various East African tribes, e.g. the Kamba. His epithet is *mumbi*, i.e. 'creator'. Etymologically, the name Mulungu is connected with Bantu words meaning 'ancestral domain' or 'ancestral soul'. It is probable that in origin Mulungu figured as ancestral chief or progenitor.

Mummu   The adviser of the old Mesopotamian primeval god → Apsu. Both were overcome by → Ea, who stripped Mummu of his radiance, thereby appropriating his being for himself.

Mundilferi → Mani

Murukān Ancient Dravidian deity, whose name means 'the youthful one'. He is also known as Cēyōn ('the red one'). He is the divine hunter and warrior, and therefore identified with the Hindu → Skanda. He rides on an elephant or a peacock. His banner is adorned with a cock, and as attribute he carries a spear along with a garland of red flowers of the Katampu tree. Murukān's own epithet was *katampan* = god of the katampu tree.

Muses (Musae) The daughters of the Greek father of the gods → Zeus and of → Mnemosýne. They dwell on Olympus and regale the gods with their song, led by → Apóllon. Later, each Muse was given a specific field of art and science: thus, to → Erato was allotted love poetry, → Eutérpe playing the flute and lyric poetry, → Kalliópe epic poetry and philosophy, → Klio history, → Melpoméne tragedy, → Polyhymnia, song accompanied by musical instruments, → Terpsichore dance, → Thalia comedy and → Urania astronomy. Here and there the Muses were revered as nymphs of wells and springs, and the Kastalia spring on Mount Parnassus was particularly sacred to them.

Musisi A god of the Ndonga people in Angola; the only son of → Kalunga. Musisi acts as an interceder for mankind: a proverb says, 'What Musisi asks on your behalf, Kalunga will give you.'

Mut An ancient Egyptian goddess. The consonantal writing of her name is *Mw.t*; the etymology of this is not clear. It has been linked with the word for 'mother', but it could also mean 'vulture', in which form the goddess was originally revered. Later, she is anthropomorphized and retains only the vulture's crest. In Thebes, she was regarded as the spouse of → Amun and mother of → Chons. Mut was equated both with the sky-goddess → Hathor and with the snake-goddess → Uto.

Mūtu In Modern Assyrian verse the god of the underworld and the personification of death. He can be recognized by his head which is that of a reptilian dragon.

Mutunus Tutunus A Roman god, re-presented as ithyphallic or as a phallus. Women brought their offerings to him in the hope that they would thereby be blessed with children.

N

Nabu (Ancient Babylonian Nabium; in the Old Testament Nebo) Babylonian god of writing and of wisdom, the son of → Marduk and of → Sarpanitu. His attribute is the writing stylus. As scribe of the tablets of destiny, he occupied a high rank in the Babylonian pantheon. The city of Borsippa was the centre of his cult, as of that of his wife → Tašmetu.

Nāga (snake) In Indian belief, demonic beings, some of whom, however, achieved immortality. They are in the form of snakes and have usually five or seven heads. In art, they are often shown in human form as far as the navel, snake-like below it. The snake Ananta is the symbol of eternity; under the name of Śeṣa it bears the world. Another Nāga, Vasuki, served as a rope at the churning of the milk-ocean, and is then used by → Śiva as a girdle, which can scare off demons. In Indian popular belief, the Nāgas are venerated as fertility bearers (stone plinths decorated with snakes). In Buddhism, they play a part in the life-story of → Gautama.

Nāgakumāra ('snake-prince') In Jainism, a sub-divison of the → Bhavanavāsin gods. They can generate rain and thunder, and were originally deities associated with water.

Nagual (Aztec *naualli*, *nahualli* = mask, disguise) In Central America, a personal tutelary spirit, which may take the form of an animal or, sometimes, of a plant. A man and his *nagual* are bound together by a mystical sharing of destiny. The Mexicans believed that even the gods had their *nagual*: that of → Huitzilopochtli manifested itself as a humming-bird or an eagle, and → Quetzalcoatl's was the green feather-snake.

Naḫḫundi (Nachunte) The sun-god of Elam which lies north-east of the point at which the Tigris-Euphrates debouches into the Persian Gulf.

Nahi A Thamudic (ancient north Arabian) god, whose function was in general helpful and protective.

Naiads (Naiades) → Nymphs who dwell in springs, pools and rivers.

Nainuema A mythical primeval being in the belief of the Uitoto in South America. He attached the world (that which is) to an empty delusion; then he descended on to this dreamed-up earth and tramped it flat and firm. Finally he spat on it so that the forest should grow.

Namita (Namite) Certain Papuan tribes in New Guinea believe in this primeval female deity who impregnated herself with her own big toe and bore twins, whom she initiated in the arts and crafts useful to man. One tribe regards the cassowary as her representative bird. Put to death at her own behest, her blood engenders the first men.

Nammu A Sumerian goddess: the primeval mother who 'has given birth to heaven and earth'. She also appears as the creator of mankind.

Namtar The Sumerian name means 'that which is cut off', and it designates the personification of fate in Sumerian thought. It is the divine (perhaps demonic) messenger of the underworld goddess → Ereškigal, charged with bringing death to mortals.

Nana An Armenian goddess, daughter of → Aramazd, and taken by the Greeks as equivalent to Athená. The etymology of the name is not certain: one plausible line of argument connects it with an Indo-Germanic word for 'mother', attested in Sanskrit. It has also been suggested that Nana is the Armenian form of the Phrygian → Kybéle. In the Parthian period her cult reached Palmyra and the east Iranian Kushan Empire. Another divine Nana is also known to us – the daughter of the river-god → Sangarios in Asia Minor.

Nanāja Ancient Mesopotamian goddess of sex, who, like → Ištar, had a war-like function into the bargain. At a later period she was equated with → Tašmetu. In the Hellenistic period her cult spread to Syria and Iran.

Nandin ('he who pleases') A white bull in the retinue of the Hindu god → Śiva, whose virility and fecundity it incorporates. In the Purāṇas, Nandin is invoked as a divinity.

Nang Lha A Tibetan house-god, to whom beverages are ceremonially offered. He is usually depicted in human form, but with a pig's head.

Nanna (1) Sumerian moon-god, whose cult had its main centre at Ur. He was regarded as 'lord of destiny' and his epithet was *ašimbabbar*, i.e. 'whose ascent is radiant'. Nanna corresponds to the Akkadian → Sin.

Nanna (2) The wife of the Germanic god → Balder, the mother of → Forseti. When Balder is slain, she dies of grief. In Old Norse, the word is used as a poetic designation for a young woman.

Nanše The local goddess of Lagaš in Sumeria. As the daughter of the god of wisdom → Enki she is the goddess of soothsaying and interpretation of dreams, and the divine will is promulgated through her as harbinger.

Nantosuelta A Gallic goddess. She is linked with → Sucellos, which seems to suggest a goddess of the dead; while her attribute – a cornucopia – points rather in the direction of a goddess who provides the good things of life. In the country of the Mediomatrici she is portrayed with a small, round house in her hand, from which we may infer a domestic trait in her make-up – perhaps she was a kind of protective deity.

Napir The moon-god of Elam, Babylon's Iranian neighbour state.

Narasimha ('man-lion') The fourth incarnation of the Indian god → Viṣṇu: in this *avatāra* he liberates the world from its tribulations under the demon king Hiranyakasipu.

Nārāyana ('son of the primeval man') In India, this name is associated with the concept of a supreme being, understood as a manifestation of → Brahma or of → Viṣṇu. According to one tradition he drifted on a banana leaf and sucked his toe (a symbol of eternity) until he had shaped the universe out of his own creative energy. A well-known iconographic representation shows Viṣṇu-Nārāyana during the universal night, mounted on the snake Ananta; from his navel there grows a lotus bearing the god → Brahman.

Nareau The creator-god of the inhabitants of the Gilbert Islands in Melanesia. He formed heaven and earth from a mussel. Then he caused sand and water to mate, and from the union came forth Nareau the Younger. The latter conquered darkness by forming the sun and the moon from his father's eyes; from the flesh he created rocks and stones, and from the backbone the 'tree of the forefathers', from which came the ancestors of the human race.

Nari Among the Slavs, demonic beings who seem to have been in origin the souls of dead children. The Bulgarians imagine them in the shape of birds. In the Ukraine they are reckoned as belonging to the domestic goblins.

Narisah The Manichaean 'god of the world of light', the father of the twelve 'light-virgins' (dominion, wisdom, victory, conviction, purity, truth, belief, patience, uprightness, kindness, justice and light), corresponding to the twelve signs of the Zodiac. Narisah may also appear as 'virgin of light', and is then essentially androgynous.

Narkissos (Latin Narcissus) Son of the Greek river-god Kephissos and the → Naiad Leirope. In unrequited love for his own image reflected in the water, he wasted away until he was transformed into the flower which now bears his name.

Nasr (also Nusur) Ancient Arabian god whose name means 'eagle'. Apart from this, little is known about him.

Natha (Sinhala = protector, master) One of the four chief gods of Ceylon (Sri Lanka), equated with the Bodhisattva → Avalokiteśvara: subsequently also identified as the future Buddha

→ Maitreya. The Buddhist goddess → Tārā is supposed to be his spouse.

Naunet In the ancient Egyptian cosmogony of Hermopolis, Naunet belongs to the → Ogdoad, and is the female counterpart of → Nun, the personification of the primeval deep. In old religious texts Naunet figures as an underworld complement to heaven (→ Nut), thus becoming a kind of counter-heaven which the sun traverses during the night.

Ndjambi Sky-god of the Herero people in south-west Africa, the source of all good deeds. Whoever dies a natural death is borne aloft by him. It is not permissible to utter his name except on certain very special occasions.

Nebtuu (Nebetu = 'queen of the fields') A local goddess venerated together with → Chnum in Esneh, the ancient Latopolis.

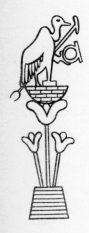

Nechbet Upper Egyptian tutelary goddess of the monarch, represented as a woman with a vulture's skin on her head, or as a vulture. Her attributes are the rod of authority and the eternity symbol. Her sacred creature, the vulture, became symbolical for the whole of Upper Egypt, and entered the Pharaonic regalia together with the snake representing Lower Egypt (→ Uto). In popular belief in the days of the New Kingdom and later Nechbet was revered as a goddess of birh.

Nechmetawaj (Nehmet-awai) An ancient Egyptian goddess venerated in Hermopolis. Her name means 'she who takes the part of the robbed'. She is the female counterpart of → Thot, who is of course a protector of justice: their son is → Neferhor. At a later date, the goddess merged with → Hathor. Plutarch mentions her under the name of Dikaiosyne.

Neferhor (Greek form Nephoros or Nopheros) Ancient Egyptian god, forming a triad with → Nechmetawaj and → Thot. The name means 'he who is fair of face'.

Nefertem (Greek form Nephthemis) Ancient Egyptian god of sweet savour: actually, the deified lotus flower which he bears on his head or carries in his hand in his anthropomorphic guise. In one Pyramid text he is described as the 'lotus-bloom on the nose of Re'. In his solar aspect, Nefertem himself becomes the sun-child on the lotus blossom, and the victorious god of light. He is often shown with a lion's head: after all, his mother → Sachmet was a lion-goddess.

Nehalennia A Germanic goddess, evidence of whose cult has been found in the Low Countries. It is not clear what her name means: and it has been variously suggested that the references to her identify her as a goddess of fertility or as a goddess of the dead. Altars dedicated to her show her with fruit (or a basket of fruit) and a dog; often the bows of a ship appear which may show her in another light, as a tutelary goddess of seafarers.

Nehebkau A snake-demon in ancient Egyptian belief. He serves the sun-god, whom he accompanies in his barque; and he is a kind of watchman at the entrance to the beyond. Finally, he assumes the stature of a primeval god, and becomes, as lord of (everlasting) time, the hope of the dead.

Neith ('the terrible one') This is the Greek transliteration of the name of the local goddess of Sais, the consonants of which are N.t. She was essentially a goddess of war: her cult symbol which she bears on her head consists of a pair of crossed arrows, often with a shield as well. Her epithet is 'she who opens up the ways', indicating that she marches ahead of the monarch and his army. The location of her cult – in the delta of the Nile – explains her close relationship with the crocodile-god → Suchos, who is described as her son. Sometimes Neith appears as a primeval goddess, who may even have androgynous features. She is a goddess of the dead along with → Isis, → Nephthys and → Selket.

Nemesis A Greek goddess who saw to it that justice and luck were evenly distributed in human life and who meted out due punishment for misdeeds and arrogance (*hubris*). The name is connected with the root *nemein* in the sense of 'apportionment of what is proper, due'. The cult of Nemesis centred round Rhamnus in Attica and in Smyrna. In the Hellenistic period, Nemesis was regarded as the goddess of the *agone* (sporting competitions of all sorts) and under the Roman Empire she was honoured in amphitheatres and at racecourses.

Nemetona A Celtic goddess, who was often coupled with the Gallic → Mars. Her name is derived from the word *nemton* = shrine, sanctum, and means something like 'she who is revered in the shrine'.

Nenun (Nenwen) Ancient Egyptian local god of Kus. He was a falcon-god, later equated with Haroeris.

Neper This old Egyptian word means 'corn, grain', and it is also the name of the god personifying grains. He is regarded as the son of the 'food-snake' → Renenutet, and offers hope to the dead as 'he who lives, after he has died'.

Nephthys (Nebthut: her name in hiero-glyphic consonantal spelling is Nb.t-hw.t = 'mistress of the house') Ancient Egyptian god-dess, who seems to be associated with → Seth, but who is functionally on the side of → Osiris, whose corpse she guards together with her sister → Isis. In this way, she becomes a goddess of the dead. Nephthys and Isis are of the east and they receive the rising sun.

Nepit The female counterpart of the ancient Egyptian corn-god → Neper. She is usually shown in human form, carrying a sheaf of corn on her head; but sometimes she appears in the form of a snake.

Neptunus (Neptune) Old Italic god of flowing water. The people celebrated his feast (the Neptunalia) on 23 July, the aim being probably to ward off the high summer drought. Neptune was equated with the Greek sea-god → Poseidon, and he was, in addition, the god of race-courses.

Nereids The fifty daughters of the Greek sea-god Nereus. As → Nymphs dwelling in the sea they form the retinue of → Poseidon. Two of them, → Amphitríte and → Thetis, deserve special men-tion. The Nereids live on in the Greek mind today as gentle fairies.

Nereus The Greek god of water, especially of the sea; the son of → Pontos and the earth-goddess → Gaia, and father of the → Nereids. Like other sea-gods, he has the gift of prophecy, and is able to change his appearance at will.

Nergal (Sumerian, Nerigal) An ancient Mesopotamian god of the underworld, the hus-band of → Ereškigal. He was particularly venerated in the city of Kuthu, whose name, significantly, served as a synonym for the realm of the dead. Other names given to the god were Lugalgirra and → Meslamta'ea. In origin, Nergal was an earth-god incorporating the burning heat of summer, and who brought fever and pestilence to human beings.

Nerthus The Roman historian Tacitus records the existence of this Germanic goddess, whom he calls Mater Terra, 'mother earth'. Archaeological and toponymical evidence suggests that her cult was mainly centred in Denmark. She is described as travelling through the land in a wagon drawn by cows and covered by a cloth; when she returns to her shrine, the wagon and the cloth, and even her image, are washed in a sacred lake. In Norway and Sweden, Nerthus is transformed into the figure of the male → Njörd. It is likely that both Nerthus and Njörd are later versions of an originally androgynous fertility deity.

Nethuns The Etruscan god of water, especially of wells and springs, later of the sea also. The name corresponds to the Latin → Neptunus. Like Neptune, Nethuns is shown as naked and bearded, with a wreath of leaves in his hair.

Neto(n) An ancient Hispanic war-god with astral character. The name is probably connected with the Celtic word *neto* = warrior.

Ngai The supreme god of the Masai people in East Africa. The name means 'rain' and indicates that Ngai was originally seen as a weather-god. When a male Masai dies, Ngai is invoked as follows: 'Oh god, I pray, give health, give possessions, give children.' Ngai is also revered as supreme god by the Bantu Kikuyu people: he lives in heaven, and lightning is visible evidence of his presence.

Niamye The supreme god of the Baule people in the Ivory Coast. He was born from the mother of the gods. The first thing he did was to create a wife for himself, and then he turned his hand to creating men and animals. To begin with, they all lived in heaven but it became over-crowded – so the god created the earth. When people misbehave and refuse to live in peace, he hurls his thunderbolts on earth.

Nidhöggr ('Envy-dragon') A corpse-eating demon in Nordic mythology. He is a demon of the underworld who gnaws unceasingly at a root of the world-ash Yggdrasil, thus threatening the whole of creation.

Nike Greek goddess mentioned first in Hesiod. She is the personification of victory which is given by → Zeus or by → Athená. She is mostly portrayed as a winged messenger of the gods, with laurel wreath, girdle and palm-leaf. Her Roman counterpart is → Victoria.

Nikkal A Syrian goddess taken over from the Mesopotamian pantheon. She had a lunar aspect (→ Ningal) and was wife of the moon-god → Jariḥ.

Ninazu Sumerian god of the underworld. In contrast with the terrifying → Nergal, Ninazu appears sympathetic. As his name suggests ('Master physician') he is a god of healing.

Ningal (Sumerian = 'great queen') The wife of the ancient Mesopotamian moon-god (→ Nanna or → Sin), and mother of the sun-god. She appears in Syria under the name of Nikkal.

Ningirsu ('lord of Girsu') A Sumerian god belonging to the Lagaš pantheon, the husband of → Baba. He is probably identical with → Ninurta, and like the latter he appears in two distinct functions: he is first a god of fertility and vegetation, and in this function his epithet is 'lord of the ploughland'; second, he has a military side and strikes terror into foreign lands. His symbolical animal is the lion-headed eagle Imdugud.

Ningišzida (Ningizida, 'lord of the right tree') Chthonic god of the Sumerians. His symbolical creature is the horned snake. According to Akkadian incantations, he watches over the demons who have been exiled to the underworld; while other traditions present him rather as a god of healing, akin to his father → Ninazu. Finally, he also figures as custodian at the entrance into heaven.

Ningyo A mermaid in Japanese popular belief. She has a human torso and a fish's tail. She wards off misfortune and preserves peace in the land.

Ninhursanga (Sumerian = 'queen of the mountains') A mother-goddess: many Mesopotamian rulers – e.g. Hammurabi and Nebucadnezzar – called themselves 'children of Ninhursanga'.

Ninigi → Takamimusubi

Nin'insina The Sumerian local goddess of Isin; in the Babylonian period she acted as a goddess of healing. At times, identified with → Inanna.

Ninlil (Sumerian = 'queen breeze') Ancient Mesopotamian goddess, wife of → Enlil and mother of the moon-god → Nanna. She is a compassionate goddess with maternal traits. The Assyrians took her to be the wife of the tutelary god of the empire → Assur.

Ninmah The Sumerian name means 'most great queen' and refers to an old Mesopotamian mother-goddess. She is also called Dingirmah ('most great divinity') or simply Mah.

Ninsun(a) Ancient Mesopotamian goddess, wife of Lugalbanda. In the epic of Gilgameš (whose mother she is) she figures as an interpreter of dreams. Her name is Sumerian in origin and means 'queen of the wild cow'.

Ninšušinak (also Inšušinak; Akkadian form Šušinak) The national god of Elam; the name is actually Sumerian and means 'lord of Susa'.

Ninurta (Sumerian = 'lord of the earth') Ancient Mesopotamian god, the son of → Enlil, husband of the goddess of healing → Gula. It is Ninurta that is thanked for flourishing herds and fertile fields. He also displays warlike traits, and he it is who hunts down the storm-bird → Zu and retrieves the stolen tablets of destiny. Ninurta is probably identical with the → Ningirsu worshipped in Lagaš.

Nirah Old Mesopotamian god who incorporates the snake in its apotropaic aspect. He is represented as a snake on Babylonian border-markers.

Nirrta → Nirrti

Nirrti (Nirriti = annihilation) Indian goddess of destruction, who threatens both living and dead. In sacrificial ritual, she is allotted the colour of black, and her messenger is the dove. Her husband is Nirrta (Nirrita) who is lord of the south-west precinct.

Nisaba Sumerian goddess of the art of writing and of knowledge, daughter of the sky-god → An. She 'opens men's ears', i.e. she gives them understanding. As in the case of → Nabu, her emblem is the writing-stylus. In origin, Nisaba was a corn goddess.

Nixe (Water-sprite) (Old High German *nihhus* = crocodile; related to Sanskrit *nijanas* 'washing oneself') The male Nix (Nicker) was originally a water-monster of an animal nature, regarded as malicious and dangerous. In Sweden, it is known as Näck. The female Nixe is a water-sprite with a human torso and the tail of a fish. There are similar beings in the folklore of many nations: cf. the → Rusalka of the Slavs and the → Ningyo of the Japanese.

Njörd A Germanic god, descended from the → Vanir but resident with the Aesir (→ As) until the end of the world. He rules over wind, sea and fire. He is enormously rich, gives the peasants good harvests and helps the fishermen to land good catches: that is to say, he behaves as a god of fertility. In west Norway, Njörd was especially venerated as a god of the sea. His children are → Freyr and → Freyja. His female counterpart is → Nerthus, whose name is an allomorph of his.

Nommo In the cosmogony of the Dogon people in west Africa, a designation for primeval beings who existed along with the creator god → Amma. They are thought of as life-giving forces belonging to the day and the sky, who are particularly associated with rain and fertility. Certain Nommo brought specific knowledge and skills to man, e.g. weaving.

Nona A Roman goddess of birth, so-called because of the nine-month term of pregnancy.

Norns (Old Norse *norn* = she who whispers) In Germanic mythology, spae-wives who determine a person's fate on earth the moment he or she is born; like the → Disir, they also play a part in the actual process of birth. To begin with, there seems to have been a plurality of Norns, but in the end they were reduced to a triad, perhaps under the influence of the → Parcae. In the Völuspa they are named as Urd, Verdandi and Skuld: that is to say, the past, the present and the future, or what has been, what is and what will be. The thread of fate which the Norns are spinning is only occasionally mentioned. In essence, the Norns are closely related to the → Valkyries.

Nortia Etruscan goddess of fate and fortune. Her attribute is often a large nail. In her temple at Volsini it was the custom to hammer in a nail at New Year; this may have been a sort of expiation rite – the nailing down of the defunct year – or it may have symbolized good wishes for the coming one.

Notos Greek god representing the south wind. Like his brothers → Boréas, → Euros and → Zéphyros, he is a son of the morning red (→ Eos). His Roman equivalent is Auster.

Nott (Old Icelandic = night) In Nordic mythology, the daughter of a giant: she drives her chariot across the sky, and the leading stallion (Frost-mane) bedews the earth. Her son is Dag (= day).

Nuadu Irish god (king) who lost his hand in the mythical battle of Mag Tured, but had it restored to him by → Dian-Cecht. He is the god of regal authority and as such the progenitor of the Irish royal lines.

Nü-gua Ancient Chinese creator divinity, variously regarded as male or female. She formed the first human beings out of yellow clay, and she invented the flute. Like the mythical cultural hero → Fu-xi, Nü-gua is depicted with reptilian lower half.

Num Sky-god and supreme deity of the Samojedic people; the word *num* also denotes the visible sky. The god is the creator of the sun, moon and earth, but he delegates the running of the world thus ordered to inferior deities. His epithet *jilibeambaertje* identifies him as the protector of herds and flocks. Reindeer are sacrificed to him and hung up on trees or poles.

Num-Torum Sky-god of the Mansi (Vogul) people: he lives in a resplendent golden house in the seventh heaven, with an iron (or silver) pillar in front of the door which signifies the *axis mundi*. The bear is closely associated with Num-Torum, and bears are regarded as the god's children.

Nun Ancient Egyptian god, the personification of the primeval deep, the waters from which all that is has arisen. Like the ocean, he embraces the earth, but is at the same time underneath it. As the primeval god who was existent in the time of Chaos, he bears the epithet 'father of the gods'. On occasion he is represented – like the other male gods of the → Ogdoad – with a frog's head. His female counterpart is → Naunet.

Nusku Old Mesopotamian god of light and fire, the son of → Enlil, and father of the fire-god → Gibil. He is the enemy of witches and demons. A lamp is shown as his symbol on Babylonian border-markers.

Nut Sky-goddess of the ancient Egyptians. In the evening, she swallows the sun in the west, only to eject it next morning in renewed vigour in the east. She is the 'sow who eats up her piglets' – that is to say, she subsumes all the heavenly bodies in her own being. In the Egyptian cult of the dead, she is connected with the concept of resurrection; and the coffin is regarded as the symbol of heaven, indeed of Nut herself, from whom the dead awaken to new life.

In art, she is shown being raised by the god of the air, → Šu, above the earth-god → Geb.

Nyama (Bantu = animal, game, fish) A designation for a class of wild animal which is rich in magic power, and which incorporates a force which is partly spiritual and partly physical. The word can be used to denote spiritual powers (e.g., the capacity of a dead person to avenge himself, to take reprisals); and among the Mandingo it is a circumlocution for certain deities.

Nyame The supreme being of the Akan (in the south of Ghana). It is Nyame who sends the soul into the embryo, and who determines individual destiny. Temples are erected to him, in which priests spend their lives in his service. His sacred number is five. His male aspect appears in the sun, his female aspect in the moon. Being essentially androgynous, Nyame can also appear as a goddess. He corresponds to → Niamye of the Baule.

gNyan Tibetan spirits who live in trees and stones, and who can send illnesses (especially plague and pestilence) and death to man. As they move about in the mountains as well, they are considered to be close to the gods.

Nymphs (Greek *nymphe* = young woman) For the Greeks, these were female nature deities of a lower order than gods; but they were sometimes regarded as demons also, especially when accompanied by satyrs and → Silene as their male partners. They dwelt in the mountains and in caves (*oreades*), in the sea (→ Nereids), in springs and pools (→ Naiads) and in trees (→ Dryads). In Greek myth they are called 'daughters of Zeus', and in popular belief they were regarded as conferring fertility. As a rule, they appeared in groups, often in the retinue of → Dionysos and sometimes led by → Hérmes, whose own mother was a nymph (→ Maía). In the Hellenistic-Roman period they were regarded mainly as water-spirits, and duly represented with water-pot or mussel shell. The building concerned with the provision of water in a Greek city was called the *numphaion* (Latin *nymphaeum*).

Nyrckes

Nyrckes figures on an old Finnish list of gods as the one who gives 'squirrels from the forest'. In magic formulae used by hunters he appears as lord of the forest animals, and as the son – but sometimes the wife (!)- of the forest god → Tapio.

Nyx

In Greek cosmogony, the personification of the night. She was regarded as a primeval goddess in whose presence Zeus himself was awe-struck and apprehensive. She was derived from Chaos, and gave birth to the heavens (*aither*) and day (*hemera*). Her sons were sleep (→ Hýpnos) and death (→ Thanatos).

Nzambi

The supreme god of the Bakongo people in the Congo area of Central Africa. He is invisible and has created all men and all things; and he punishes those who transgress his commands. He is inaccessible to man, and accordingly no cult surrounds him. One tradition tells how Nzambi was born as a three-headed androgynous being. Among the Equatorial African Pangwe (Fang) the god figures under the name Nzame; he is invoked only when people want rain.

O

Oannes This is the Greek form of the name of an old Mesopotamian god, perhaps a corruption of the Akkadian *ummânu* = master. The name is mentioned in the historical writings of the late Babylonian priest Berossos; it denotes a culture-hero, half-man, half-fish, who instructed mankind in handicrafts, building and applied science.

Odin (Low German Wodan; south German Wuotan) Germanic god, described in the Edda as the chief of the Aesir (→ As) the husband of → Frigg. He is god of war, patron of heroes and 'father of the dead' (Walvater). He is served by the → Valkyries. Sacred to the god are the wolf and the raven; and two ravens, Hugin and Munin, whisper into his ear what they have seen on their flight through the world. The name Odin/Wodan is connected with the German word *Wut* = rage, fury. Wodan is the god of ecstasy, of

magic (runic magic) and of the art of poetry; and to achieve wisdom he sacrificed one of his eyes. In saga and in popular belief he appears as a one-eyed warrior armed with a spear, or as a wanderer in a blue mantle with a floppy hat. Finally, he is also the leader of the 'wild army' of peregrinating souls. One of his epithets is Grimnir ('the masked one') – this because of his fondness for changing his outward shape (e.g. into eagle or snake) and for disguises. Other specific epithets are Hangagud ('god of the hanged') and Bölverkr ('harm-bringer'). In Scandinavia and in England, the third day of the week is called after him – English Wednesday. In the myth, Odin is swallowed by → Fenrir at Ragnarök, the destruction of the world. Early medieval bracteates show the god threatened by a monster; he is accompanied by two birds and sometimes by a deer as well, as in our illustration.

Odqan Mongolian fire-spirit. The name is borrowed from Turkish and means 'fire-king'. The female version *Yal-un eke* is older; it means 'mother of fire'.

Odudua An earth-goddess of the Yoruba people in Nigeria. In her aspect as a fertility bringer she is also a goddess of love. Her sacred colour is black.

Oengus (Angus) An Irish god. Through cunning he acquires the palace of his father → Dagda by asking if he may have it for one day and one night: to the Celtic mind, this is a way of saying 'for ever', and the father has been ousted for good. The full name of the god is *Oengus ma ind Oc*, which means 'he who alone is powerful'.

Ogdoad A group of four pairs of gods venerated in Hermopolis, whom the Egyptians called Šmun = the eight. They are the personifications of the primeval forces of Chaos: → Nun and his wife → Naunet symbolize the primeval waters, → Kuk and Kauket darkness, Huh and Hauhet the eternity of space, and → Amun and → Amaunet represent invisibility. As cosmic gods they are represented in anthropomorphic form; individually they also appear as apes who are seen greeting the rising sun (a symbol for the creation of the world). They are also sometimes conceived as chthonic animals, the male gods appearing as frogs, the female ones as snakes.

Ogma Chief god of the Irish pantheon. In the battle against the demonic → Fomore, he is able to take their king's sword away from him. One of his epithets is 'he whose visage is like the sun'. One of his most signal achievements was to invent the Og(h)am script which is used in the oldest texts in the Irish language.

Ogmios A Gallic god, corresponding, as his name suggests, to the Irish → Ogma. Lukianos (second century AD) equated him with → Heraklés. Bald-headed and wrinkled, carrying a bow and a club, he is supposed to symbolize the power of speech. It may be Ogmios who is portrayed on coins in the shape of a head, out of whose mouth an intertwined chain of tiny human heads proceeds. Ogmios has also been interpreted as Psychopompos, he who leads the dead.

Okeanides The sons of the Greek water-god → Okeanos; they are principally river-gods, as, e.g. → Acheloos.

Okeaninai The daughters of → Okeanos and of → Tethys. The best-known of them are → Styx, and Doris, who provided the sea-god → Nereus with fifty daughters.

Okeanos The designation of the representative of the waters which girdle the earth, and from which all springs, rivers and lakes derive. The etymology of the name remains a mystery. Okeanos was supposed to be the son of the sky-god (→ Uranós) and the earth-goddess (→ Gaia) and husband of → Tethys. He is portrayed as bearded and carrying a water-pot or urn.

Okeus (Oke)   For the Indians living in the Virginia area, this was the evil counterpart to the great god → Ahone. The European colonists and missionaries declared him to be a devil.

Okuninushi   Japanese god of the art of healing and of magic. Once upon a time, it is related, he descended to the underworld, over-came the storm-god → Susanowo, and robbed him of his weapons.

Olifat (other forms of the name are Olafat or Yelafath)   In the belief of the Caroline Islanders, a superhuman figure, part culture-hero, part rogue. His father was the sky-god, his mother was a mortal woman. On the one hand, he gave mankind fire – but on the other, he gave the shark its teeth so that it could eat men.

Olmai (Olmay)   Among the Lapps, this word denotes divine properties: thus, *biegg-olmai* is the wind-god, and → *waralden olmai* is a god of universal significance.

Olokun   In Yoruba cosmogony, the god of wealth and of the sea. He is often to be seen on Benin bronzes; he has legs like fish, and in each hand he holds a lizard. In days gone by, human sacrifice was made to Olokun, it is said, to placate the anger of the god. Among the Ika Ibo, Olokun was worshipped in the form of a water-jug. One Yoruba myth tells how he once wanted to sink the earth in the ocean but was prevented by the

creator god Obatala (Aubatala) from carrying out his threat.

Olorun The supreme god of the Yoruba people. He 'it was who charged the sky-god → Orisa Nla to create a fundament, and then he sent the rain vitally necessary for the growth of plants. The god has neither temples nor priests, and he can only be invoked as a last resort in the direst of circumstances.

Ometeotl (also known as Ometecutli, Tloque Nahuaque or Citlatonac) A high god in Aztec religion, who played little part, however, in cult and religious observance. He is 'he who is in the centre-point', the god who embraces all things. He is immediately and directly present but remains invisible. He is the originator of all things: according to one tradition, indeed, he thought himself up. His Maya counterpart is → Hunab Ku.

Omichle → Pothos

Onuris   The Greek form of the god Anhuret, worshipped in the Upper Egyptian city of This (Thinis). The name Anhuret means something like 'he who brings the faraway'. He is portrayed in human form with four feathers on his head; in one hand he holds a lance. He is a deification of the royal hunter and warrior, a function which is underlined by his epithet – 'lord of slaughter'. In the late period he merges with → Šu, who brings back the faraway eye of the sun.

Ops   Roman goddess of seed-growth and harvest, the wife of → Saturn. It was in her honour that the harvest festival was celebrated on 25 August. The cult of Ops found a foot-hold in North Africa (among the ancient Berber tribes).

Ora   In Albanian popular belief, a female protective spirit. Every one of us is equipped with an *ora* from birth, which may have a white or a black visage according to whether the *ora* has a brave and industrious person to look after or a lazy, cowardly one.

Orahan   The sole god worshipped by the Canary Islanders on the island of Gomera; he is enthroned in heaven, and his implacable enemy is the demonic, woolly-haired Hirguan.

Orcus   A Roman god of the underworld, lord of the realm of the dead, equivalent to the Greek → Hades. He appears as a fierce fighter who strikes the valiant to the ground and who runs down the cowardly fugitive. In popular belief he also appears as a demon with black wings.

Ördög In ancient Hungarian belief, the deity controlling the dark forces of the world; after Christianization, a designation of the devil.

Oreades In Greek mythology → nymphs who lived in the mountains and in caves.

Orion Son of the Greek sea-god → Poseidon. He was a mighty hunter who was abducted by → Eos to be her lover. But the Olympians begrudged Eos her possession of the beautiful youth, and he was killed by an arrow from → Artemis; according to another version, however, he was slain because he made sexual advances to the goddess herself or to one of her nymphs. Orion was elevated to the stars, where his constellation is still to be seen.

Orişa Nla The sky-god of the Yoruba people in Nigeria; he is delegated by the supreme god → Olorun to create the earth, the other gods and the first men.

Oro War-god in Tahiti who ousted the ancient war-god → Tu from this office. His father is → Tangaroa. An image showing him in anthropomorphic form had a girdle of red feathers, a sign of highest rank.

Orotal(t) Herodotus has given us this name of an ancient Arabian god, who may have corresponded to the Nabataean → Dusares. The Greeks took Orotal to be equivalent to → Dionysos.

Orpheus The son of the Thracian river-god Oiagros and the Muse → Kalliópe. Apóllon is often said to be his father. Orpheus can charm plants and animals with his singing and his lute-playing. When his wife Eurydice died, he moved the gods of the underworld so deeply with his singing that they restored her to him – but she had to go back to the underworld again because Orpheus disobeyed the command of the gods and looked round at her. Later, he was torn to pieces by Thracian Maenads and interred by the → Muses.

Orunmila
Among the Yoruba people in Nigeria the god of compassion, who comes down to earth to help people.

Osiris
(the consonantal script form is *wsjr*; the Coptic form is Usire) In ancient Egyptian religion, the son of the earth-god → Geb and of the sky-goddess → Nut. The main centres of his cult were, in Lower Egypt, Busiris (Dedu) where he merged into the figure of the ancient tutelary god Anezti, and, in Upper Egypt, Abydos, where he was equated with the god of the dead → Chontamenti. The myth tells how Osiris was murdered and cut into pieces by his brother → Seth: the remnants were collected by his sister → Isis and given new life so that she could receive from Osiris her son → Horus. Horus took over the royal inheritance of Osiris, while the latter acts as regent and judge in the realm of the dead, and causes the plants to sprout forth from the surface of the earth. This shows him as a fertility god, an aspect which is underlined by his connection with the annual flooding of the Nile. As the 'eternally good being' he appears under the name of Wennofer. As lord of the underworld, Osiris represents the sun in its nocturnal transit. He was even seen in certain circles as a moon-god, the lunar phases being taken as tokens of the god's death and resurrection. His attributes are the crooked staff and the so-called scourge.

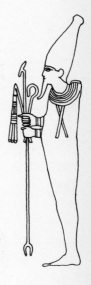

Ostara
A Germanic goddess who has given her name to the Easter festival. She is identical with the Anglo-Saxon goddess Eostra mentioned by the Venerable Bede. In name and function the

269

goddess parallels the Greek → Eos and the Roman → Aurora. She is the personification of the rising sun, associated by the Germanic peoples not with a time of day (dawn) but with a season – spring.

Otos → Aloádes

Ouiot The primeval father and moon-god of the Luiseño Indians in south California. He told his people that three days after his death he would return to them, and this is said to have happened. Since the departure of Ouiot, men too must die.

Oya Mother-goddess of the Yoruba people in Nigeria. She is the 'good mother', but as goddess of storms she has her terrifying aspect as well. She can even bend the spirits of the dead to do her bidding. She is goddess of dancing and is accordingly represented on the rods carried by Yoruba women in folkdances.

P

Pabilsang A Sumerian god, the son of the god-king → Enlil, and husband of → Nin'insina, the goddess of healing. In Babylonian times he was equated with → Ninurta.

Pachamama A fertility goddess in the Inca Empire, and still revered in some of the Andean valleys. The name means 'earth-mother'.

Pachet ('she who scratches') An ancient Egyptian goddess of the desert, in the form of a lion. She was thought of in connection with the crown-goddess → Urthekau.

Padmanarteśvara ('lord of the dance, with the lotus') A form of the Bodhisattva → Avalokiteśvara. He is invariably depicted with one head, but he may have from two to eight or ten arms. In his two-armed form he is red in colour: in his left hand he holds a red lotus, with his right hand he makes a gesture associated with dancing.

Padmasambhava ('he who is born from the lotus') A Buddhist teacher (*guru*) from north India who spread Tantric Buddhism in Tibet in the eighth century AD. Tradition makes him out to have appeared in a lotus blossom, having been created by → Amitābha. He preferred to meditate in places of the dead. In Tibet, he is said to have changed many demons into → Dharmapālas.

Padvāxtag → Xrōštag

Pajainen In the Finnish myth of the slaughter of the great bull (or pig), this is the god who figures as the slaughterer. An attempt has been made to derive him from the Lappish god of thunder → Pajonn, with the hammer or the axe of Pajonn acting as the instrument of slaughter.

Pajonn The Lappish god of thunder. The name comes from *pad'd'i* = 'above': the god is 'he who dwells above in heaven'.

Pales A Roman goddess who appears as a guardian of flocks and herds, a function she shares with → Inuus: she is the Pales Panda, i.e. the Pales 'who is to offer fodder'. Her feast-day – 21 April – was celebrated as the birthday of Rome, in token of the city's founding by herdsmen.

Palk The sun-god in the religion of ancient Korea, the founder of the realm of light and the adversary of → Kud. His cult was practised on mountain tops: here sacrifice was made to him, with stringent attention paid to the correct easterly orientation.

Pan A god of fields and woods originating in Arcadia; the son of the god of herds → Hérmes and a nymph. He was represented with the horns and legs of a billy-goat, and it is in the guise of a randy goat that we see the mythical Pan pursuing → Nymphs. One of them, called Syrinx, changed herself into a reed to escape his clutches – so Pan cut several reeds and made himself the pan-pipes (*syrinx*). He had a habit of appearing out of the blue, especially in the hush of the noonday heat, and this caused panic among men and animals. The tale that Plutarch tells about the death of Pan shows that he was a vegetation-god. The name 'Pan' was not been satisfactorily explained; it has been connected with the Greek word *pan* meaning 'all', which would elevate Pan to the

status of an omnipotent or all-embracing deity. His counterpart among the Roman gods was → Faunus. In late medieval speculation he was seen simply as the devil.

Pañcarakṣa ('five-fold protection') A group of five Buddhist goddesses who were invoked to grant longevity and to protect certain villages or areas. They arose through the personification of five magical protective formulae (*rakṣā*) which, it is alleged, were once uttered by → Gautama Buddha himself.

Pāndarā ('the white one') A Buddhist goddess, the partner (*prajñā*) of → Amitābha. Her element is fire and the passion of love. Iconographically, she appears in various forms.

Pandora Created by → Hephaistos at the behest of → Zeus, and equipped with every seductive gift, she was despatched to earth as the first woman. With her she had a box (really a barrel: in Greek *pithos*) containing sorrow and misfortune. It is possible that she is a later version of an ancient earth-goddess, as the name, which means 'she who gives all' or 'she who is rich in gifts' has been applied to such a goddess also.

Panku (Pan-gu) A primeval giant in Chinese mythology. He was born from the five basic elements, and he used a hammer and chisel to form the heaven and the earth. According to another version of the myth, Pan-gu arose from the world-egg in which *yin* and *yang* were as yet undivided; and from these components he formed the earth (*yin*) and the heavens (*yang*). After the death of the giant, the sun arose from his left eye, the moon from his right eye, the rain from his sweat; his flesh decomposed and fell apart to form the arable land, and the plants grew from his hairs.

Papa → Atea

Papaja → Išduštaja

Papas A Phrygian god, equated by the Greeks with → Zeus. He is said to have impregnated a stone which then gave birth to the hermaphrodite → Agdistis.

Papsukkal An ancient Mesopotamian god: the messenger of the gods who also acts as watchman or gate-keeper.

Para Goblin-like creatures in Finnish folk-belief; they are thought of as domestic spirits who take the form of snakes, frogs or cats, and who increase one's supply of corn, milk, butter and money. Among the Baltic peoples a similar role is played by → Pukis.

Paramāśva ('noblest of horses') Both the name of this Buddhist god and the horse's head he bears in his iconographic representation, remind us of → Hayagrīva. He is red in colour, with four faces and eight legs which he uses to trample on Hindu gods.

Paraśu-Rāma ('Rama with the axe') The sixth incarnation of → Visnu, who took this form to break the tyranny of the warrior caste (the ksatriyas) and help the Brahmans to take power. At the behest of his father he used the axe (*paraśu*) to kill his mother: this done, he pleaded successfully for her reawakening.

Parcae (Latin root *parere* = to bear, give birth) Originally, a pair of Roman goddesses of birth, named Decuma and → Nona; later, under the influence of the Greek → Moirai, a triad was formed by the addition of the goddess of death Morta. Together, the three were thereafter seen as the decisive influences on one's personal fate in life.

Pariacaca The god of rain, water and thunder in the belief of the pre-Inca Indians in the central Andes. His sacred creature was the falcon. In myth, he is the adversary of the fire-god Caruincho.

Parjanya ('rain-cloud') Old Indian rain-god and, accordingly, generator of vegetation. The fertilized earth is thought of as his wife. In the Rigveda he is represented in the form of a bull.

Parnaśavari In origin, this is a goddess once worshipped by aboriginals in the sub-continent and who was then taken over by Buddhism. The name means 'Savari of the leaves', i.e. Savari who has a loin-cloth of leaves. She occurs in two forms, one yellow and one green. Her garments consist of bunches of leaves, or she may be shown wearing a tiger-skin with a wreath of leaves. She is regarded as the goddess who routs all epidemics.

Pārśva The penultimate in the series of the 24 → Tīrthaṁkaras. According to the legend he was protected by the seven-headed snake-king Dharana from the attacks launched against him by the demonic Meghamalin. Hence, his symbolical creature is a snake, and on his head he wears a seven-fold snake's hood. It is probable that Pārśva is based on a real historical personality – a prince who lived some 250 years before → Mahāvīra and who founded the order of the Nirgrantha, that is, 'untrammelled', those who have freed themselves from the bonds of Karma.

Pārvatī ('daughter of the mountains') The wife of the Hindu god → Śiva, the daughter of → Himavat, king of the mountains. Her son was the war-god Karttikeya (→ Skanda). Pārvatī merges into the better-known goddess → Durgā.

Pasiphae In Greek mythology, the wife of the Cretan king → Minos. She was supposed to be a daughter of the sun-god → Hélios, and was also interpreted as a moon-goddess because of her name ('she who shines on all'). The fruit of her union with a bull sent by → Poseidon was → Minotauros.

Paśupati ('Lord of cattle') Seals belonging to the ancient Indus cultures show this ithyphallic deity seated in the Yoga posture, surrounded by animals (especially snakes as symbols of fertility). In the Veda, Paśupati is one of the names of → Rudra; later, the name was used for → Śiva in his aspect as a god of fertility. *Paśu* not only means 'cattle', 'beasts', but is also a designation for the soul; as 'Lord of the soul' the god leads his devotees to the 'end of sorrow', that is, to liberation. The cult of Paśupati is particularly wide-spread in Nepal. In one tradition, the god is said to have appeared in the shape of an antelope, and one of his horns, which was broken off when he was being hunted, was revered as his linga (phallus).

Patecatl Aztec god of medicine and 'lord of the pulque root'. His wife is the pulque-goddess → Mayahuel.

Pateke (sing: patek) According to Herodotus, protective whose images the Phoenicians fastened to the bow of their ships; in the light of this usage, the name was also applied to certain dwarf-like male beings in the late Egyptian period. These were supposed to be mainly a form of protection against wild animals, and images of them were worn as amulets round the neck to ward off evil. They were called the 'sons of → Ptah'. The youthful Ptah could himself figure as a Patek; and, imported in this guise from Egypt, he was a popular figure in Carthage.

Pattini The most important female deity of the Singhalese. She watches over marriage and keeps epidemics at bay; and she is said to have brought the cultivation of rice into Ceylon. The myth tells how she was born from a mango which had been struck by a divine arrow. 'Fire-walking' is a practice bound up with her cult.

Pax Roman goddess of peace, equated with the Greek → Eirene. It was during the rule of Caesar Augustus that she first acquired an altar on the Field of Mars (Ara Pacis Augustae). On coinage she appears as a youthful woman, with a garland of corn, a cornucopia and an olive-branch.

Pazuzu An Old Mesopotamian (Assyrian) demon with four wings and a scowling visage. He was the representative of the stormy winds from the south-east, and he was feared as a bringer of illnesses. Our illustration shows his general appearance but does not show his scorpion's tail. His power to harm could be countered by various spells and incantations.

Peithó A Greek goddess, the personification of persuasion. She appears in the retinue of → Aphrodíte.

Pekar (Pehar) A Tibetan demon-prince who probably played a part in the pre-Lamaist Bon religion, and who may also appear as a divine figure. He rides on a white lion, and is regent of the northerly quarter.

Pele Volcano goddess on Hawaii, unpredictable and liable to sudden outbursts of anger. Traditionally, she came originally from Kahiki (Tahiti), expelled by her divine brothers who could no longer put up with her insubordination. Pele is also called Hina-ai-malama ('Hina who eats the moon'). It is possible that she is the Hawaiian form of the common Polynesian moon-goddess → Hina; and both goddesses are also in control of lightning.

Pellonpekko Finnish god of barley; his name comes from *pelto* = field. To him is due the first beer brewed from barley. In Estonia, Peko is a corn-god, a waxen image of whom is kept in the corn-chest. St Peter is called Pekka in Finnish, and it was on St Peter's day that the festive beer used to be brewed; taken together, these points suggest Christian influence.

Pemba (Bemba) Creator-god of the Bambara in West Africa. When he was let down by the world-spirit → Yo on to the earth, a tree grew out of him, under which the humans who had been created by → Faro, sought refuge. The divine primeval tree was tireless in coupling with women to engender living creatures. In order to strengthen the tree people sacrificed their blood to it.

Penates (Di Penates) In ancient Rome, originally the divine protectors of the store-room (*penus*) and the supplies therein; later widened to signify house and family spirits in general. They were venerated, together with the Lares, at the household hearth. These spirits had no proper names. The domestic *penates*, the protective spirits of the family, were paralleled by the *penates populi Romani*, the protectors of the Roman people.

Peneios A Thessalian river and its god who was a son of → Okeanos and of → Tethys. His daughter was → Dáphne.

Perchten (Berchten) Demonic creatures in myth and folktale, especially in Alpine areas. They form the retinue of Frau → Bercht, who sallies forth in deep midwinter. In folk-tale it is claimed that the devil mixes with the eerie throng, in the hope of grabbing a victim incognito. The old beliefs linger on in the Perchten processions with their grotesque demonic disguises.

Perendi Old Illyrian name for God, related to the Lithuanian → Perkunas, the god of thunder, and the Greek word *keraunos* = lightning. That is to say, Perendi was a storm-god. With the coming of Christianity, his name was retained in Albanian as the ordinary designation for God.

Perit In Albanian folk-belief, female mountain-spirits clad in white. They punished anyone who was wasteful with bread by making him a crooked hunchback.

Pērkons Latvian god of thunder, armed with sword, spear, iron arrows and an iron rod. As the bringer of rain he fosters fertility. In myth he also appears as the smith of heaven and in folk-tale he fights the devil. → Perkunas is his Lithuanian equivalent.

Perkunas Lithuanian god of thunder, bringer of rain and of fertility. He protects law and justice, and pursues demons. Sacred to him are the oak-tree and fire. He drives in his chariot over the clouds, holding an axe, which returns to his hand after he has hurled it at a target. He disguises himself as a hunter in order to hound the devil.

Persé (Perseis) The wife of the Greek sun-god → Hélios. She embodies the underworld aspect of the moon-goddess. Another name for her is Neaira = the new one, i.e. the new moon. Her children were → Kirke and → Pasiphae.

Persephóne (also Persephassa; in Latin Proserpina) In Greek myth, the daughter of → Zeus, and wife of → Hades, who abducted her as a small girl (hence her name of Kore). Thereafter, she spends one-third of the year in the underworld (during this time the plants wither) and two-thirds of the year with her mother, the earth-goddess → Demeter. Both Demeter and Persephone were venerated as goddesses of vegetation, and their myth was solemnly enacted in the Eleusinian mysteries. The plants consecrated to Persephone are the ear of corn and the pomegranate.

Perses (Persaios)   A Titan-like god of light, the son of → Perseus. From his union with Asteria, the stellar goddess, was born → Hekáte.

Perseus   Son of → Zeus, who united with Danae in the form of a golden rain. Perseus was charged by Polydektes, king of Seriphos, to bring him the head of the → Gorgon Medusa, whose glance turned all those who met it to stone. The → Nymphs gave him winged sandals and a cap which conferred invisibility, and from the gods he received a sickle-shaped sword with which he struck off the gorgon's head. On the way back to Seriphos, he rescued Andromeda from a sea-monster.

Perun   A Slavonic god of thunder, especially venerated in old Russia. His name is taken to mean 'striker'; the Polish word *piorun* means 'thunder'. Among the images of gods erected at Kiev, Perun was shown with a club as attribute. In the Balkans, bulls were sacrificed to him. It is doubtful whether Perun can be connected with the thunder-god of the Baltic peoples. Whether Perun is etymologically connected with the Lithuanian word → Perkunas is not certain.

Petbe   Old Egyptian god of retaliation, whose cult was known in the Ptolemaic-Roman period. The word *petbe* means 'the retaliator' and was also used as an epithet denoting one of the specific aspects of death.

Petesuchos   Old Egyptian crocodile-god, venerated in Fayum in the Graeco-Roman period.

Pēy   Among the Tamils, demonic beings who are thought to have something to do with necrophagia. They are pictured as wild creatures with tousled hair who drink the blood of dead and wounded warriors, and who bring misfortune to the living. The word *pēy* means 'devil' or 'goblin'.

Phaéthon ('the shining one')   The son of the Greek sun-god → Hélios, who once allowed him to drive the sun-chariot. But Phaéthon was too weak to control the fiery solar steeds: he came too close to the earth and caused a terrible fire. Whereupon → Zeus hurled him in a flash of lightning into a stream, on whose banks his grieving sisters, the Heliades, were transformed into trees which drip amber tears.

Phanes (Greek = he who appears)   In Orphic teaching regarding the creation, the first god who arose from the primeval egg which emerged from → Chronos. An older source has him sitting 'in the untrodden (space) of the cave of the night'. Yet another tradition says that holy night (→ Nyx) is his daughter, and from their union heaven and earth were generated. In a sense, then, Phanes is the solar potentiality breaking forth from primeval darkness, and thus semantically coincident with → Mithras.

Phorkys (also Phorkos)   A Greek sea-god, whose epithet was *krataios* = 'the strong one'. He was the husband of Keto (*ketos* was a sea-monster), and their children were the hideous → Graii and the terrifying → Gorgons. Hesiod says that Phorkys was a son of the earth-goddess → Gaia and the sea-god → Pontos.

Phosphóros ('he who brings light': also known as Heosphoros)   The Greek god of the morning star. He was represented as a naked, winged youth hurrying ahead of his mother → Eos, or the sun-god → Hélios, with a torch in his hand. In Latin he was called Lucifer.

Picullus Old Prussian god of the under-world, who came to be identified with the prince of hell. In Old Prussian *pickuls* means 'devil'.

Picus (Latin = woodpecker) In origin, per-haps, a soothsaying forest demon; later, the patron of husbandmen. The woodpecker was the creature sacred to → Mars, and was sometimes equated with the god. His son was said to be → Faunus.

Pičvu'čin The god of hunting and of wild creatures among the Chukchi in east Siberia. He is so small that he can ride on a tiny grass sledge drawn by mice; but he has the strength of a giant. He derives his nourishment not from solid food but from odours – probably those of the sacrifice.

Pidrai The consort of the Phoenician god → Baal. She probably represents some sort of meteorological phenomenon.

Pinikir (also Pinenkir) A mother-goddess revered in Elam, comparable to the Babylonian → Išar. It is uncertain whether Pinikir corres-ponds to the Kirišša who is often mentioned in invocations to the gods.

Pirwa (Peruwa) A Hittite deity, whose name is derived from *peruna* = cliff. An associated epithet is 'queen', but otherwise the deity is considered to be male. His attribute is the horse.

Pistis Sophia Female abstract redeemer figure in a Gnostic work of the same name dating from the third century AD. Pistis Sophia claims equal status with God the creator, and describes herself as 'The First and the Last'. The gnostic movement known as the Sethians called her Barbelo.

Pitaras ('the fathers') In India, the venerable dead who were the first to follow the path to heaven found by → Yama. The Atharvaveda describes them as immortal and divine beings, yet their world is not that of the gods.

Pleiades In Greek myth, the seven daughters of → Atlas, who were pursued by → Orion the hunter, and who were, for their own protection, placed by Zeus in heaven as a constellation.

Plutos The Greek god of riches: first and foremost, the benefactor who gave mankind the boon of farming, and, as such, the son of the earth-goddess → Demeter and of the mortal Iasion, who was said to be the first sower of seed. Plutos had a temple in Eleusis but seems to have played no other role in ritual observances. In one of Aristophanes' comedies, the god appears as an old blind man who distributes his gifts in a very haphazard and unfair way. In sculpture he is usually portrayed as a boy with a cornucopia, often on the arm of → Eirene.

Podaleirios The son of the Greek god of healing → Asklepiós. He was a doctor in the Greek army besieging Troy, and was revered as a Great Healer in Asia Minor and in Thessaly.

Polydeukes → Kastor

Polyhymnia (also Polymnia) The → Muse of grave and solemn song accompanied by instruments. Her name means 'she who is rich in songs'. She is generally represented without any sort of attribute, in a posture of earnest meditation.

Polyphem (Greek Polýphemos) The one-eyed son of the sea-god → Poseidon, and the nymph Thoosa. He was one of the → Cyclops, in whose cave Odysseus and his companions find themselves.

Pomona A Roman goddess of ripening fruit, the wife of the vegetation-god → Vertúmnus; she is often presented as the beloved of → Picus. Her name comes from Latin *pomum* = fruit (of a tree).

Pon The sky-god of the Yukagir who live in east Siberia. He causes day and night to succeed each other, and he gives the blessing of rain. The name means something like 'some(thing)'. If any cult attaches to his name, nothing is known of it.

Pontos The classical Greek word for 'sea', and the name of a sea-god. His union with his mother → Gaia produced the sea-gods → Nereus and → Phorkys.

Porenutius A Slavonic god worshipped on the island of Rügen; he was depicted as having four heads.

Portúnus Roman god of the house-entrance (Old Latin *portus*); subsequently, the god of the Tiber basin, the 'exit port' for Rome. On the day of his feast – the Portunalia, held on 17 August – people threw their door-keys into the fire in order to make them immune to misfortune.

Poseidon Greek sea-god, the son of → Kronos and of → Rhea. The name is already attested in Mycenaean times, but the etymological meaning is not clear. In Homer, he rates as one of the most powerful gods along with the lord of heaven → Zeus, and the god of the underworld

→ Hades. He sends storms and earthquakes, but he may also favour the traveller with a good voyage. In origin, Poseidon was possibly an old fertility god, in the shape of a horse, and venerated as the patron of horse-breeding; later on, the horse figured as his sacred animal, and in Corinth horse-races were held in his honour. As the god of earthquakes, he bore the name Enosigaios, 'earth-shaker'. Originally he was armed with lightning flashes, later replaced by the trident – the symbol of fishing. As Phytalmios, promoter of growth, he was close to the earth-goddess → Demeter, and as sea-god he had → Amphitríte to wife. Among his many children borne by various wives are → Antaíos, → Orion and → Polyphem. His Roman counterpart is → Neptunus.

Pothos A personification of a divine primeval force in late Phoenician cosmogony. Pothos is primeval desire which unites with Omichle, darkness. Their offspring are Aër, the 'unsullied of the spiritual', and Aura, 'the living exemplar moved by the spiritual'. According to Philon of Byblos, Pothos moved as a 'dark' wind over the face of Chaos, and impregnated himself.

Prahlada → Daityas

Prajāpati ('Lord of the creatures') In the Rigveda, the name of the divine creator of the world. In the Atharvaveda he is said to be the creator of heaven and earth. The world arises as an emanation from his inexhaustible being. His function as a progenitor is underlined in the Mahābhārata where he appears as protective lord of the sexual organ. Occasionally, he takes the place of → Varuṇa, whose sacred animal, the tortoise, can be one of the forms Prajāpati may assume. In Hinduism, Prajāpati is understood as one of the names of the god → Brahman.

Prajñā In Buddhism, the female principle: on the spiritual way, it is the intuition which complements the male technique of meditation. The meaning of the word *prajñā* is 'wisdom' or 'insight'. The law of polarity specifies that *prajñā* can be paired with certain male partners as their necessary complement. The personified *prajñās* form the passive components in this partnership; and accordingly, in iconographic representation, they are always shown smaller than the god so complemented. When both are shown in the Yab-yum position, the polarity is integrated.

Prajñāpāramitā (Perfection of insight) The personification of a text of the same name, in which → Gautama Buddha is supposed to have set out his teaching. As a female deity she figures in iconography from India to south-east Asia and Java, hardly changing in appearance and usually equipped with the text in question. To those who worship her she gives insight and learning. Contemplation of her symbolizes the insight of

transcendence, 'insight which has reached the farther shore'.

Preas Eyn God of the Khmer people in Kampuchea: he rides a three-headed elephant, hurls bolts of lightning and corresponds to the Indian → Indra. We are assured in ancient tradition that it was Preas Eyn himself who built the great temple complex of Angkor Wat, thus giving mankind on earth an image of the heavenly city.

Preas Eyssaur A god of the Khmer people; he is a destructive god, but from death he engenders new life, and in this he corresponds to the Indian → Śiva. The upright stone pillar which the ancient Khmer kings adopted as the symbol of their authority is, in fact, a version of the linga symbol, characteristic of Śiva.

Preas Prohm A mythical primeval god of the Khmer, himself uncreated but containing within himself all power. Preas Prohm expressed no wish, but all that was hidden within him was revealed, and thus arose the world of appearances. Preas Prohm is represented as having four faces: he corresponds to the Indian → Brahma.

Prende (north Albanian Prenne) Old Illyrian goddess of love, the female partner of the thunder-god → Perendi. Today, she is nothing more than a Catholic saint, but in Albanian folk-belief she still rates as *zoja e bukuris*, 'queen of beauty'. As is usual in many cultures, here too Friday is the day sacred to the goddess of love.

Preta (Pali Peta) Spirits of the dead in Hindu and Buddhist belief. As befits the damned, they have ugly bodies and live in Yamaloka, the realm of → Yama. In Buddhist iconography, certain deities (e.g. → Mahākāla) are often shown standing on a Preta, thus symbolizing the power of the teaching.

Priapos A Phrygian god of fertility, of gardens, bees, goats and sheep. In Greece, he was unknown until the Macedonian hegemony, and his cult never assumed significant proportions, either in Greece or in Rome. His father was said to be → Dionysos, and his mother → Aphrodíte, the goddess of love. His cult was most honoured in Asia Minor, and in Lampsakos, on the Hellespont, he is even supposed to have been the most important figure in their pantheon. He was represented as an ugly, satyr-like man with exaggerated genitals. Priapos played a second part too, as the patron of fishermen and sailors.

Priśni → Maruts

Prithivī ('the wide (earth)') In India, the earth, felt as a mother and symbolized in the form of the cow; in Vedism, revered together with the god of heaven → Dyaus. Among her children are the dawn (→ Uṣas) and fire (→ Agni). When she gave birth to → Indra, the earth quaked.

Prometheus ('he who thinks things out in advance') The son of the Titan → Iapetos, who stole fire from the gods and gave it to man. As a punishment, he was chained to a rock in the Caucasus, and an eagle fed daily on his liver, which was self-restoring. Finally he was released by → Heraklés. Prometheus was a culture-hero who brought man not only fire but also handicrafts and art, and he was revered in Athens as the patron of craftsmen, particularly potters. One tradition makes him out to be the actual creator of the human race, as he formed men and women from clay and water.

Proteus A divine 'old man of the sea' in Greek mythology. He was able to assume various shapes. He had oracular powers, and anyone smart enough to get hold of him could benefit from these.

Pryderi → Pwyll

Psezpolnica 'Lady Midday' in Wendish (Serbian) folktale: her counterpart in Poland is Poludnica. She appears round about midday during harvest time, when the day is at its hottest, and drives people off their heads, weakens their limbs or cuts their heads off with a sickle. She is pictured as a woman with black hair, but sometimes as a whirlwind.

Ptah Ancient Egyptian god who was particularly venerated in Memphis. As a god of handicrafts he soon acquired the status of a creator-god, whose instruments of creation were his heart and tongue; and through the power of the word he created the world. He is 'the primeval one', who contains within his own being the essence of the male → Nun and the female → Naunet. In popular belief he was the 'sculptor of the earth' who like → Chnum, created all beings on a potter's wheel. Finally he came to be seen as 'Lord of world-order', and as 'chief of Duat', i.e. of the underworld. In the Ptolemaic period, Ptah had the status of a tutelary god of Egypt, and the monarch was crowned in his temple.

Puck In north Germany and Scandinavia a kind of goblin (the Norwegians call him Pukje); in English popular belief an evil spirit. The word was taken over by the Baltic peoples: → Pukis.

Pudicitia (Latin = modesty) A Roman goddess, the personification of chastity and demureness, represented as a matronly figure, veiled or heavily cloaked. With the increasing erosion of morality in the Empire, her cult went out of fashion and was forgotten.

Pugu The sun-god of the Yukagir in eastern Siberia. He is a champion of righteousness, and punishes all deeds of violence.

Pukis A kind of dragon in Latvian folk-belief. The name may well be of German origin (cf. → Puck). As a rule, Pukis is not malevolent, indeed he may even help you to amass riches. In Lithuania, Pukys appears as a goblin-like domestic spirit: then again as a dragon bringing treasure.

Pultuce → Castur

Purá (also under the name of Poré) The supreme god of the Indians in Guyana, also connected with the moon-god. The word is also used to denote a supernatural (divine) power of a general nature.

Puruṣa ('human being') In India, the primeval man. The Puruṣa hymn in the Rigveda tells us that three quarters of him are immortal and belong to heaven; one quarter is mortal. From this mortal quarter he released his wife → Virāj, and then he himself was born from her as universal spirit. Puruṣa assumed the form of a giant and was sacrificed by the gods: that is to say, he was ritually slain and separated into his constituent manifestations: head = heaven, navel = atmosphere, feet = the earth. In the Brahmanas and the Upaniṣads, Puruṣa serves as a designation for → Prajāpati, and in Buddhist texts the name is applied to → Buddha.

Pūṣan ('the prosperer') Old Indian god, who is described as radiant and toothless. He is married to the sun-maiden, and confers growth and prosperity through light. He watches over roads, protects travellers and guides the dead. His car is drawn by goats.

Pwyll (Welsh = understanding, judgment) A god of the underworld worshipped in ancient Wales. It is told of his son Pryderi that he brought pigs from the underworld to Wales.

Python A dragon which guarded the oracle of its mother, the earth-goddess → Gaia, in Delphi. It was finally slain by → Apóllon.

Q

Qandiša A female demon who lives in springs and rivers in popular belief in the north of Morocco. She is particularly on the look-out for young men whom she first seduces and then robs of their reason. In one locality, sacrifice is made to her on the day of the summer solstice. It is possible that she is an up-dating of an ancient love goddess, possibly → Astarte, who may have reached these parts via Carthage.

Qaynān A god in pre-Islamic south Arabia. The arabic word *qain* means 'blacksmith' so Qaynān may well have been a god of smiths and their craft.

Qormusta (Chormusta) Among the Mongolians, the highest of all the → Tengri, i.e. the heavenly ones. As king of the gods he dwells in the centre of the world, and is connected with the genesis of fire.

Quat The creator-god of the Banks Islanders in Melanesia. Out of boredom he created people, pigs, trees and rocks.

Quetzalcoatl ('feathered snake') Originally, an ancient Mexican local god, possibly based on a historical priest-king; subsequently, the culture-hero of the Toltecs. The Aztecs furnished him with various offices: god of the wind, god of the zodiac (the feathered snake was a stellar symbol) and lord of knowledge. Born into the world by parthenogenesis (→ Coatlicue) he is said to have been seduced by → Tezcatlipoca; whereupon he burned himself to death and was transformed into the morning star. He was also

seen as a moon-god who burns himself in the sun's fires in order to reappear in renewed youth. As divine priest, Quetzalcoatl is the counterpart of the divine warrior Tezcatlipoca. He is also the creator of the first humans, whom he kneaded together out of the meal of the rubbed-down 'jewel-bone', mixed with his own blood.

Quilla (Mama-Kilya = mother moon) The moon-goddess who was especially deeply venerated in the Inca Empire. She was closely associated with the Inca calendar, as feast-days were nominated according to the phases of the moon.

Quirinus This god was revered along with → Jupiter and → Mars as the third member of an ancient divine triad. Originally, he was the local god of the Sabines dwelling on the Quirinal; thereafter he appeared in a military function, defensive rather than offensive. He is therefore depicted peaceably disposed, as a bearded man in garments which are partly clerical and partly military. His sacred plant was the myrtle which was regarded in antiquity as the symbol of bloodless victory. Later, his cult fused with that of the deified → Romulus.

Quiritis The protective deity of motherhood in the Sabine pantheon, corresponding to some extent to → Juno.

Quzah An ancient Arabian god of storms and thunder, who was worshipped in the neighbourhood of Mecca. His weapon is a bow which he uses to shoot the arrows of hail.

R

Rādhā In Indian tradition, a cow-girl who
was the beloved and/or wife of → Kṛiṣṇa. Their
love for each other symbolizes the relationship
between the deity and the individual soul. Rādhā
is accorded divine status and accordingly worshipped by certain Vishnuite sects.

Rahab A monster of chaos in the Old
Testament, the exemplar of powers inimical to
God (Job 9: 13; 26: 12). Visualized as a sea-
serpent.

Rāhu The Indian demon of eclipses: in
cosmogony, the ascending node in the lunar path.
He drives in a car drawn by eight black horses,
and pursues sun and moon with his jaws open.
Whenever he succeeds in swallowing one or the
other, there is an eclipse. He is also portrayed on
the chariot of the Buddhist goddess → Mārici.

Rakṣas (Sanskrit *rakṣasas* = malignant demon)
In Vedism, nocturnal demons who go about in the
shape of dogs or birds, harming people. Their
king is → Rāvaṇa, who abducts → Sītā, the bride
of → Rāma.

Raluvimbha The supreme god of the
Baventa who live in the north of the Transvaal in
South Africa. The god's name contains the word
luvimbha = eagle. All natural manifestations such
as thunder, earthquake, drought and flood are
regarded as his handiwork, and so are epidemics.
The tribal chief is permitted to speak with
Raluvimbha, whom he addresses as 'grandfather'.

Rāma ('The dark-coloured one') Also called Rāmacandra ('Rāma the moon'). He corresponds to the seventh incarnation of the Indian god → Viṣṇu. In the Rāmāyana, the heroic saga of India, it is told how Rāma conquers the king of the demonic → Rakṣas, and frees his wife → Sītā. In iconography, his attributes are a bow and arrows. A cult of Rāma is attested from the eleventh century onwards, and in Vishnuite north India his name is a designation for the supreme god. More than one north Indian royal dynasty saw Rāma as their divine progenitor.

Ran A sea-woman in Nordic mythology, the daughter of → Aegir. She possesses a net with which she fishes up all those who have been drowned. Later, she acquired the status of a goddess of the dead ruling over her own necropolis.

Ran-deng (Chinese = burning lamp) In Chinese legend, a beggar-woman who saved up her money until she could afford to light a lamp at Buddha's altar: whereupon it was prophesied that, as a reward, she would be a future Buddha. According to another tradition, Ran-deng was a celebrated Taoist teacher who introduced Buddha to the teaching that leads to perfection.

Rangi A Polynesian sky-god. For the Maori in New Zealand he and the earth-goddess Papa form the divine primeval pair from whose warm embrace all living beings arose, led by the gods such as → Tangaroa and → Tane.

Raphael (Hebrew = blessing from God) In the Old Testament Apocrypha, the angelic travelling companion of the young Tobias. Later, he became the patron saint of pilgrims and travellers – indeed, the embodiment of the protective angel in general. He is regarded as one of the four (or seven) archangels. It has been suggested that his name is connected with that of the → Rephaim.

Rapithwin
Old Iranian god of midday, lord of summer and of the southerly quarter.

Rašnu
In old Iranian religion, the personification of righteousness, the god of Ordal and guardian of the Cinvat bridge which leads to the beyond. He also makes an appearance at the last judgment, where he weighs our good and bad deeds in golden scales. Under the name of Rajña he was also known in north India.

Rati → Kāma

Ratnapāni
A → Dhyāni-Bodhisattva of minor importance. He is green in colour; in his right hand he holds the jewel, in his left the moon-disc on a lotus.

Ratnasambhava
('born of a jewel'; in China, known as Bao Sheng Fo) A → Dhyāni-Buddha; he is yellow in colour, his heavenly quarter is the south and his season is spring. His car is drawn by a pair of lions or by a horse. His left hand reposes in his lap with the palm turned uppermost.

Rātrī
In Indian mythology, the night, sister of the dawn (→ Uṣas). As a benevolent goddess, she is invoked for protection against robbers and wolves.

Rat-taui
(Rait-taui, 'Sun of the two lands') Ancient Egyptian goddess, wife of → Month, mother of → Harpre. She was represented in human form with a vulture's crest, and cow's horns with the sun's disc. The Greeks tran-

scribed her name as Ratus, and identified her with → Leto.

Raudna A Lappish goddess, wife of the thunder-god → Horagalles. Her name means 'rowan' (mountain ash), and could be related to the Finnish → Rauni.

Rauni Finno-Ugrian philologists disagree as to the exact identity of this figure in Finnish mythology: some regard her as the wife of the thunder-god → Ukko, others take her to be a male deity. In any case, it seems clear that he/she has something to do with fertility. Etymologically, equation of the name with the Lappish → Raudna ('rowan') has been suggested. The figure of Rauni has also been connected with the rainbow which is, of course, associated with rainstorms.

Rāvaṇa The ten-headed and twenty-armed prince of the demonic → Rakṣas, in Indian mythology. It was in order to break his power that Viṣṇu was born as the prince → Rāma.

Re (Ra; in Middle Babylonian texts Ria) The old Egyptian name of the sun and of the sun-god, whose cult was already established at an early date in On (the Greek Heliopolis, 'sun-city'). He united with → Harachte, from whom he took the falcon-head which accompanies his anthropomorphic guise. Through his union with → Atum, he became the creator of the world; and he was also identified with other gods, e.g. with → Amun and with the crocodile-god → Suchos. From the fourth dynasty onwards the Pharaohs describe themselves as 'sons of Re'. In his barque, the sun-god and guider of worlds fares across the ocean of heaven, accompanied by his vizier → Thot and his daughter → Maat, who personifies cosmic order. The orb of the sun was taken to be the visible body of the god, but it was also

regarded as his eye. Symbols of his cult were the obelisks whose pinnacles (often gilded) were struck by the first rays of the rising sun.

Reahu The name given by the Khmer people to the dark demon who pursues the sun and the moon through the heavens in order to swallow them (cf. → Rahu).

Remanta In Buddhism, king of the horse-gods and lord of the easterly quarter of heaven. He rides on a red horse and holds a red banner; he is accompanied by birds like falcons and vultures.

Renenutet Ancient Egyptian goddess of agriculture and harvest. When the crops were being gathered in and the grapes were being pressed, sacrifice was made to the goddess who was then represented in the image of a snake. Her name consists of two components: *renen* = food, nourishment and *utet* = snake. One of her epithets was 'queen of the orchards'. The Greeks called her Thermuthis.

Rephaim (root RP: the *m* is the plural marker) Ancient Syrian chthonic beings, bound up with the concept of fertility. It is not clear whether they rated as 'divine beings' or as 'spirits'; and there is some evidence to suggest that they were denizens of the underworld. In the Old Testament, certain giants are called Rephaim.

Reret Ancient Egyptian hippopotamus-goddess, whose name really means 'sow': an indication of maternal fecundity which tirelessly creates new life.

Rešef The Canaanite-Phoenician god of lightning and of plagues; identified by the Greeks with → Apóllon. His name means 'fire' or 'plague', and the word *rešep* is used in both meanings in the Old Testament (Deuteronomy 32: 24; Psalm 76: 4). Rešef is the god of pestilence who spreads death around him and who bears the epithet 'lord of the arrow'. He was taken over by the Egyptians who made him into a war-god, represented with shield and club (or ball-axe?); instead of the uraeus in his Upper Egyptian crown he has the head of a gazelle.

Rhadámanthys The brother of the Cretan king → Minos: he rules over the Islands of the Blessed, whither are sent the souls of heroes beloved of the gods.

Rheia (Rhea) The daughter of the sky-god → Uranós and the earth-goddess → Gaia, sister and wife of → Kronos and mother of → Zeus, → Poseidon, → Hades and → Hera. She was later equated with the Anatolian mother of the gods → Kybéle.

Ribhus A triad of Indian gods of somewhat inferior rank, named Ribhu, Vaja and Vibhvan; they were the sons of → Indra and of Saranyu, a daughter of → Tvaṣṭar. According to one tradition they were of human descent and their promotion to divine status was a reward for their skilful work – for example, they provided Indra and the → Aśvins with the vehicles they ride in.

Rigenmucha The supreme being of the Papuan tribe of the Baining (in the Gazelle Archipelago of New Guinea). He is conceived as a lone, disembodied being above the clouds. He created the world and from him come both life and death.

Rind (Rinda, Old Icelandic Rindr) A north Germanic goddess. Her name has not been satisfactorily explained, but it may be connected with the word *rind* = ivy, an etymology which would associate the goddess with the generative powers of growth. She has also been interpreted as an earth-goddess. A liaison between her and → Odin produced → Vali.

Riṣabha The first herald of salvation (→ Tīrthaṁkara) in Jainism. He is golden in colour and is symbolized by the bull.

Riṣis ('seers') In Vedism, the singers of holy songs before the dawn of time: holy ones raised to supernatural status who form the seven stars of the Great Bear. In the post-Vedic age, other Riṣis are mentioned, including → Dakṣa and → Kāśyapa.

Romulus Son of the vestal priestess Rhea Silvia and the war-god → Mars. Romulus was exposed in the Tiber along with his twin brother Remus; they were suckled by a wolf and reared by a herdsman. When Rome was founded, Romulus slew Remus and became the first king of the thriving city. At the close of his life he is supposed to have journeyed up to heaven in a fiery chariot; later, he was revered as the god → Quirinus.

Rongo (known in Tahiti as Ro'o, in Hawaii as Lono) Polynesian god of peace and agriculture. It is he who causes the food plants to grow. He abominates blood sacrifice. On Mangareva he is the rain-god who manifests himself in the rainbow. Rongo loves song and festivities. The name means 'sound', 'noise'; he is therefore 'the sounding one', represented by the islanders on Mangaia as a large Triton's horn.

Rosmerta A goddess of fertility and riches who was particularly venerated in north-east

Gaul, among the Lingones, the Treveres and the Mediomatrikes. Iconographically she is shown with cornucopia and caduceus, the staff with two snakes. The presence of the latter attribute has led some scholars to identify the goddess as the female counterpart of the Gallic → Mercurius.

Rudā (also in the form Radū, from the root RDW = to be gracious)   A pre-Islamic deity revered in north Arabia, sometimes male, sometimes female and usually associated with the evening star. In Palmyra, Rudā was known under the name of → Arsū.

Rudianos   A Gallic local god of warlike character, a manifestation of the Gallic → Mars. The name is related to the root *rudio* = red.

Rudra   Indian god of storms, father of the → Maruts. In the Rigveda he appears as a vengeful archer, who fires his arrows of sickness at gods, men and animals. In his terrible aspect he appears as ruddy or blackish, but he can also be a benign god who shines like the sun and whose epithet is *śankara* = he who does good deeds. He is a ready helper of the sick and a lord of animals; in this latter capacity he appears in the form of a bull. In older periods of Hinduism. Rudra is identified with Śiva. The name Rudra is interpreted as meaning 'the howler' or 'the red one'.

Rugievit ('Lord on Rügen')   A god who was once worshipped on the island of Rügen by the Slavs who originally lived there. His function was probably warlike. According to the ancient Danish historian Saxo Grammaticus he was portrayed with seven heads and a sword in one hand.

Rundas Hittite god of hunting and good fortune. His emblem is a double eagle with a hare in each of its talons.

Rusalka Demonic female beings among the east Slavs. They are water-nymphs who dance in forest clearings and meadows on the night of the new moon. Their shrill laughter can be fatal to men.

Ru Shou → Gou Mang

Ruti A pair of lions revered in the ancient Egyptian city of Letopolis. They were early identified with → Šu and → Tefnut. Among their functions was the nourishment of the dead.

S

Sabazios (Sabos)   Phrygian god of agriculture and midwifery, whose figure merged to some extent with that of the Jewish Zebaoth (→ Jahwe). The cult of Sabazios spread by way of Thrace to Greece and Rome. His epithet Bassareus identifies him as one 'clad in a long fox-skin'. Ceremonial contact with a snake formed part of his rites. The orgiastic nature of his cult, rich in nature symbolism, sometimes caused him to be equated with → Dionysos. The Romans identified him with → Jupiter.

Sachmet ('she who is powerful')   Old Egyptian goddess of war, completing, along with her husband → Ptah and her son → Nefertem, the triad of Memphis. She accompanied the Pharaoh (as whose mother she figured) to war, and spread fear and alarm everywhere. She was armed with arrows 'with which she shoots through hearts'. The hot winds of the desert are the fiery breath of the goddess. She was also associated with the fire-spitting uraeus of the monarch, thus becoming the 'eye of → Re'. She was represented as a lioness or as a woman with a lion's head. Sachmet was regarded as a mistress of magic who put her supernatural skills at the service of the healer's art and craft.

Śacī → Indra

Šaddai   In the Old Testament, a very obscure epithet of → Jahwe: in the combination 'el šaddai' it is usually translated as 'God the almighty' or 'most high God'.

Šadrapa An ancient Syrian god of healing; in Palmyra he was represented as a youth with a snake or a scorpion. He was also venerated in Carthage and in the Roman city of Leptis Magna and further, under the name of Satrapas, in some coastal areas of Greece.

Safa The god of weapons among the Ossetians (in the Caucasus): in particular, the tutelary spirit of the chain associated with the household hearth. Children and newly-married couples were commended to his care – always in connection with the chain.

Šai (the Greek form is Psais) In ancient Egypt the personification of destiny and its shaping. He is the beneficial power which co-operates with → Renenutet to make human life possible. Like the Greek → Agathós Daímon he can be represented as a snake.

Šaitan The Arabic form of the name → Satan. In pre-Islamic writings the name is found as a synonym of → Jinn.

Sajigor A god in the pantheon of the Kalaš people in the Hindu-Kush, possibly with a military function. His cult symbol is a knife.

Śakra ('the powerful one') One of the divine princes in the Jain pantheon. In canonical scripture he is called Devadhipati = Lord of gods. In his choice of riding animal (the elephant Airāvata) and weapon (*vajra* = thunderbolt) he corresponds to → Indra in the Brahmin-Hindu pantheon. In Buddhist texts, Śakra (in Pali Sakka) is the name of the Hindu Indra, but is construed as a purely Buddhist figure. As divine king, Śakra leads the fight against the demons.

Śakti ('power') Female creative energy, usually personified in Hinduism as a goddess. Śakti is allotted to the male creative principle as consort, a role in which she appears as → Durgā, as → Lakṣmī or as → Pārvatī. In popular belief → Kāmākṣī is venerated as the supreme Śakti. The Tantric symbol of Śakti is the *yoni* (womb) which unites with the *lingam* of → Śiva to express the unity of all opposites.

Šala(s) Old Mesopotamian goddess, the wife of the Akkadian weather-god → Adad, or of → Dagan, who was taken over from the west Semites.

Šalim → Šar

Salmān (Šalmān) Pre-Islamic god revered in north Arabia; his name means 'peace', 'blessing'.

Salus (Latin = salvation, rescue) A Roman goddess personifying the general welfare of the state (*salus publica*); later identified with the Greek → Hygíeia, and revered as the protector of health. She is accompanied by a snake. Another of her attributes is a bowl.

Samael (Sammael, Samiel) The name of an angel in apocalyptic writing. From the third century onwards, a Jewish designation for → Satan, who leads men astray into all sorts of evil doings. He is best known for his erotic relationship with → Lilith. Samael is also occasionally taken to be an angel of death.

Sāmantabhadra ('he who is completely fortunate') One of the eight great → Bodhisattvas; he was an emanation from → Vairocana. Only in Tibet, under the name of Kun-tu-bzan-po, did he assume greater significance as the primeval Buddha (→ Adhibuddha). In oriental art he is shown enthroned on a white elephant, the symbol of strength and wisdom. In China he is known as Bu-xian, in Japan as Fu-gen.

Šamaš The Semitic word for the sun became the name of the Babylonian sun-god; during the day he sees all things, and hence is the god of justice and of the oracle. He is symbolized by the sun's disc and a four-pointed star, surrounded by rays. In Assyria, the emblem was the solar disc with wings. Otherwise, he is represented as a king seated on a throne. Šamaš is 'judge of the heavens and of the earth': justice and righteousness, Mešaru and Kettu, are in fact hypostatized into personifications who accompany him at all times. By night the sun-god moves through the underworld, bringing light and nourishment to the dead.

Sämpsä A Finnish god of vegetation, whose name means 'sedge'. When Sämpsä lies idle in bed, enjoying his winter sleep, neither rye nor oats can prosper. So the god must be roused. Before sowing, he celebrates marriage with his step-mother. Sämpsä is also seen as a sower who sows pines, fir and juniper.

Šams A pre-Islamic deity whose Arabic name means 'sun'. In north Arabia, the deity was conceived as male (like the Mesopotamian → Šamaš); but as female in south Arabia. The south Arabian sun-goddess has the epithet *aliyat* = she who is lofty.

Samvara (also Cakrasamvara) A god of initiation in Tantrism. His mandala shows him as four-faced and with twelve arms; his sacred cord is a snake, and his crown consists of five skulls. His female consort is → Vajravārāhi.

Šanda   An ancient Luvian god in Asia Minor, the associate of → Kubaba. On occasion, he appears as → Marduk, an import from Babylon. He was also known in Cilicia and Lydia under the name of Sandas.

Sangarios   An ancient Anatolian (Phrygian) river-god. His daughter Nana (an epiphany of the Magna Mater) is impregnated by the fruit of an almond tree, and gives birth to → Attis.

Şango   God of thunder among the Yoruba in Nigeria. On his head he bears a large axe with six eyes. The thunder is represented by the bellowing of the ram, the animal sacred to the god.

Saošyant (a later form is Sošāns)   In Iran, originally the title of the eschatological hero and coming saviour. According to the Avesta, he renews the world and resurrects the dead. He carries out the sacrifice of the bull Hadayoš, and from its fat mixed with Haoma juice he prepares a draught of immortality for all of mankind.

Šapš   The goddess of the sun in Ugaritic myth. She is called 'the light of the gods'.

Saptākṣara ('seven-syllabled')   A form of the Buddhist god → Heruka. He is blue in colour, six-armed and three-headed, each head having three eyes. His plaited crown is adorned with a double thunderbolt and the sickle moon. On his knee is seated his → prajñā who is embracing him. He is surrounded by six other goddesses who form his mandala.

Šar and Šalim   Old Syrian deities representing morning and evening, or perhaps the morning and the evening star. The word šar or šachar really means 'dawn', and is found in the

Old Testament (Isaiah 14: 12). It has been suggested that the place-name Jerusalem – in Hebrew *jerušalajim* – means the place 'founded' by the god Šalim.

Šara The ancient Mesopotamian god of the town of Umma; he was said to be the son of → Inanna.

Sarasvatī In origin, an ancient Indian river goddess. In the Brahmanas, she is identified with speech, whence she is promoted to become goddess of eloquence and wisdom, identified with → Vāc. The Hindus venerate her as Vāgdevi, 'goddess of language'. She is regarded as both the creation and the wife of → Brahma, and as the mother of the Vedas. She rides on a swan (less frequently on a peacock) or sits on a lotus. In her manifestation as Vajrasarasvatī she is three-faced and six-armed.

Sárkány A weather-demon of the ancient Hungarians: he had seven or nine heads, lived in the underworld and was armed with a sabre and the morning star. Seated on his charger he rides along with the thunderclouds, often accompanied by a magician. Sárkány can turn people into stones. In Hungarian folktale the name is applied to a dragon.

Sarpanitu (Akkadian = 'she who shines silver') The wife of the Babylonian chief god → Marduk. Under the epithet of Erua she figured as the goddess of pregnancy.

Šarruma (Sarrumma) Old Anatolian god (Hurrian): the 'king of the mountains', the son of the weather-god → Tešub, who appears in the form of a bull, and → Hebat. Thus, Šarruma is also known as 'bull-calf'. He rides on a panther, and he is armed with an axe.

Śāsana-deva, Śāsana-devī ('gods and goddesses of the teaching') Jainist divinities who accompany each Tīrthamkara. While they are redeemed and raised above all earthly things, the gods are still accessible via prayer. Among their names are many which occur also in the Brahmin-Hindu pantheon, e.g. → Brahmā, → Kubera, → Varuṇa, → Kālī, → Gaurī.

Satan (Hebrew = the adversary; Greek form Satanas) In the Old Testament, Satan appears as the 'prosecutor' before the heavenly court (Zechariah 3: 1 ff.; Job 1: 6; 2: 7 ff) but he also figures as the chief seducer and tempter (1 Chronicles 21: 1), while in the Christian scheme of things he is the embodiment of evil (Mark 4:15). In the apocryphal book of Henoch it is told how Satan rebelled against God and was hurled by the angel → Michael into the abyss. Satan is the devil pure and simple, the 'prince of this world'; and he can be imagined in the form of a snake or a dragon. Other names for him are → Beelzebub and → Belial.

Sataran (Ištaran) Ancient Mesopotamian god who appears both as judge and as doctor. As regards the latter aspect, it is fitting that the snake-like → Nirah should figure as his messenger.

Sati In Indian mythology, the daughter of → Dakṣa, and the wife of → Śiva. Grief-stricken by reason of her husband's dispute with her father, she seeks release in death. Her corpse is dismembered by → Viṣṇu, but the goddess is reborn as → Pārvatī.

Satis The wife of the ancient Egyptian creator-god → Chnum; the 'Queen of Elephantine' and donator of the cooling waters of the cataract. She was represented anthropomorphically with the crown of Upper Egypt on her head, flanked by two curved antelope horns.

Satúrnus The Roman god of agriculture, presumably taken over from the Etruscans. As early as the fifth century BC his temple stood on the Forum, acting as the Roman treasury (the *aerarium*). At his feast, the Saturnalia, held on 17-19 December, it was the custom for masters to serve their slaves; and people gave each other candles as presents, whose light was supposed to be a magical contribution to the failing powers of the winter sun. In Roman myth, Saturnus appears as husband of → Ops and father of → Jupíter. His name is connected with the concept of a golden age. From the third century AD onwards, Saturn was identified with the Greek → Kronos.

Satúrnus Africánus This god was revered in Roman North Africa. In some respects, he is reminiscent of the Punic → Baal. He appears as a bearded old man, and is regarded as lord of heaven, of time and of agriculture. His attributes comprise sickle, honey-comb or fir-cone and a lion. He is the 'holy god' (*deus sanctus*) and 'god of fruits' (*deus frugum*).

Satyr The satyrs were the licentious and lecherous crew who accompanied the Greek god → Dionysos. They were thought to be hybrid creatures, half-man, half-horse, with animal ears, a rough tousled pelt, horns and a tail, and they were usually depicted as ithyphallic. They were related to the → Silenes as demons of fertility, indeed often hardly to be distinguished from them.

Saule The Latvian sun-goddess; in mythology and in folktale she is hailed sometimes as 'sun-virgin' and then again as 'mother sun'. She is wooed by the sky-god → Dievs and the moon-god → Mēness. Saule herself was thought of as dwelling on her farm or estate on top of the mountain of heaven, and she was invoked in prayer to foster the fruits of the earth. Among the Lithuanians, Saule (the sun) figures less prominently as a deity, having been set in heaven by the divine smith; but here too we find the tradition that sun and moon (→ Menulis) form a conjugal couple.

Saules meitas These were the 'daughters of the sun' in ancient Latvian mythology, and are often mentioned together with the → Dieva dēli. While the daughters of the sun sow roses, the sons of the sky-god strew golden dew.

Săuška (Šawuška, Sausga) A goddess worshipped by the Hurrians who lived in Asia Minor; functionally, she is comparable to the old Mesopotamian goddess of love → Ištar. Like Ištar, Šauška not only confers health and fertility: she has warlike traits as well, and her name means 'she who is armed'. She is portrayed wearing the cap normally reserved for male deities, and a slit skirt which leaves her legs free. Wings sprout from her back. Her sacred animal is the lion. Šauška's reputation as a goddess of healing reached as far afield as Egypt.

Savitar The Vedic god who oversees the whole span of heaven, and who drives man and animals to activity (Savitar means 'stimulator'). He drives in a golden chariot and has golden arms which reach to the frontiers of heaven: in other words, a solar god.

Saxnot ('sword-companion': cf. Old High German *sahs* = knife, sword) Originally, the tribal god of the Saxons, who is mentioned in an old Low German manuscript along with Donar and Wodan (→ Odin). He is probably a local form of → Tyr.

Sebettu (Akkadian = the seven) Designation of a group of demons, some benign, others malignant. The seven malevolent demons are in fact the progeny of the sky-god → An, but that does not prevent them from helping the plague-god → Erra; they also encircle the moon, thereby causing an eclipse. The benign seven appear as adversaries of these malignant spirits. Sebettu was also the Akkadian name for the Pleiades.

Sechat-Hor

('she who remembers Horus') Ancient Egyptian cow-goddess, queen of herds and foster-mother of the infant → Horus. She was particularly venerated in the third nome of Lower Egypt.

Securitas

The personification of security, revered by the Romans as the goddess in whose hands the permanence of the Empire rested.

Šed

A popular god in ancient Egypt. The name means 'saviour' and identifies the god, who often figured on amulets, as one to whom men could turn in their hour of need. Above all, he was supposed to offer protection against wild animals.

Šed → Šedim

Šedim

In the Old Testament, devils or demons to whom the apostate Israelites made sacrifice (Deuteronomy 32: 17; Psalm 106: 36). In some translations of the Bible they appear as goblins. They are probably connected with the Mesopotamian → Šedu. In rabbinic literature, the word *šed* denoted a dangerous type of demon with magical powers.

Sedna

Sea-goddess of the Eskimos in Baffin Land. In east Greenland, she is known as 'mother of the sea' (Immap ukua), while the polar Eskimos refer to her as Nerrivik, i.e. 'the eating-place', a very apt description of the sea as a source of nourishment. Sedna is queen of the sea-creatures.

Šedu In the days of the Babylonian Empire, a kindly and helpful demon. In the late Assyrian period, Šedu and the female Lamassu (→ Lama) were winged bull-beings who protected the palace entrances.

Se'irim (Sahirim) The Se'irim are mentioned in the Old Testament as demons in the shape of goats. The name is derived from the word *sā'ir* = hairy. In Leviticus 17:7 the children of Israel are forbidden to make sacrifice to the Se'irim (goat-spirits).

Šelardi The moon-god of the Urartian contemporaries of the Assyrians, who lived in what is now Armenia.

Seléne (from Greek *selas* = light, radiance) Greek goddess of the moon, the daughter of the Titan → Hyperion and sister of the sun-god → Hélios. She drives in a chariot drawn by two horses or rides on a mule. The goddess, who was also called Mene = moon, was regarded as tutelary deity of magicians and sorcerers. In the Hellenistic period she fused with → Artemis or → Hekáte; the Romans equated her with → Luna.

Selket The name of this old Egyptian goddess is really Serket-hetu which means 'she who lets throats breathe'. She is the tutelary goddess of the dead, and uses her magic spells to help the sun-god against his enemies. Her symbolical animal, which she wears on her head, is the scorpion. The Greeks called her Selkis.

Selvans An Etruscan god: the similarity in name has led scholars to compare him with the Roman god of field and forest → Silvanus.

Semele In origin, Semele was probably a Thracian-Phrygian earth-goddess. In Greek myth she appears as the daughter of the Theban king Kadmos. When → Zeus, who was wooing her, revealed himself to her in all his divine majesty, she was burnt by the lightning emanating from him. Zeus rescued the unborn child by sewing the embryo into his thigh, and in due course → Dionysos was born. Later, Dionysos descended to the underworld and led his mother back to Olympus where she took her place among the immortals under the name of Thyone.

Semnai Theai ('exalted goddesses') In origin, typical earth-goddesses of fertility who were worshipped in a cave on the Aeropagos. Later, they were identified with the → Erinyes.

Semnocosus A war-god worshipped in northern Hispania, whose cult became popular among Roman troops. Prisoners, horses and goats were sacrificed to him.

Senmurw A mythical winged monster in ancient Iran. In one tradition it is described as a bat combining the natures of dog, bird and musk-ox. In Sassanid art it is represented as a sort of peacock dragon with a dog's head. Fancies relating to Senmurw were later transferred to the modern Iranian wonder-bird, the simurgh: it is supposed to be so old that it has seen the destruction of the world three times already.

Šentait An ancient Egyptian goddess in the form of a cow. She was taken into the circle of deities concerned with the protection of the dead; as an exemplar of maternal fertility she merges in the late period into the figure of → Isis.

Sepa (Sep) The Old Egyptian word means 'centipede'. It is the name of a god who was invoked in charms and spells against dangerous animals and enemies of the gods. As a chthonic being, he was identified with → Osiris, the god of the dead.

Sequana A Gallic goddess of the river Seine and the tribe of the Sequanae. The duck is sacred to her.

Seraphim (Serafim, Hebrew *saraph* = to burn; then, fiery 'snake') In the Old Testament, spirits with three pairs of double wings, seen by Isaiah in the vision which launched him on his career as a prophet (Isaiah 6: 2). In the divine hierarchy of Dionysius the Areopagite they form the highest of the nine angelic choirs: the → Cherubim are ranked below them. The seraph was an oft-recurring motif in romanesque art.

Serapis (Sarapis) The Greek form of Osiris-Apis: i.e. the bull-god → Apis as raised to fusion with → Osiris. This is the designation given to a god first introduced into the Egyptian pantheon by King Ptolemaios I who came from Macedonia. As lord of generative fecundity he bears a *kalathos* (a basket-shaped head-dress) entwined with ears of corn. Otherwise, he has the status of a universal god, uniting in his person traits of → Zeus and → Hades. From his temple (Serapeum) in Alexandria, his cult spread to every corner of the Roman Empire.

Šeri and Hurri Divine bulls and companions of the old Anatolian weather-god (→ Iškur, → Tešub). The names mean 'day' and 'night'. Both names figure in lists of gods to be invoked when making a vow or taking an oath.

Šeṣa An Indian snake-demon, who bears the earth or enfolds it. He is the king of the Nāgas; under the name of Ananta he is the symbol of eternity, and ranged under → Viṣṇu.

Sešat Ancient Egyptian goddess of writing. She is 'she who presides over the house of records' and 'queen of builders'. Her most important function is recording the Pharaonic years of rule and jubilees. She is regarded as the sister or daughter of → Thot.

Šesmu (Šesemu, Šezemu) Ancient Egyptian god of oil and wine pressing. To the dead he proffers wine as a sustaining draught; as for sinners, he tears their heads off and presses them in his wine-press.

Seth (Setech, Sutech) The shady god in the ancient Egyptian pantheon. As lord of the desert he is the adversary of → Osiris, the god of vegetation, and the fight between the two brothers reflects the permanent struggle between these two aspects of nature. As Seth murders his brother, he came later to be regarded as the embodiment of evil, and the Greeks equated him with →

Typhon; and it is significant that Seth was also regarded as the god of non-Egyptian lands. The horse, the antelope, the pig, the hippopotamus and the crocodile were regarded as sacred to Seth. Seth had a positive aspect as well, appearing as the Upper Egyptian partner of the Lower Egyptian tutelary god → Horus. Standing on the bows of the sun-barque, Seth fights off the → Apophis-snake.

Sethlans Etruscan god of fire and blacksmiths, in iconography equated with the Greek → Hephaistos.

Shang-di (also known simply as Di) The supreme god in ancient China. He rules over heaven in the same way as the dynastic ruler is supreme on earth. Because he exercises control over such natural forces as thunder and lightning, wind and rain, he is also regarded as the god of agriculture.

Sheila-na-gig A female demon known in the British Isles from early Celtic times onwards. She displays her pudenda in an apotropaic gesture, thus providing a parallel to the Baubo of antiquity. During the Middle Ages, Sheila-na-gig was represented on the walls of various churches in England as a way of warding off evil.

gShen-Lha-od-dkar A Tibetan deity in the ancient, pre-Lamaist Bon religion. He is 'god of the white light' from whom all other gods have emanated. Lamaism took him over as god of wisdom.

Shen-nong Chinese culture-hero, known as the 'divine husbandman'. He has the head of an ox, and it is he whom mankind has to thank for agriculture and the knowledge of healing and curative herbs. As god of the hot winds, however, he can also be harmful to peasants. His wife is the goddess of silk-worm culture.

gShen-rab The founder of the Bon religion. In art he is represented as a supernatural being remote from the world, seated on a lotus: in his right hand he holds the swastika sceptre.

Shen Yi Chinese sun-god, known as the 'divine archer'. Once upon a time, it is said, there were ten suns in heaven whose heat threatened all life on earth. Shen Yi shot down nine of them and became the lord of the remaining one. In terms of Chinese *yin-yang* symbolism (the polarity between the male and female principles) Shen Yi incorporates male *yang*, while his wife → Heng E represents female *yin*.

Shichi-fukujin The Japanese deities of good fortune, usually shown as seven in number: → Benten, → Hotei the friend of children, → Jurojin, → Fukurokuju, Bishamon (missionary zeal), Daikoku (riches), and Ebisu the patron of fishermen. They are sometimes portrayed all together in a treasure-ship.

Shi-jia-mu-ni → Fo

Shi-tenno The name applied to the four Shintoist gods who guard the heavenly quarters. One of these 'kings of heaven' is → Zocho. Their Indian counterparts are the → Lokapālas.

Shosshu The god of blacksmiths and metal-workers among the Abkhaz people who live in the Caucasus. Oaths were sworn and pledges made over the anvil which represented the god.

Shou Lao (Shou Xing Lao Tou-zi) In China, the 'god of long life', also called Nan-ji Xian-weng, 'the ancient of the South Pole'. Originally a stellar deity, he became the president of that department of heavenly administration which fixes our life-span. His sacred creature is the white crane, a symbol of longevity. He is often shown holding a peach in his hand.

Shurdi A god of thunderstorms whose ante-cedents go back to the ancient Illyrians who once lived in the area of present-day Albania. The name is interpreted as meaning 'the deaf one' and may be connected with the name of the Thracian thunder-god Zibelthiurdos.

Si A moon-god heading the pantheon wor-shipped in the ancient Chimu Empire of Peru. On vases, he is shown in the sickle-moon with a crown of feathers joined to an armoured back-plate (see illustration).

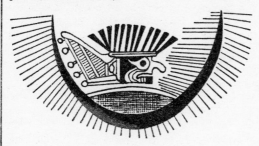

Sia → Hu

Sif The wife of the Germanic god → Thor. It has been suggested that her golden hair is a poetic image for waving fields of corn. However speculative this is, it does seem very probable that Sif played the part of a goddess of vegetation.

Sigyn The wife of the Germanic god → Loki. For his share in the murder of → Balder, Loki is punished by having a poisonous snake suspended over his head – but his faithful wife collects the venom in a bowl as it drips down.

Sihai → Sirao

Sila (or Silma inua) The divine ruler of the universe in the belief of the Eskimos: some tribes imagine him as an airy spirit, others think of him as the god who rules the souls of man and beast and whom the shamans invoke.

Silene Two-legged half-human horse-like beings in Greek mythology. Silenos (in the singular) is the ringleader of the → Satyrs, and also appears as the tutor of the young → Dionysos: he is portrayed as bald-headed and pot-bellied. → Marsýas also belonged to the Silene.

Silewe Nazarata A goddess revered on the island of Nias (Indonesia). She represents life in all of its forms. She is regarded as helpful to mankind, nevertheless she bears the epithet 'she who is feared'. The moon is often said to be her dwelling-place; otherwise, she sits with her husband → Lowalangi in the loftiest sphere of heaven.

Silvanus Roman god of fields and woods. He was portrayed as a peasant, either naked or clad in a tunic tucked up round his legs; in his long hair he wears a wreath of pine twigs, and he has a goat-skin over his shoulders. Silvanus had no official cult, but he was very popular among the common people. It is possible that he can be traced back to the Etruscan → Selvans, whose name would be understood, by popular etymology, as meaning 'he who lives in the woods (*silva*)'.

Šimigi A sun-god of the Hurrians in ancient Anatolia. In significance and mode of appearance he coincides with the Hittite → Ištanu.

Simurgh → Senmurw

Sin (1) (older form Suen; Old Assyrian, Suin) Babylonian moon-god. His symbol is the sickle-moon which can be construed as a boat, and the god himself was called 'shining boat of heaven'. But the moon-god was also thought of as a bull, whose horns are formed by the sickle of the moon. Sin was revered as an ancient and wise god, as lord of destiny and – like the sun-god → Šamaš – as judge of heaven and earth. The number associated with him was 30.

Sin (2) A god of the moon and of riches revered in pre-Islamic times in Hadramaut (south Arabia).

Singbonga The chief god of the Mundas, who speak an Austro-Asiatic language and live in eastern India. The word *sing* may mean 'sun', and *bonga* originally meant 'spirit' or 'higher being'. In the Ho tribe, the god is called Sirma Thakur = Lord of Heaven. White goats and white cocks are sacrificed to Singbonga.

Sipe Gyalmo In the Bon religion of Tibet, a goddess who is 'queen of the world'. In art, she is represented as having a head with three eyes, and six arms in which she holds the following attributes: banner of victory, sword, royal sunshade, swastika, skull-bowl and trident. She rides on a red mule.

Sirao An ancient tradition among the island-ers on Nias (in Indonesia) tells us that Sirao was the first of the gods, who created the earth, and then the first existent being, named Sihai. The world tree sprouted from Sihai's heart (according to another version of the myth, from that of his son); from his right eye came the sun, and from his left eye the moon. Among other names, that of → Lowalangi is mentioned as the son of Sirao.

Sirens (Greek seirénes) Divine hybrid creatures, half-bird, half-maiden, gifted with the power of bewitching song. They dwell in Hades or in the heavenly fields; but, as the daughters of → Phorkys they may live on an island, beguile passing mariners with their song and then suck their blood. In this, they are close to the old demons of death like the → Harpies; and they were often represented on funerary monuments as symbolic figures of mourning.

Sirona A Celtic goddess revered in the Mosel Valley and often connected with the Gallic-Roman Apóllon. As to her function, there are conflicting theories – she may have been a goddess of springs and wells, or possibly a stellar goddess.

Sītā An incarnation of the Indian goddess → Laksmi. By her own wish she was born from a freshly ploughed field – hence her name, which means 'furrow'. She became the wife of → Rāma. Abducted by the king of the → Raksas (→ Rāvana) she was, after her release, suspected of adultery, whereupon she returned to her mother earth.

Sītalā ('the cool one') Bengali goddess of smallpox, depicted as an ugly woman with a switch, riding on an ass. In south India she is revered under the name of Mariamma.

Šiuš A sky-god and sun-god of the Hittites who invaded Asia Minor. Subsequently, he had to relinquish his solar aspect to other deities (→ Ištanu, the sun-goddess of Arinna).

Śiva ('the friendly one', 'gracious one') This deity can be traced back to the Indus Valley cultures which preceded the Aryans in north India. Very early on, Śiva began to take on characteristics of the Vedic → Rudra, forming a triad (→ Trimūrti) together with → Brahma and → Viṣṇu. In his dark and destructive aspect he is Ugra ('the violent one'), Mahākāla ('death') and → Bhairava; and in this aspect he is portrayed as either naked or clad in a skin, smeared with ashes and adorned with a wreath of skulls. In his benign aspect he appears as Mahāyogin ('the great yogi') and as Naṭarāja ('King of the dance'). As Ardhanariśvara he combines in himself male and female characteristics. Among his attributes are the sickle moon and the trident (*triśūla*) and a third eye. In south Indian art he is shown with an axe and a gazelle in his hands. Śiva is the great god of generation, revered under the symbol of the *linga(m)*, and in this connection the bull → Nandin on which he rides should also be mentioned. His wife is → Durgā; in the epics, → Pārvatī also appears in this role. His devotees see Śiva as the supreme being, the embodiment of cosmic power in all of its aspects, destructive as well as creative. In Ceylon, he is known as → Iśvara. For his relationship with Viṣṇu see → Harihara.

Šiwini The Urartian sun-god; known as → Šimigi among the Hurrians.

Skadi In Germanic myth, the daughter of the giant → Thiassi and wife of the god → Njörd. Njörd and Skadi fall out with each other as to where they should live: Njörd would like to live by the sea, but Skadi prefers the mountains. Later, according to Ynglingasaga, Skadi entered into a new marriage with → Odin. Any connection between the name Skadi and the word Scandinavia is hypothetical.

Skan The sky-god of the Sioux Indians. He was revered as the source of all power and strength and as the creator of the world, which he has ordered *modulo* 4. Skan is judge over the gods and over the souls of men.

Skanda Indian god of war, the son of → Śiva: another version of the myth makes him the progeny of the seed of → Agni, cast into the sacrificial fire. Reared by the six-starred constellation of the Pleiades (Kirttikah) he was given the name Kārttikeya. As a handsome young man he is also known as Kumāra ('youth'). He rides on the peacock Paravani, has six heads and twelve arms, and carries spear, bow and arrows. In south India, Skanda is worshipped under the name of Subrahmanya ('favourable to Brahmins').

Skuld → Norns

Skylla (Greek = bitch; Latin Scylla) In the Odyssey, a monster lurking by certain straits which devoured passing seamen; it was imagined as having twelve feet and six heads which were canine or lupine. Later, Skylla, and Charybdis lying opposite it, were identified as the whirlpool, dangerous to shipping, lying in the Straits of Messina.

Smertrios War-like deity of the Gauls, especially of the Treveres. On a relief discovered in Paris he is portrayed as a bearded athlete, using a club to dispatch a snake.

So The name given to their god of thunder by the Ewe people who live in Togo and Ghana. He is in fact a *mixta persona* – the male Sogblā and the female Sodza, both of whom are manifest to us in a thunderstorm. Sogblā dwells in heaven and is surrounded by flames; he is revered above all by hunters, and feared by evil-doers. Sodza is the donor of rain and fertility. Ewe people are forbidden to drink rain-water, as this is water of So.

Sokar (Seker, Sokaris) A falcon-god of the dead revered in the area of Memphis in ancient Egypt. As lord of the necropolis he became patron of the craftsmen working there, and was equated with → Ptah; later, also with the god of the dead → Osiris.

Sol (1) Roman sun-god, corresponding to the Greek → Hélios. His temple stood on the Quirinal, and as patron of the chariot teams he had a second temple in the Circus Maximus. During the Empire period, the designation *Sol invictus* was transferred to various oriental sun-gods, e.g. to the Syrian → Elagabal. Under the Emperor of the same name, Elagabal became the supreme tutelary god of Rome.

Sol (2) (Old Icelandic *sol* = sun) The daughter of Mundilferi, sister of → Mani. Her car is drawn by two horses called Arvakr ('he who is early awake') and Alsvidr ('swiftest of all') across the sky. The personification of the sun is also found in the second Merseburg spell, under the name of Sunna.

Soma In ancient India, the intoxicating drink made from the soma plant, which played a crucial role in the Vedic sacrificial rites and which was personified as a deity. Soma was regarded as the vital sap in all living beings, and its ritual extraction was a symbol of cosmic processes. The gods drink soma from the bowl of the moon, and soma confers immortality (*amrita*). In the post-

Vedic age, Soma is a customary name for the moon-god.

Somtus (better known as Harsomtus = 'uniter of the two lands')   A god revered in the ancient Egyptian city of Dendera: creator and child of the sun. Late temple pictures show him as a snake or a lotus blossom.

Sopdu   Ancient Egyptian god of the frontier and of the east, revered originally in the twentieth nome of lower Egypt, then later in the Sinai Peninsula.

Sothis   The Greek name of the ancient Egyptian goddess Sopdet, the incorporation of the Dog Star, Sirius. As the heliacal rising of Sirius once coincided with the onset of the Nile flood, it was believed that the goddess herself was to be thanked for the life-giving waters and the fertility they engendered. Later, Sothis merged into the figure of → Isis, who, as Sirius, follows → Osiris, embodied in Orion.

Spandaramet   Armenian   earth-goddess, whose name comes from the Iranian *spenta Armaiti*. She is the goddess of 'those who are asleep', i.e. the dead. With the coming of Christianity, the word Spandaramet took on the meaning of hell.

Spenta Mainyu (Spēnāk Menoi)   In Old Iranian myth, the constant adversary of Angru Mainyu (→ Ahriman). Where Spenta Mainyu creates life, Angru Mainyu is responsible for death. Throughout the whole of world history the two remain active as good and evil principles. In Pahlavi literature, the figure of Spēnāk Mēnoi merges into the figure of Ormazd (→ Ahura Mazda).

Spes Roman goddess, the personification of hope, not excluding the plant world. This made her a goddess of gardens, who had her temple in the vegetable market, and who was represented as a girl bearing flowers or grain.

Sphinx The (male) Sphinx of Gizeh was worshipped as → Harmachis. Later, the form of the Sphinx was attributed to the king of the gods, the sun-god → Amun-Re. In Greece, the (female) sphinx – originally *phix*, which became *sphinx* = the strangler, by popular etymology – is to be interpreted as a kind of demon of death. She is the daughter of → Typhón and of → Echidna. To every passer-by she gives a riddle – and swallows those who cannot solve it.

Sraoša (Modern Persian Sroš) In Old Iranian religion, a figure belonging to or close to → the Ameša Spentas: a personification of the 'ear' of → Ahura Mazda, through which the faithful have access to the god. After sunset, he guards creation from the demonic powers. Through cock-crow he calls men to their religious duty. In Manichaeanism the name is transferred to a cosmic luminosity with eschatological function.

Šrat A domestic demon of the West Slavs which can fly and which appears as a fiery figure. The name is Germanic (cf. Old High German *scrato* = forest spirit).

Sri Demonic beings in the old Bon religion of Tibet. They dwell below the ground, chase little children and behave as vampires in places where corpses are laid out.

Śridevi One of the terrifying goddesses of Lamaism, whose Tibetan name is dPal-ldan Lhamo. She exercises a special tutelary function for the Dalai Lama, but she also plays a part in the judgment of the dead, and keeps a record of our sins. She is portrayed as mounted on a mule; she has an eye in her forehead, and in her left hand she carries a bowl made from a skull.

Stihi A female demon in south Albanian popular belief. As a fearsome dragon breathing fire it guards a treasure.

Stribog East Slavonic god mentioned in the Nestor Chronicle and elsewhere. The phrase 'Stribog's grandchildren' referred to the winds, and the god himself has accordingly been seen as ruler of the winds.

Strigae (sing. *striga* = she who screeches) In Roman popular belief bird-like demons who stole children. Sometimes they were said to be old women who had turned into birds.

Styx (from Greek *stygein* = to hate) The name
of the river in the Greek underworld, and of its
tutelary goddess. Hesiod says that she is the most
powerful of the daughters of → Okeanos and of
→ Tethys. The gods swore their most solemn
oaths by the water of the Styx (the river itself is
masculine in Greek). Among the children of the
goddess were → Bia and → Nike.

Šu (Greek transcription Sos) In ancient
Egyptian myth, Šu came forth as breath from the
nose of the primeval god → Atum. His name
means 'emptiness' and identifies him as a god of
the space between heaven and earth, which he is
said to have separated, the one from the other.
Together with his sister → Tefnut (moisture), Šu
(air) incorporates the forces which are necessary
for life. The identification of Atum with the sun-
god → Re makes Šu the 'son of Re' and he is
then entitled to be represented wearing the lion's
head.

Suaixtix A designation of the sun and the
name of the sun-god of the ancient Prussians
(Pruzzen). A connection has been suggested with
the word *svaistikas* ('he who shines around').

Succubus (from Latin *succumbere* = to lie
under) A female demon who besets a man
sexually during sleep. In other words, the succubus is a kind of → Alp. Women on trial as
witches were often accused of being the devil's
succubus or paramour.

Sucellos (Celtic = he who strikes well
home) A Gallic god with markedly syncretic
traits. His chief attribute is a hammer, and Celtic
philologists refer to him therefore as the
'hammer-god'. His rather more haphazard attributes are a club and a purse, reminiscent of
figures like → Heraklés and → Mercurius. Often
he holds in his hand a vase or a drinking-bowl

(*olla*), which may be symbols of plenty and which may identify him as a god of fertility. He has also been interpreted as a god of the dead, and evidence for this theory is provided by the dog allotted to him on an altar.

Suchos This is the Greek reading of the name of the old Egyptian crocodile-god: in script SBK, vocalized as Sobek. The main centres of his cult were Krokodilopolis in Fayum and Kom Ombo in Upper Egypt. In the myth he appears as the son of → Neith. Representations showing crocodiles with falcon heads and the double crown are based on an approximation of this god to → Horus. Further identification with → Re led to the solar disc being added to the crocodile's head. The Greeks depicted Suchos as a radiant → Hélios, and gave him a crocodile in one hand as an attribute.

Sugaar A male snake-like spirit of the Basques: it lives under the ground but can also traverse the heavens like a fiery sickle. In one district he is regarded as the spirit → Maju, in another as the devil.

Sul A Celtic goddess worshipped in Bath (in southern England). Eternal fire burned in her temple; her name means 'sun'. During the Roman occupation she was identified with Minerva.

Šulmanu The Assyrian god of war and of the underworld.

Šulpa'e An old Mesopotamian god whose Sumerian name means 'youth who appears in radiance'. He may appear as the husband of the mother-goddess → Ninḫursanga. He was regarded as the representative of the planet Jupiter.

Sumbharāja One of the Buddhist →
Krodhadevatās, and guardian of the mandalas.
He has three eyes and six arms, and in his crown
he bears the image of → Akṣobhya.

Summamus An Etruscan god who hurls
down lightning by night. He received his own
temple in Rome and the *fratres Arvales* sacrificed
black wethers to him.

Sun Hou-zi A divine ape in Chinese
mythology, also known as Sun Wu-kong, i.e. 'he
who awakens to nothingness (Nirvana)'. He was
born from an egg fertilized by the wind. Skilled in
various magic arts and crafts, he was finally
able – against the will of the gods – to eat of the
peaches of immortality and the pills of eternal
life.

Supārśva The seventh → Tīrthaṁkara in
Jainism. Its characteristic emblem is the swastika
symbolizing the four planes of existence – the
world of the gods, the world of men, the world of
animals and hell.

Surt(r) In Germanic mythology, an opponent
of the gods at the time of the destruction of the
world. He rules over Muspelheim and possesses a
glowing-hot sword with which he will set fire to
the world at the end of time. In the last battle he
slays → Freyr.

Sūrya Indian sun-god and guardian of the
south-west quadrant. His father is the sky-god →
Dyaus or → Indra; one myth tells how he arose
from the eye of the world-giant → Puruṣa. Sūrya
has golden hair and golden arms. He drives in a
chariot drawn by a team of four or seven horses;
in his hand he holds a lotus flower, often a discus
(*cakra*) as well. The daughter of the sun-god is
also called Sūrya.

Susanowo (Susanoo) Japanese god of the winds and lord of the ocean. It is said that he arose from the nose of → Izanagi. In his capacity as god of thunder he is associated with snakes and dragons.

Svantevit (Latinized form Svantovitus) A war-god revered by the Slavonic inhabitants of the island of Rügen. He was also a protector of their fields, and the harvest festival was dedicated to him. The early Danish historian Saxo Grammaticus relates that his main attributes were a cornucopia and a white horse.

Svarog (Svarožič) Slavonic fire- and sun-god, equated by Greek-Christian writers with → Hephaistos. The divine smith was also regarded as the founder of the institution of marriage. Originally, Svarog was at the summit of the Slavonic pantheon, but he ended up as a sort of fire-spirit. In Russia, his place was taken by → Perun.

Syrinx → Pan

T

Tabiti Goddess of fire and queen of animals of the Scythians who once lived in south Russia. She was the 'great goddess' represented as winged and surrounded by animals. The Romans took her to be identical with → Vésta.

Tages In Etruscan tradition, a youth who had the wisdom of age: it is said that he suddenly emerged from a furrow one day when a field was being ploughed, and proceeded to expound the practice of *haruspicina* – prognostication by the inspection of entrails. Tages, the child of earth, begotten by a → Genius, is represented on bronze mirrors with two snakes forming his lower limbs.

Tailtiu An Irish goddess, embodying tellurian and natural forces. In Irish myth, she figures as the nurse of → Lug. At her request, a festival is instituted for her after her death – the *Lugnasad*, i.e. 'the espousal of the god Lug'. It has been suggested that this festival represents a *hieros gamos* between the god of light and the earth goddess (Tailtiu).

Tai-sui-xing 'The star of the great year' – that is to say Jupiter which takes 12 years to complete its orbit, and which is regarded as the god of time in China.

Tai-yi ('the Great Monad') Taoist sky-god, who dwells in the 'purple palace', the constellation of Zi-gong. He was that being who was already perfected before the creation. During the Song Dynasty (960-1279) Tai-yi was revered as the highest of nine or ten stellar gods, and he was given the name of Jiu-gong Tai-yi: i.e. 'Tai-yi of the nine palaces'.

Takamimusubi ('high and sublime be-getter')

In Japan, the progenitor god of the royal family. As a sky-god he rules the world together with the sun-goddess (→ Amaterasu). It is said that his grandchild Ninigi descended from heaven and founded the dynasty of the Tenno.

Ta'lab

Sabaean (ancient south Arabian) god. The name is taken to mean 'ibex', and the god himself is seen as a moon-god. In addition, he was also a kind of oracle.

Tane (in Hawaii Kane)

Polynesian god of the forest, and patron of craftsmen, especially boat-builders. He is the god of light, and on Tahiti he is revered as the god of all that is beautiful. People turn to him when they are in trouble. The name 'Tane' means 'man'. The Maoris say that 'Tane's way' leads westwards – that is to say, it follows the path of the sun. His entrance into the underworld (his night voyage) is described in the myth in terms of his relationship to → Hine-nui-te-po.

Tang

In Chinese mythology, the heavenly swallow in its function as Messiah and redeemer. In order to help mankind, it sacrificed its own body in the mulberry-tree copse. Tang's most signal achievement is his victory over the prince of hell.

Tangaroa (Tangaloa)

Polynesian sea-god, and creator of all things. In the Marquesas Islands he appears as god of the winds and of fishing, under the name of Tana'oa. At the same time, it is related of him that he dwelt in heaven at the beginning of time, and that he ruled over the night until → Atea was born from him.

According to Tahitian tradition, the god resided in a dark mussel-shell, from which he finally fashioned heaven and earth. Tangaloa's messenger is the bird Tuli.

Ta Pedn The god of the Semang negritos in Malaysia: the name can be translated as 'old man Pedn' or 'grandpa Pedn'. He is enthroned on a many-coloured mat in the heavens, with his wife sitting beside him. The god loves his grandchildren, the human race.

Tapio East Finnish forest spirit or god, often invoked in hunters' prayers. With the coming of Christianity he turned into a patron saint of hunting: he is supposed to have a daughter – St Anna (Anniki).

Tārā (less frequently Tārini) The most important Buddhist goddess; her name means both 'she who delivers' and 'star'. The legend goes that she was born from a tear shed by → Avalokiteśvara. The earliest representations of the goddess date from the sixth century AD. Tārā incorporates the very concept of female divinity, and her name can therefore be added as a generic term to the names of other goddesses: indeed other goddesses often appear as specialized forms of Tārā. Altogether, 21 forms of Tārā are distinguished, divided into the white forms (in these her left hand usually holds a lotus) and the coloured forms (blue, yellow, red).

Taranis (Celtic *taran* = thunder) Gallic thunder-god and lord of heaven, equated by the Romans with → Jupiter. It is possible that he is the god shown in Gallic art as bearing a wheel, which is taken to be a symbol of thunder or of the sun. The Gallic hammer-god has also been connected with Taranis, but he usually has a lightning flash in his hand.

Tarhunt An ancient Anatolian (Hurrian) weather-god. The name means 'mighty one, victor'; he corresponds to the Hittite → Iškur.

Taru Ancient Anatolian (Hattic) weather-god; his Luvian name is → Tarhunt. His son is the vegetation-god → Telipinu.

Tašmetu Ancient Mesopotamian goddess, who in her function as 'she who hears prayer' personifies divine accessibility; she is the spouse of → Nabu.

Tašmišu Ancient Anatolian god, who figures repeatedly in myth as the brother and helper of the weather-god → Tešub.

Tate The wind-god of the Sioux Indians. He orders the seasons, and allows only those souls to take the path of the spirits, whom → Skan regards as worthy.

Tatenen (Tenen, Ten) The name of this ancient Egyptian god means 'the raised land' – a reference to the primeval hill, the earth as it rose in the beginning from the primeval waters. Tatenen is primeval god and god of the earth; in Memphis he was coupled with → Ptah, under the name of Ptah-Tenen. He is represented in human shape with the horns of a ram and a crown of feathers.

Tawa Among the Pueblo Indians of North America, the great sun-spirit, who has created men.

Tawiskaron ('fire-stone') An evil spirit in the mythology of the Mohawk, Huron and Onondaga Indians in North America. He steals the sun, creates monsters with human faces, lets a toad drink up the fresh water which humans need, and wreaks havoc among the good works of his creator-brother → Teharonhiawagon. In ritual, Tawiskaron figures as the great magician to whom the nocturnal ceremonies are dedicated, and who was credited with being able to ward off illnesses.

Tecciztecatl ('he who comes from the land of the sea-slug shell') Aztec moon-god, so-called because of the similarity between the moon and the slug.

Tefnut (Greek form Tphenis) Old Egyptian goddess who emerged from → Atum along with the god of the air → Šu. She represented humidity, but came to be regarded subsequently as incorporating world order. At an early date, Šu and Tefnut were identified with the pair of lions → Ruti, revered in Leontopolis, and were accordingly portrayed theriomorphically. In Egyptian myth, this goddess may represent either the lunar or the solar eye: and as the latter can also appear as the uraeus snake, Tefnut may figure as the 'snake on the forehead of all the gods'.

Teharonhiawagon The good god revered by the Mohawk and the Onondaga Indians. The name means 'he who holds the heavens in his two hands'. Another name for him is Oterongtongnia, which means 'little tree'. He has created all good things, and gives health and prosperity. Morning and day are his province, while evening and night form that of his adversary → Tawiskaron.

Teisiphone → Erinyes

Telchines Demon workers in metal, gifted with the evil eye and skilled in magic, in the mythology of the Greek islanders (especially on Rhodes). In many respects they resemble the → Kabiroi. The Telchines often appear as diminutive mermen; it was to them that the young Poseidon was handed over for his bringing up.

Telipinu (Telipuna) Ancient Anatolian god of vegetation, the son of the weather-god → Taru. He brings rain, and has, like his father, control over thunder and lightning. He causes plants to grow, and confers fertility upon man and animals. Sometimes in anger or in pique he quits the assembly of the gods, and then all life on heaven and earth comes to a standstill. The *pinu* component in his name means 'son' or 'child'.

Teljavelik The heavenly smith in Lithuanian mythology. He it is who created the sun (→ Saule) and placed it in the heavens.

Tellus (Latin = earth) Roman goddess of the earth and the cornfields. In her aspect as a fertility goddess, she is related to → Ceres. Tellus was sometimes given another Latin name which also means 'earth' – Terra.

Tenenit A goddess of beer mentioned in the Egyptian Book of the Dead and in some texts dating from the Ptolemaic period.

Tengri Among the Turkish tribes and the Mongols, a designation for certain heavenly beings. The Buriats call their sky-god Esege Malan Tengri – 'Father Bald-head Tengri'. The supreme sky-god of the Mongols is called → Qormusta Tengri. His Yakut counterpart is Tangara, whose epithet is *urün ajy tojon* = wise lord creator.

Ten-gū (Tengu) Mountain and forest goblins in Japanese folklore; they have long noses or beaks, and figure as bogeymen. They dwell in hollow trees, and are said to be the progeny of the storm-god → Susanowo.

Tepeyollotli This earth and cave god was originally native to the Indians in the Central American isthmus. He was the 'heart of the mountain' and the source of earthquakes. His symbolical animal was the jaguar. The Aztecs regarded him as one of the gods of night and as representing one aspect of → Tezcatlipoca.

Terminus Roman god of border markers. His feast was the Terminalia, held on 23 February.

Terpsichore (Greek = she who delights in dancing) The → Muse of the solemn and ceremonial dance. She is usually shown with a lyre in her left hand, while she plucks the strings with the plectrum held in her right hand.

Tešub (Tešup) The Hurrian weather-god, corresponding to the Hittite → Iškur. His attributes are the double-headed axe and the cluster of lightning flashes; his car is drawn by the bulls → Šeri and Ḫurri. His wife is → Ḫebat.

Teteo innan ('Mother of the gods') An ancient tellurian deity of the Aztecs, also known as Tonantzin (= 'our little mother'). Women revered her as a goddess of childbirth and childcare, while men saw her as a divine warrior – Quauhcihuatl, 'Eagle woman'. She may be transmuted into the figure of → Cihuacoatl, and then again equated with the goddess of love → Tlazolteotl.

341

Tethys Daughter of the sky-god → Uranós and the earth-goddess → Gaia: one of the → Titans. She is also the sister and the wife of → Okeanos.

Teutates A god revered in Gaul, whose name is attested in Britain as Totatis. The name is interpreted as meaning 'father of the tribe, people'. He was thought of in connection with war and fighting (that is to say, a sort of Gallic → Mars) but also appeared as a god of fertility and plenty (→ Mercurius, Gallic). His importance may be gauged from the epithets applied to him: Albiorix ('King of the world'), and Loucetios ('the shining one'), while Caturix ('lord of the battle') points to his warlike aspect.

Tezcatlipoca (Tezcatl = mirror, popoca = smoking) Aztec tutelary god of warriors, and avenger of misdeeds. One of his epithets was Moyocoya = the omnipotent. He represents the stars (→ Mixcoatl), the night sky, the winter, and the north, and is thereby the adversary of → Huitzilopochtli. The animal sacred to him is the jaguar, whose spotted coat is reminiscent of the night sky. On the other hand, Tezcatlipoca may also embody the sun. It is typical of his divisive and divided being that he is able to lead → Quetzalcoatl into temptation. Each year, a prisoner of war was chosen as the earthly representative of Tezcatlipoca, and sacrificed by having his heart torn from his breast.

Thab-lha A hearth-god in the old Tibetan Bon religion. Condign punishment awaits anyone who defiles his domestic fires. He is imagined as a red man who holds a snake aloft in the form of a noose.

Thaleia → Charites

Thalia (Greek *thaleia* = she who blossoms)
The → Muse of comedy, the light-hearted art of
letters. Among her attributes are a comic mask, a
wreath of ivy and a crooked staff.

Thallo → Horae

Thalna An Etruscan goddess of birth, depicted as a sumptuously clad young woman; she is
often shown in the company of the sky-god →
Tin.

Thanatos In Greek mythology, the son of
Night (→ Nyx) and twin brother of → Hypnos.
At a later period he was portrayed as a beautiful
winged youth, bearing a lowered torch in one
hand.

Theandr(i)os A pre-Islamic god revered
in north Arabia, and known to us from Greek and
Latin inscriptions.

Theia In Greek mythology, one of the →
Titans, wife of → Hyperion: their children are
the sun-god → Hélios, the moon-goddess →
Seléne and the goddess of dawning → Eos. The
name Theia means 'the divine one'; another of
her names – Euryphaessa = she whose rays shine
afar – underlines her character as a goddess of
light.

Themis Greek goddess of justice, order and
morality. She was supposed to be the daughter of
the sky-god → Uranós and the earth-goddess →
Gaia; she was the wife of → Zeus and the mother
of the → Horae and the → Moires.

Thesan Etruscan goddess of dawning, who
not only ushers in the day but also, according to

evidence from Greek sources, was regarded as a goddess to invoke in childbirth.

Theseus Athenian cult figure and national hero. His father is variously given as the sea-god → Poseidon, and as the mythical King Aigeus, from whom the Aegean Sea gets its name. One of his most outstanding feats was to conquer the monster → Minotauros.

Thetis Daughter of the Greek sea-god → Nereus and wife of the mortal Peleus; their son was → Achilleus.

Thiassi (Thjazi) A giant in Nordic mythology, the father of → Skadi. He was slain by → Thor, and his eyes were thrown into the skies where they became stars.

Thor (Old Saxon *thunar*: Donar, etymologically cognate with German *Donner*) Germanic god of thunderstorms and of fertility, belonging to the race of the Aesir (→ As); the son of → Odin and the divine personification of the earth (→ Jörd). He drives in a chariot drawn by two goats, and possesses the throwing-hammer Mjölnir. In the Edda, he is described as the strongest of all the gods whom he protects, along with the human race, against the giants. At Ragnarök, the twilight of the gods, he slays the → Midgard-snake, but is himself done to death in the moment of victory. It was to Thor that men turned for happiness in marriage, and for protection of herds and crops. His sacred tree was the oak (the Donar-oak at Geismar, felled by Boniface). The Romans took him to be equivalent to → Hercules or → Jupiter, and the fourth day of the week is named after him.

Thot (Dehuti) Ancient Egyptian god of the moon, of the calendar and of chronology. His attribute is writing materials or a palm-leaf (as a year/date marker). His ibis head identifies him as native to the delta, and in Hermopolis he soon fused with the figure of the peacock-headed god → Hez-ur. In myth we are told how Thot searches for and finds the lost eye of the moon, which he heals with his spittle. Another tradition relates how Thot was born from the head of → Seth. He is 'representative deputy of → Re' and versed in very powerful magic skills. As protector of → Osiris he came to be seen as a guide and helper of the dead; and in due course this led to his identification with the Greek escort of souls → Hérmes.

Th'uban A fire-spitting, dragon-like demon in Islamic literature, known to the Arabs under the name of Tinnin. It is likely that a pre-Islamic snake-deity underlies the figure.

Thunupa Ancient Peruvian culture-hero, who can transform himself into the figure of → Huiracocha and who also shows signs of Christian influence. Thus, it is said of him that he came from the north, carried a cross and expelled the old gods.

Thursir In Germanic mythology, giant demonic beings with big ears and covered with rough hair. They can cause illnesses and rob men of their understanding. In myth, the Thursir were present at the beginning of the world: the world-giant → Ymir is the progenitor of all the Hrimthursir, the giants of frost and rime.

Tiamat (Akkadian = sea) In old Mesopotamian myth, the name of the universal mother, the personification of salt water and spouse of the god of fresh water → Apus. Tiamat is the primeval dragon-like monster of original chaos, which is defeated by the god → Marduk, and from whose two halves he forms heaven and earth.

Tian The Chinese word denotes both the sky and its personification. Tian fused partly with the ancient sky-god → Shang-di, partly with the supreme being of Taoism → Yu-di. From the Zhou Dynasty (*c.* 1050-256 BC) onwards, the Chinese Emperor was regarded as the 'son of heaven'. In the meaning of 'supreme ruler' the characters *tian* and *di* are interchangeable.

Tian-long → Di-ya

Tian-zhu ('lord of heaven') The designation chosen for 'God' in the Chinese Catholic catechism.

Tiberínus The most important river-god of the Romans, whose temple stood from the very earliest times on an island in the Tiber. In order not to provoke the god, bridges across the stream had to be made of wood only, with no iron parts; a constraint which lasted right into the republican period. In myth, his bride is the vestal virgin thrown into the Tiber, Rhea Silvia.

Tiki (known as Ki'i in Hawaii) The Polynesian designation either for the god who first created man, or alternatively, for the first man himself. Furthermore, Tiki also denotes anthropomorphic images of gods fashioned out of stone or wood.

Tilla A bull-god of the Hurrian people in ancient Asia Minor. Yoked with the bull → Šeri he sometimes pulls the chariot of the weather-god.

Tin (Tinia) Etruscan sky-god, depicted some-times bearded, sometimes unbearded, but always with a cluster of lightning flashes. His attributes may also include a spear or sceptre. The Romans equated Tin with → Jupiter.

Tinirau East Polynesian god of the sea and of fish, depicted sometimes in human, sometimes in fish form. He is of terrifying appearance as is indicated by his epithet 'the swallower'. There are several versions of the myth relating his love affair with the lady in the moon → Hina.

Tinnit (also Thinit; an earlier reading of the name was Tanit) Supreme goddess of Carthage with the constant epithet of 'face of Baal'. She is queen of heaven, virgin and mother, and she confers fertility. In this latter capacity she bears the name Nutrix ('foster-mother', 'she who nourishes'), and has such attributes as a pome-granate, figs, ears of wheat and, from the realm of creatures, the dove. Her special symbol is the so-called Tinnit emblem: a triangle with horizontal beams placed on it, on which a disc lies. In her capacity as Dea Caelestis she seems to have had some sort of relationship with the moon.

Tir Armenian god of writing, wisdom and oracles. His epithet 'clerk of Ormizd' suggests Iranian influence. In the → Mithraic mysteries, Tir corresponds to → Hérmes/Mercurius.

Tirawa The god of the Pawnee Indians who live in Kansas. He is the creator of all things and giver of life. The wind is his breath, and lightning is his glance; but no one knows what he really looks like. Tirawa is the power that has ordered all things and given man everything he needs.

Tīrthamkara ('ford-maker': that is to say, he who finds a ford through the stream of the

rebirth cycle)   A saviour in Jainism. Jains believe that there have been 24 such saviours, of whom the following are treated in this book: Riṣabha, Supārśva, Pārśva and Mahāvīra. The symbol of all Tīrthaṁkaras is the mystic syllable *hrim*, where the nasal marker takes the shape of the sickle moon in token of deliverance.

Tišpak
The Babylonian tutelary god of Esnumma. It is possible that he was taken over by the Hurrians (weather-god → Tešub).

Tištriya
Iranian stellar god (Sirius) who engages the forces of evil in combat, as leader of the armies of Angru Mainyu (→ Ahriman). He also sends rain and the seed of useful plants. In Armenia, Tištriya appears in a different capacity under the name of → Tir.

Titans
The secondary race of gods in Greek mythology, comprising the six sons and the six daughters of the sky-god → Uranós and the earth-goddess → Gaia. According to Hesiod they form six sets of pairs; among the best known of these pairs are → Okeanos and → Thetys, → Hyperion and → Theia, → Kronos and → Rheia. Others are Koios and Phoibe, Kreios and Eurybie, → Iapetos and Klymene. Led by the youngest son Kronos, the Titans topple their father Uranós; later, however, they too are overthrown by → Zeus with the help of the → Cyclops.

Tiwaz
In Luvian (a language related to Hittite) the name of the sun-god. The name appears in Palaic in the form Tijaz. Both in function and in appearance the god corresponds to the Hittite → Ištanu.

Tlahuizcalpantecutli
('lord in the house of twilight')   Aztec god of the morning star.

Under the calendar name of *ce acatl* ('one-reed'), he figured as a mystic hero born of the virgin Chimalman (a personification of the earth).

Tlaloc

Aztec rain-god, whose dwelling was supposed to be partly in the cloud-capped mountains and partly in springs and lakes. As he often conceals himself behind a dark storm-cloud, he is portrayed in manuscripts as black of body and with a painted face. In his hand he carries a staff which is the symbol of lightning; it may be toothed, or may have snakes entwined round it. His Maya counterpart is → Chac. Those who are drowned or struck by lightning, and those who have leprosy are admitted to Tlalocan, the kingdom of Tlaloc, where they will never again suffer any need.

Tlazolteotl

The love-goddess of the Nahuatl people in Mexico, the mother of the maize-god Cinteotl. Her epithet Ixcuinan ('queen of cotton') comes from the Huastec people. Her forehead is bound and she has cotton ear-rings. The Aztecs identified her with their older earth-goddess → Teteo innan, and regarded her as the mother of the maize-god. The name Tlazolteotl ('goddess of filth') seems to be a reference to illicit sexual relationships; adulterers came to her priest to confess.

Tnong

The sun-god of the Menik-Semang people in the Malacca Peninsula. He is supposed to take the shape of a dragon-fly.

Toar

→ Empung Luminuut

Toeris

(Thoëris, Ta-uret, 'she who is great') Old Egyptian hippopotamus-goddess, who is portrayed as upright with human arms and breasts. In her capacity as a protective deity she was depicted on beds, head-rests and in vignettes

in the Books of the Dead. As an attribute she holds the Sa-loop, an emblem of protection; often also a torch to ward off demons. Toeris is especially helpful to women in childbirth.

Tomam A bird-goddess of the Ket people in Siberia. She is queen of the migratory birds.

Tomor(r) A divinity whose antecedents go far back into Illyrian times; father of the gods and of men, and also known as Baba Tomor. He is flanked by two female eagles with long beaks. The winds are his servitors. Even today, Albanian peasants swear by him. His spouse was supposed to be → Bukura e dheut.

Tonacacihuatl ('queen of our flesh') An Aztec goddess who co-operates with her husband → Tonacatecutli in the task of transferring infant souls from heaven to the maternal womb. For this reason she is known as Omecihuatl ('queen of duality').

Tonacatecutli ('lord of our flesh') A supreme god of the Aztecs. He bears this name because it is he whom we have to thank for our food which builds up our bodies. Together with his wife → Tonacacihuatl he sits enthroned in the loftiest of heavens, and together they are engaged in promoting generation and birth. In this capacity, he bears the name Ometecutli ('lord of duality').

Tonatiuh ('soaring eagle') Aztec sun-god, usually represented with a crown of eagle feathers. His house (*tonatiu ichan*) offered hospitality to those who had died in battle and to women who had died in childbed. Tonatiuh could also be worshipped in the form of → Huitzilopochtli.

Tore   God of the forest and lord of animals in the belief of the Bambuti pygmies in the Ituri area. He manifests himself in wind and storms, and may appear as a leopard. He may present himself in his theriomorphic guise at initiation ceremonies for boys.

Tork   A mountain god in Old Armenian literature. His antecedents go back into the farthest Anatolian past, and subsequently he acquired demonic traits. Originally, he was the mountain itself, and only thereafter the patron and protector of the mountain world and the animals living in it. He was of hideous appearance, but nevertheless a being endowed with superhuman powers.

Torto   A fearsome spirit in Basque folklore. He has only one eye in the middle of his forehead, and he likes to abduct young people whom he dismembers and devours.

Triglav (Trigelawus)   A god of the Slav peoples who lived in the Baltic area; presumably, he had a warlike function. The name means 'three-headed', and according to medieval chronicles he was represented as three-headed at various sites in Stettin and Brandenburg. In Stettin he was regarded as the supreme god. Some sort of horse-oracle was connected with his cult. A south Slavonic god Triglav has also been postulated on many occasions, but there is no convincing evidence for this – in spite of the mountain with the same name in Slovenia.

Trimūrti ('having three forms'; trinity)   The Indian trinity consisting of the world creator → Brahma, the sustainer → Viṣṇu, and the destroyer → Śiva. According to the Samkhya school, the three are manifestations of one essential unity. In popular belief they are often regarded as manifestations of the supreme god → Iśvara.

Triphis The Greek name given to the Egyptian Repit ('she who is exalted'). Essentially, an honorary title, referring in particular to → Hathor. However, it is also a proper name for a lion-goddess worshipped in the ninth nome of Upper Egypt, where Athribis was the cult-centre.

Triton Greek sea-god, half-man, half-fish. His parents are → Poseidon and → Amphitríte. Later pluralized, so that now we speak of Tritons, meaning the male companions of the female → Nereids, who are shown blowing on their conch shells.

Troll (Old Norse = fiend) In Scandinavian folk-belief, trolls are demons who may be male or female, giants or dwarfs. They are endowed with magic powers during the hours of darkness, and this is why they fear daylight.

Trowo (the singular is *tro*) The Ewe people in Togo believe in these as God-created beings who represent various cosmic objects or phenomena – the sky, stars, lightning. Oldest among them is Anyigba, the earth, whose constituent parts – mountains, streams, forests, ant-hills – form their own series of *trowo*, who give children, cause the yams to flourish and induce or cure illnesses.

bTsan (bCan) Tibetan demons whose realm is in the air. They appear as fierce ruddy huntsmen, riding furiously over the mountains on bright-red horses. Anyone found alone in the wilderness is slain by their deadly arrows. In ancient Tibet, the king was regarded as the earthly representative of the bTsan, and had the title bTsan-po.

Tsukiyomi Japanese moon-god. He arose when → Izanagi washed her right eye in the sea;

when she washed her left eye, the sun-goddess →
Amaterasu was born.

Tu (1) (The Hawaiian Ku) Polynesian war-
god; his name means 'he who stands'. He was
also the great master-craftsman engaged in the
creation of the world. On Mangarewa Tu is
invoked to make the bread-fruit trees flourish. In
ancient times, human sacrifice was made to the
Hawaiian god 'Ku with the maggoty mouth'.

Tu (2) A god-like earth-spirit in ancient
Chinese religion. It was also called *she*, and was
the object of a fertility cult. *She*-altars in phallic
form were made out of pounded earth on fields
belonging to the ruler and his vassals.

Tuatha De Danann ('the people of the
goddess Dana') A clan of Celtic gods in Ireland,
to whom belong → Dagda, → Lug, and → Ogma
inter alia. In myth and in cult, these heroic deities
appear as the partners of human beings.

Tuchulcha Etruscan demon of the underworld. Its head looks like that of → Charun,
while its arms are entwined with snakes.

Tupa Among the Guarani in South America,
this is the favourite son of the supreme god. The
name was taken over by Christian missionaries
working in Brazil and in Paraguay to translate
'God'.

Turan Etruscan goddess of love. Her attributes are a swan and a dove, often accompanied
by a twig or a blossom. She is usually portrayed as
winged, conforming in this to the general type of
the ancient Mediterranean Great Mother. Turan
was also the tutelary deity of the town of Vulci.

Turms An Etruscan god with the function of a *psychopompos*, guider of souls to the underworld. As such, he takes on the iconographic characteristics of → Hérmes, and is shown naked with a backwards-streaming shoulder cloak (*chlamys*), winged shoes and *kerykeion* (the herald's staff).

Tursas In Finnish folk-poetry, a deep-sea monster which raises its head from the sea. The name probably derives from the Germanic *thurs* = giant, monster (→ Thursir). It is not clear to what extent Tursas is connected with the Turisas mentioned in a sixteenth-century list of gods.

Tvaṣṭar (Tvastri; Sanskrit, 'he who forms') Indian craftsman-god who gave all things their forms, his principal achievements being the soma cup of the gods, and the thunderbolt (*vajra*) for → Indra. In the earliest traditions he appears as the creator who gave heaven and earth their shape, and who gave life to mankind. In Hinduism he is reckoned as one of the twelve → Ādityas.

Tyché Greek goddess of fate and fortune. In Hesiod's Theogony she appears as one of the daughters of → Okeanos. Pindar calls her a daughter of → Zeus. As a representative of the unpredictable way of the world, Tyché became particularly popular at the time of the Sophists, when belief in other gods was at a low ebb. Several Hellenistic towns, such as Antiochia on the Orontes, chose Tyché as their tutelary goddess. In art she is shown with a helmsman's rudder (as director of fate) and cornucopia (as bringer of good fortune). The wheel and the globe point to inconstancy and transitoriness. Her Roman counterpart was → Fortuna.

Typhón (Typhoeus) The progeny of the underworld (Tartaros) and the earth (→ Gaia). A monster with a hundred dragon-heads and snake's feet. From his union with → Echidna came → Kerberos, → Ladon and the Chimaira. The name Typhón (or Typhos) means 'whirlwind', and later the giant was taken to be a demon which causes storms and earthquakes.

Tyr The original form was Tiwaz, Anglo-Saxon Tiw, Old High German Ziu, cognate with Greek → Zeus. To begin with, a sky-god of the early Germanic peoples, till he was ousted by → Odin. The Romans were quick to identify him as a god of war, and the week-day dedicated to Mars became Ziu's day (Tuesday; Alemannic Zischdi). Tyr/Ziu was not only god of war but also of justice, and his spear was an emblem of judicial authority as well as being a weapon. At Ragnarök the god falls in battle with → Garm.

U

Uacilla Among the Ossetians who live in the Caucasus, the spirit ruling over thunder, lightning and rain. The *illa* component in the name is derived from Elias (Elijah), the Old Testament prophet who is regarded in Eastern Europe as the lord of thunder and storm.

Udu(g) (Akkadian Utukku) An ancient Mesopotamian demon, regarded for the most part as malevolent. The terrifying Utukku can turn into the evil → Sebettu.

Ugar An Old Syrian god. The name is probably derived from the Akkadian *ugar* = field, and indicates the agricultural nature of the god. It is not clear whether or not the name of the town, Ugarit, is connected with him.

Uji-gami ('clan-chief') A Japanese designation for ancestral or progenitor deities.

Ukemochi A kind of fertility goddess in Shintoism; after she was slain by the moon-god → Tsukiyomi, rice, oats, beans, a cow, a horse and silk-worms were found beside her corpse.

Ukko ('old man') The Finnish god of thunder, also known as Isäinen ('grandad'). When he drives his wagon along a stony path in the heavens, sparks fly from the hooves of his horses. When it thunders, people say that Ukko is rolling big stones or grinding corn. In incantations and magic spells he is described as having such attributes as a blue cloak, a fiery pelt, a sword, an axe and a hammer. In Karelia and in Ingermanland, the prophet Elias (Elijah) takes the place of Ukko.

Ülgän
The sky-god of the Altai Tatars. He it is who sends the saviour Maidere to earth, to teach men to respect and fear the true god, but Maidere is slain by the evil → Erlik. From Maidere's blood there arises a fire which roars up to heaven, whereupon the sky-god causes Erlik and his followers to be destroyed.

Ull(r)
A north Germanic god, whose name may be connected with the Gothic word *wulthus* = splendour. He is closely associated with the administration of justice (oaths were sworn over his ring) and he was invoked for protection in duels. He was reckoned to be a skilful archer and skier. On the one hand he has all the traits of a god of winter, but on the other he is connected with the forces of fertility, and in place-names his name is more often than not combined with words meaning 'field', 'meadow', etc. In myth, Ull is the son of → Sif and the stepson of → Thor.

Ullikummi
Ancient Anatolian demon, created by the dethroned king of the gods → Kumarbi, by making a stone pregnant, in order to help him to get back his kingdom in heaven.

Umā
In India, the personification of light and beauty; also venerated under the name of → Gaurī. She is the Devi (goddess) allotted to → Śiva, and, as such, can turn into → Durgā or → Pārvatī. The main centre of her cult is in Bengal.

Umvelinqangi
The creator god of the Zulu people in South Africa. He caused trees and grass to grow and created all animals. Finally, he fashioned a reed or cane, out of which the god → Unkulunkulu emerged.

Uneg A plant-god mentioned in the Pyramid texts, companion of the sun-god → Re, and bearer of the heavens.

Ungud Aboriginals in north-west Australia believe in this divine creative power which takes the form of a snake and which can be thought of as male, female or androgynous. It may also represent the rainbow. Medicine-men believe that their erect penis is identical with Ungud.

Uni Etruscan goddess, corresponding in terms of Greek myth to → Hera, and accordingly allocated to the sky-god → Tin. In addition, she was the tutelary goddess of Perugia. It is probable that the name Uni is not Etruscan, but connected with the Italic-Latin name Iuno (→ Juno).

Unkulunkulu The supreme god of the Zulus in South Africa, said to have emerged from a 'primeval cane'. He and his wife of the same name (together forming an androgynous unity?) then generated the first human beings.

Unumbotte A mythical god of the Bassari people who live in Togo. He first created human beings, and then the animals.

Unut A goddess in the form of a hare who was worshipped in the fifteenth nome of Upper Egypt (Hermopolis). Later, she took on the lineaments of a lioness. She was finally ousted as a figure of any significance by → Thot, and was reduced to playing the part of a protective goddess armed with knives.

Upelluri In Hurrian belief (ancient Anatolia) a world-giant, whose torso sticks up out of the ocean and bears heaven and earth.

Upuaut (Wep-wawet; the Greek transcription is Ophois)   Ancient Egyptian god of Siut, in the form of a black jackal or wolf. The name means 'he who opens up ways, paths' and may refer to a successful military campaign. His standard accompanied the king as a sort of battle ensign. His attributes as a god of war are the club and the bow. In processions he precedes the god → Osiris, just as he precedes the king. In Abydos he became, as 'lord of the necropolis', a god of the dead.

Upulevo   The sun-god in the Indonesian island of Timor. No image is made of him, and he is worshipped in the form of a lamp made from woven coconut leaves. He comes down over a fig-tree to his wife, mother earth, in order to fertilize her. Pigs and dogs are sacrificed in front of this tree.

Upulvan (short form Pulvan)   The highest of the four great gods in the Singhalese pantheon. His name means 'the water-lily coloured one'. According to the tradition, he was the only god who stood by → Gautama Buddha in the latter's fight with → Māra. In recent times the god has tended to fuse with the Hindu → Viṣṇu.

Urania ('the heavenly one')   One of the nine → Muses, she who comforts mortals by pointing to the harmony of heaven. She represents astronomy, and her attribute is the heavenly sphere.

Uranós ('heaven', 'sky')   Greek god of the sky, the husband of the earth goddess → Gaia; their progeny are the → Titans and the → Cyclops. When Uranós driven by hatred and fear banished the Cyclops to the underworld (Tartaros), Gaia incited the youngest son (→ Kronos) to attack his father, castrate him with a sickle and topple him from his throne. From the drops of blood which fell into the sea → Aphrodíte was born.

Urăs An old Mesopotamian form of the earth goddess, espoused to the sky-god → An. Their child was the goddess of healing → Nin'insinna.

Urd → Norns

Uriel (Hebrew = 'my light is like God') In the Old Testament apocrypha, an angel who reveals secret things to Esdras (4:4). In Christian angelology, an archangel.

Urme (Also known as *ursitory*) Polish, Russian and Serbian gipsies believe in these female spirits who determine people's fate. They are thought of as three in number.

Uršanabi (Sursunabu) In the Gilgameš epic, the ferryman of the underworld stream.

Urthekau (Werethekau = 'she who is rich in magic') A personification of mysterious supernatural powers, which the ancient Egyptians imagined as inherent in the crown. The lion-headed crown goddess dwelt in the state sanctuary. Urthekau could also figure as an epithet for other goddesses, e.g. of → Isis.

Urtzi (Ortzi, Urcia) A Basque word meaning 'firmament' and, by extension, the sky-god, who also acted the part of the 'thunderer'.

Ušanas In India, the divine regent of the planet Venus. He is white in colour and holds a staff, a prayer-ring and a water-pot in his hands. This deity may also be portrayed as a woman sitting on a camel. Uśanas was supposed to be the tutor of the demons (→ Daityas).

Uṣas Indian goddess of the early dawn, daughter of the sky-god → Dyaus, and beloved of → Sūrya. In the Vedas she is described as a delicate bride in rose-red garments with a golden veil. She drives in a car pulled by reddish cows (an image of the morning clouds).

Usinš A Latvian deity with somewhat indeterminate functions. In part it has the characteristics of a god of light, with special reference to the morning or the evening star; in part, again, it is connected with spring, and, finally, appears as a sort of tutelary deity of bees. With the coming of Christianity, the figure of Usinš was transmuted into that of St George.

Uṣṇīṣavijayā ('the victorious one with the head-band') A particularly popular Buddhist goddess, white in colour with a white mandala; she has three faces and eight arms. → Vairocana is visible in her crown. She possesses the virtues of all the Buddhas.

Utgard-Loki In Nordic mythology, a demonic giant to whom even the gods → Loki and → Thor succumb in competition. Thor tries in vain to overcome the giant's foster-mother (a personification of old age) in a wrestling bout, and to lift his cat (the → Midgard-snake) from the ground.

Uto (Wadjet) The name of the old Egyptian snake-goddess of Buto (in the sixth nome of Lower Egypt). Her name means 'she who is papyrus-coloured' – i.e. 'the green one', and the goddess is bound up with the regenerative forces of vegetation. As the tutelary goddess of Lower Egypt she is the counterpart of the Upper

Egyptian vulture-goddess → Nechbet. Uto is equated with the uraeus of the monarch, thus becoming a manifestation of the solar eye.

Utu Sumerian sun-god. His main role is that of a guardian of justice. In other respects he falls short of the Akkadian sun-god → Šamaš in importance and significance, and this is evident from the fact that he is classified under the moon-god (→ Nanna) who was his father.

Uzume Japanese goddess of jollity, whose obscene dancing entices the goddess → Amaterasu from her cave, thus ensuring the return of the spring sunshine bringing life and fertility.

al-Uzza The Bedouin tribes in ancient central Arabia regarded al-Uzza as the youngest daughter of Allah (the other two being → Allat and → Manat). She dwells in an acacia-like tree. Her cult can be shown to have spread to north Arabia where she is known as Han-Uzzai. Her identification with the morning star is also attested.

V

Vāc (Vak = speech) In India, the deified personification of speech, which is believed to be invested with magical powers. In the Rigveda, Vāc is the world principle which underlies all action by the gods. The goddess is regarded as the wife of → Prajāpati. In Buddhism, Vāk is a name of → Mañjuśri; he sits in the meditative posture, with his hands in his lap.

Vadātājs An evil being in Latvian folklore. It may appear either as an animal or in human form and it tries to lead travellers astray at cross-roads.

Vahagn Armenian god of bravery and victory, corresponding to the Iranian → Verethragna. His epithet, Višapakal, has not been satisfactorily explained: it may mean 'dragon-strangler' (dragon-slayer) or 'drawer up of dragons', in the sense of a god of thunder-storms. In Armenian myth, Vahagn arises from fire and has flames for hair.

Vahguru ('Great guru') The name of the one true God in the Sikh religion which has been influenced by both Hinduism and Islam. He is also known by the Hindu names Hari ('God') and Govinda ('herdsman'). There are no images of gods in the Golden Temple at Amritsar.

Vaimānika In Jainism, a group of gods who dwell in mobile palaces in the world above. One of the most important gods in this group is → Śakra.

Väinämöinen The central figure in the Kalevala, the Finnish folk-epic: a singer of magical potency and inventor of the *kantele* (a zither-like instrument). He has all the marks of a shaman who can range through the underworld in the form of a snake; in the end, however, he is translated to the heavens where Orion is his scythe and the Pleiades form his woven shoes. In a list of gods drawn up in the sixteenth century he figures as Äinemöinen, 'he who forges poems'.

Vairocana ('sun-scion') One of the five → Dhyāni-Buddhas. Of the five world-divisions, the centre is the one allotted to him, and his season is the winter. He is white in colour, and his hands are held in the so-called sermon position against his chest. His vehicle is a pair of dragons or a lion, and his emblem is a white wheel. In Tantrism he appears as three-faced and six-armed. In China, Vairocana is known as Pi-lu Fo and may appear in the office of a world-ruler. Certain Japanese sects like the Tendai and the Shingon regard him as the universal Buddha, all other Buddhas, Bodhisattvas and gods being merely specific manifestations of him.

Vaiśravaṇa (in Pali, Vessavana; in Chinese Do Wen) One of the four Buddhist guardians of the world (→ Caturmahārājas). Vaiśravaṇa is entrusted with the northern quarter. His allotted colour is yellow, he bears a banner aloft in token of victorious belief and he is lord of the → Yakṣas who watch over hidden treasure.

Vaja → Ribhus

Vajrabhairava ('he who arouses fear') Buddhist god regarded as a manifestation of → Mañjuśri, whose function is to overcome the god of death (→ Yama). He has 9 heads, 34 arms and 16 legs. The main head is that of a bull.

Vajrapāni ('he who holds a *vajra* in his hand') Originally, in the earliest Buddhist period, a kind of protective spirit accompanying → Gautama; later, reckoned as one of the eight great → Bodhisattvas, and as an emanation of → Akṣobhya. Finally he was seen as preceptor of esoteric doctrines and 'lord of secrets'.

Vajrasattva ('Vajra-being') Revered in Nepal as the sixth → Dhyāni-Buddha. In much Tantric ritual he is regarded as a mystic Buddha. The second half of the night is allotted to him, and his season is autumn. He is portrayed balancing a *vajra* on his right hand in front of his breast.

Vajravārāhi In Buddhist belief, one of the most important supernatural female beings (→ Ḍākinī). Her name means 'diamond-sow' and this she owes to the fact that there is a growth close to her right ear which looks like a pig's head. Her naked body is red like a pomegranate blossom. In her right hand she holds a thunderbolt (*vajra*), and in the left a skull and a club.

Vajrayoginī A Buddhist goddess of initiation, one of the → Ḍākinīs. In her yellow form she is headless, and carries her head in her hand. From her rump comes a stream of blood. In her more usual red form, she has thunderbolt, cranium and club as attributes, and is functionally equivalent to → Vajravārāhi.

Vali A Germanic god, the son of → Odin and of → Rind. He was only one night old when he avenged the death of → Balder by slaying the murderer Hödur. The specification of 'one night old' probably refers to moment of initiation, not to date of birth.

Valkyries (German Walküren; also as Valkyrien; Old Norse *valkyrja* = 'she who selects the dead') Supernatural female beings commissioned by the god → Odin to intervene in battles and bring heroes doomed to die (Einherjer) up to Valhalla, 'hall of the dead'. From the names of individual Valkyries, their original function as natural demonic forces is clear: thus, for example, Wolkenthrut ('cloud-power') and Mist ('fog'). It is not until the heroic epic in Middle High German that the anthropomorphic image of the warrior maiden appears.

Vampire In south Slavonic folklore, the spirit of a dead person, or a corpse revived by an evil spirit. Vampires arise by night from graves and suck people's blood. In the literature of the nineteenth and twentieth centuries – for example, in E.T.A. Hoffmann and Gogol – vampires became more and more demonic in character: it is enough to think of the film figure of Dracula. In Greek folklore the → Lamia correspond to the vampires.

Vanir A group of north Germanic gods, including among their number → Freyr, → Freya, and → Njörd: all three of them being fertility deities. The struggle between the Aesir (→ As) and the Vanir, and the subsequent reconciliation between them, may reflect the opposition between two ways of life – that of the peasant and that of the warrior. The Vanir countenanced marriage between siblings, and they were master magicians (*seidr*).

Vanth A female demon in the Etruscan underworld. She is represented as winged, with a snake, a torch and a key as attributes. On alabaster urns from Volterra we can see that there is a large eye on the inside of each of her wings – a warning that this demonic being is everywhere present and keeps an eye on everybody. Vanth is a messenger of death and may be helpful with the quietus.

Varāha The third incarnation of the Indian god → Viṣṇu. In the form of a boar he slays the demon Hiraṇyakṣa and frees the earth which the demon had sunk in the ocean.

Varuṇa The supreme god in Vedism, creator of the three worlds, heaven, earth and air. The etymology of the name is doubtful; it may be cognate with the Greek Uranos ('sky'). Varuṇa is the guardian of order, both cosmic and moral (*rita*). He binds evil-doers with his nooses; but he can undo sin just as one undoes a noose. In late Vedic theology, Varuṇa becomes lord of the night as → Mitra is of the day. In later mythology, Varuṇa is the god of water and guardian of the westerly quarter of heaven. One of his epithets is Nāgārāja, 'King of the snakes'.

Vasiṣṭha In Indian mythology, a poet (→ Riṣi) who had access to the gods, and who may indeed have been himself of divine origin. He is provided with everything he requires by the wishing-cow Nandini. According to the Purāṇas, he is one of the → Prajāpatis.

Vasudhara ('she who holds treasure') Buddhist goddess of riches, in origin, perhaps, an earth-goddess. She is the consort of → Vaiśravana. She is portrayed as yellow in colour, aged 16, and heavily bedecked with jewellery. With her right hand she makes the gesture of donation of largesse, while in her left hand she holds ears of corn and often a vessel filled with jewels. She stands on the moon above a double lion.

Vasuki → Nāga

Vasus A group of Indian gods. In the Rigveda, their leader is said to be → Indra, whose role is later taken by → Agni. The other seven Vaşus are the deified forms of earth, wind, air, sun, moon, stars and sky.

Vata Old Iranian god of the wind (*vata* = wind). He is called Ašvara ('the truthful one') and is often mentioned along with → Mithra and → Rašnu. The god of victory → Verethragna first appeared to Zarathustra in the form of Vata.

Vāyu (Sanskrit = wind) Indian god of wind; it is related in certain myths that he arose from the breath of the world-giant → Puruṣa. Vāyu, → Agni and → Sūrya form one of the oldest triads. In the Rigveda, the → Maruts appear as his sons. In Iran too there was a wind-god called Vayu along with → Vata. The Iranian Vayu was the tutelary god of warriors, and also a deity controlling fate. In this latter capacity he can appear as either a beneficent Vayu or an evil one (then also known as Wai). This dual role is particularly marked in the Pahlavi texts. Pantheistic speculation made Vayu out to be the breath of God, or the suspiration of the cosmos.

Ve → Vili

Veive (Vetis; Latin Veiovis or Vedius) An Etruscan god, beardless, with arrows and a goat as attributes. He is of youthful appearance and is reminiscent of → Aplu, both of them having a laurel wreath on their heads. Veive was either ousted by Aplu as a cult figure, or fused with him.

Veja māte ('wind-mother') Latvian goddess of the winds, who rules the weather. When she tears across the land it is said of her, 'she is blowing her flute'. Together with → Meža māte she looks after the forests and the birds.

Veles (Volos) Slav god of the underworld. In modern Czech *veles* means something like 'devil'. In Old Russian texts, Volos has the epithet 'cattle-god', and non-Varangian Russians had to swear by him.

Velnias Lithuanian name for the devil; the name is a derivative from *vele*, *velionis* = dead person.

Velu māte ('mother of the dead') Latvian queen of the dead; she is clad in a white woollen wrap and she receives the dead at the entrance to the burial place. Her epithet is indicative: *Kapu māte*, 'graveyard-mother'.

Venus (Latin = love, sensual desire) Old Italic goddess of spring and gardens, native to Latium. It was not until the beginning of the third century BC that her cult reached Rome. Her feast – the Veneralia – was celebrated on 1 April. Under the influence of Greek literature she was equated with → Aphrodíte. Caesar, who regarded himelf as descended from → Aenéas and hence from Aphrodíte/Venus, introduced the cult of Venus Genetrix, in which the life-giving function of the goddess was stressed.

Verbti (*verbi* = the blind one) Old Albanian god of fire and of the north wind which fans fires. He hates uncleanliness and bad ways of speaking. Christianization turned Verbti into a demon, and it was spread about that anyone who invoked him would go blind.

Verdandi → Norns

Verethragna Old Iranian god of victory who manifests himself in the wind, and then again in anthropomorphic or theriomorphic form.

369

Particularly noteworthy is his incarnation as a boar which tramples opponents with its metal feet. The name contains the word *vritra* = encloser, obstruction (for the Indian form → Vritra): Verethragna is he who breaks down resistance, the victor.

Vertúmnus (or Vortumnus) In origin, an Etruscan god (→ Voltumna) who was taken over by the Romans in the third century BC. He was revered as the god of change, i.e. of the changing year (Latin *vertere* = to turn, change). His feast, the Vortumnalia, was celebrated on 13 August. The wife of Vertúmnus was → Pomona.

Vésta Old Italic goddess of the domestic hearth and its fire, and, as such, related to the Greek → Hestia. The small round temple dedicated to her at the foot of the Palatine Hill contained no image of the goddess; but there was the public hearth with the sacred fire burning. Near the sanctuary lay the *atrium Vestae* where the *vestales*, charged with the care of the fire, lived. The ass was regarded as sacred to the goddess, as one was supposed to have defended her against the advances of → Priapos. On her feast-day, asses were adorned with wreaths.

Vestius Alonieus A god once revered in north-west Hispania; he was associated with the bull, and had a military function.

Vibhvan → Ribhus

Victoria Roman goddess of victory, corresponding to the Greek → Nike. She had her own temple on the Palatine Hill in Rome. She was regarded as the maiden protector of the Roman Empire, and was often portrayed on coins.

Vidar North Germanic god, the son of → Odin and of the giantess Gridr. He is the god of vengeance, who slays the wolf → Fenrir in retaliation for the death of → Odin at Ragnarök, the twilight of the gods. After Ragnarök, Vidar and his half-brother → Vali are to rule over the rejuvenated world.

Vidyādhara ('possessor of knowledge') Semi-divine beings in Buddhist belief, who are supposed to possess a knowledge of supernatural powers. They can fly through the air and are therefore known as *vāyuputras*, 'sons of the wind'. They bear garlands of flowers and are reminiscent of flying genii. In Tibet they are Tantric divinities under the name of *rig-'dzin lnga*, i.e. they are five (*lnga*) in number.

Vidyujjvālākarāli A Buddhist goddess, a specific form of → Ekajaṭā. Her name means 'she who is as terrible as the fire of lightning', and she is indeed a fearsome figure: jet-black in colour, armed with such attributes as sword, *vajra*, arrow, spear, hammer, club, knife, noose and skull, to say nothing of her bared fangs, her 12 heads and her 24 arms. Her brown hair streams upwards like flames.

Vighnāntaka ('he who gets rid of obstructions') A Buddhist god, who also appears under the name of Vighnari, and who is a door-keeper of mandalas. He is usually represented as having one head and two arms; he is blue in colour and of terrifying appearance. In his left hand with its threatening index-finger, he holds the noose, while his right hand raises the thunderbolt.

Vili and Ve In Nordic mythology, the sons of Bor, and the brothers of → Odin. From the members of the primeval giant → Ymir, slain by them, the three brothers fashion the earth and they use his blood to make the sea. The proposed etymology of 'will' for Vili and 'holiness' for Ve (Gothic *weihs*) is not certain.

Vilkacis A werewolf in Latvian folklore, known in Lithuanian as Vilkatas. Usually a threatening figure, he may on occasion have treasures to bestow.

Víly Spirits of wind and storm in Slavonic folklore. In Slovakia they are regarded as the souls of dead girls, who lead young men to death. In south Slavonic belief, they are beautiful female beings endowed with supernatural powers: they often appear in the form of a swan, on occasion of a horse. They are in general well disposed towards humanity, but the arrows they fire may disturb one's reason. Country people used to lay food and flowers in front of caves where they believed the *vila* dwelt.

Virāj ('she who extends herself in might') In Indian mythology, a primeval being generated by → Brahman; often thought of as the primeval cow. Another tradition makes Virāj a female creative principle which has arisen from → Puruṣa.

Virtus (Latin = courage, manliness) A Roman goddess, often coupled with → Honos as the personification of virile manhood. Virtus is represented as a maiden in a short tunic, with a helmet on her head, and a sword and/or a lance in her hand.

Virūdhaka (in Pali Virulha; in Chinese Zeng Zhang) One of the four Buddhist guardians of the world (→ Caturmahārājas). He is specifically charged with looking after the southern quarter. His colour is blue, he holds a sword and is lord over the demonic Kumbhanda.

Virūpākṣa (in Pali, Virupakkha; in Chinese Guang Mu) In Buddhism, the guardian of the western quarter of heaven, one of the four great kings (→ Caturmahārājas). He is red in colour. As lord over the → Nāgas, he holds a snake in one hand; in the other he holds a pearl or other jewel. Often a pagoda is also present.

Viṣṇu Indian god; in the Vedas, the consort of → Indra. As he who takes three steps to speed through the world he is a manifestation of the sun in its daily transit – rising, zenith and setting: and here a reference is also seen to the three worlds – heaven, atmosphere and earth. In Hinduism, Viṣṇu is one of the most important gods. Indeed, his devotees, the Vishnuites, regard him as the supreme god, and he is bound up with the concept of → Nārāyana. One of his many epithets is Purusottama = 'the highest god'. He belongs to the → Trimūrti, and his main function is to sustain the world. He appears in various forms or *avatāras*, to combat demons and to restore cosmic divine order. The Purāṇas mention ten *avatāras*: as a fish (→ Matsya), as a tortoise (→ Kūrma), as a boar (→ Varāha), as a man-lion (→ Narasiṁha), as a dwarf (Vamana), → Paraśu-Rāma, → Rāma, → Kriṣṇa, →

Buddha and → Kalki. Later, further *avatāras* are mentioned, as for example, Gajarāja, 'lord of the elephants'. Viṣṇu is generally depicted as four-handed, and his attributes include club, mussel-shell, discus and lotus; he rides on the mythical bird → Garuḍa. The seven-headed world-snake (Ananta) serves him as resting-place.

Viśvakarman ('the all-creator') In India, a figure bound up with concept of a supreme god. In the Brahmanas he is identified with the creator god → Prajāpati. Under Hinduism, the god took on the functions of → Tvaṣṭar.

Viśvapāni A → Dhyāni-Bodhisattva of minor interest, an emanation of → Amoghasiddhi. His symbol is a double lotus.

Vivasvat (Vivasvant, 'he who lights up') In Indian mythology, father of the → Aśvins, of → Yama, the god of death, and of → Manu, the progenitor of mankind. Vivasvat is an aspect of the sunrise; in the Rigveda he is said to bring fire.

Vodnik (Russian *vodyanoi*) In Slavonic folk-lore a water-demon, said to arise from a drowned unbaptized child. The vodnik entices people into the water and then drowns them. To placate him, sacrifice was made to him – in Poland, for example, of a chicken.

Vohu Manah ('good thought') A hypostatization in Iranian religion, forming part of the → Ameša Spentas. Vohu Manah is, on the one hand, a specific trope of → Ahura Mazda, and, on the other hand, created by him. On earth, Vohu Manah is represented by the benign creatures, especially the cow. In Manichaeanism he is known as Wahman: he appoints the apostles, and helps in the creation of the New Man.

Voltumna   An Etruscan god, originally of chthonic nature and subsequently elevated to the status of supreme god (*deus Etruriae princeps*). For the Etruscans he was primarily the tutelary god of the Etruscan federation; some scholars believe him to be a specialized form of the sky-god → Tin. Voltumna was taken over by the Romans under the name of → Vertumnus.

Volumna   Roman goddess of the nursery, who was supposed to look after the health and welfare of her charges.

Vör (or Vara)   A Germanic goddess. In the late period – e.g. in the work of the Icelandic writer Snorri – she appears as goddess of contracts, and her name is taken to mean 'she who is cautious'. Oaths and pledges are sacred to her, and she is also the guardian of marriage.

Votan (Uotan)   Originally, it would seem, a religious reformer among the Maya in Central America, who was subsequently deified. He was given the epithet 'heart of towns', and was supposed to be the guardian of the slit-drum (*tepanaguaste*). His wife was → Ixchel.

Vritra   In Indian belief, a demon who holds the waters prisoner – hence his name, which means 'encloser'. He is the fearsome enemy of gods and of men, who is finally slain by → Indra's club. Vritra was variously imagined, as a dragon, a snake or a cloud.

Vucub-Caquix ('seven Arara')   A demon mentioned in Popol Vuh, the sacred scriptures of the Quiché-Maya. He imagined himself to be sun, moon and light, and had to be overthrown by the divine brothers → Hunapu and Ixbalanque before they could start creating the human race.

Vulcanus (Volcanus) Roman god of fire and of the blacksmith's craft, taken over from the Etruscans; later, identified with the Greek → Hephaistos. His feast, the Volcanalia, was celebrated on 23 August, at the time of greatest drought, and was intended to ward off the danger of major conflagrations; and as a further mollification of the fire-god fish were thrown live into the flames. In the seaport town of Ostia, where stores of grain were especially at risk from fire, Vulcanus was the chief deity.

W

Wadd Moon-god and tutelary god of the ancient south Arabian states of Ausam and Main (fifth to second centuries BC). The name means 'love' or 'friendship'. The snake was sacred to the god.

Wakan The name used by the Dakota Indians to designate their gods. Everything in the world has its *wakan* or spirit, which is neither born nor dies. Chief among the *wakan* beings is the sun, which is called *wakan tanka kin*. Several Sioux tribes regarded Wakan Tanka as the universal god, under whom four other deities (including the sun-god Wi) were ranked.

Wakan Tanka → Wakan

Wakonda The creator of all things in the belief of the Omaha Indians in North America. The word is now used to designate an invisible life-force which is omnipresent, and which is invoked by human beings in need of help.

Walaganda → Wondjina

Waralden Olmai One of the most esteemed gods of the Lapps. The name comes from the Old Norse *veraldar god* ('world god'), an epithet of the Germanic god → Freyr.

Watauinewa The supreme being in the belief of the Yamana who live in Tierra del Fuego. He is the primeval progenitor and lord of life and death. The god is invoked in prayers as

'Our father', but plays no part in myth. He is lord and giver of animals.

Wele The supreme deity of the Bantu Kavirondo (Vugusu). He appears in two aspects: when he has the epithet *omuwanga*, he is the benign 'white' god; with the epithet *gumali*, he is the 'black' god of disaster.

Wen-chang The Taoist god of literature, honoured in many Chinese households by having his name-tablet on the wall.

Wer (or Mer) Along with → Adad, another name for the weather-god among the Semitic population of ancient Mesopotamia. In Mari he was called Itur-mer.

We-to A divine general in Chinese Buddhism. He is portrayed as youthful and arrayed in the full panoply of war, with helmet and sword. He is seen as a protector of the teaching (→ Dharmapāla) and is also a sort of guider of souls from earth to the lowest heaven.

Whiro Among the Maori in New Zealand, the god of darkness, of evil and death. He is the adversary of the god of light and fertility → Tane. Whiro is aided and abetted by the spirits of illness.

Whope Among the Sioux Indians, the daughter of the sun-god → Wi, and wife of the south wind. She came to earth one day and visited the Sioux people, to whom she brought the pipe as a symbol of peace. But the pipe is also supposed to be an intermediary between humans and → Wakan Tanka.

Wi The sun-god of the Sioux Indians. He was supposed to be omniscient, and the defender of those who were brave and loyal. Among the animals, the bison was particularly closely associated with him; indeed, it was often regarded as a manifestation of the god himself. His daughter was the beautiful → Whope.

Wonajö (Wanajo) A culture-hero in the form of a snake in the Louisiade Archipelago in the Pacific. He lit the first fire and scattered its ashes across the heavens so that the clouds arose. He gave the islanders the pig, the dog and the taro-plant.

Wondjina Primeval beings in the belief of the aboriginals in north-west Australia. They are spirits of rain and cloud, and are identified also with the rainbow snake. Most of them were imaged in rock-paintings, while their spirit dived into a near-by pool so as to be available to man in the form of life-giving water. One of the Wondjina, named Walaganda ('he who belongs to heaven') changed himself into the Milky Way.

Wosyet ('she who is strong') Ancient Egyptian goddess, worshipped in Thebes during the Middle Kingdom period as the protector of the youthful → Horus.

Wunekau A sun-god worshipped by various tribes in New Guinea. He is taken to be the creator of all things, whose name may be uttered only with the most extreme reverence. A wind sent by him makes women pregnant. The giant snake Make is seen as a special manifestation of his divine presence.

Wuru(n)katte Ancient Anatolian (Proto-Hattic) god of war, whose epithet was 'king of the land'. In the Hittite period his role was taken over by → Zababa, the war-god borrowed from the Akkadians.

Wuru(n)šemu

The proto-Hattic name of the old Anatolian sun-goddess. In essentials she corresponds to the goddess of → Arinna. Wurušemu also figures as an earth-goddess, in which capacity she is the consort of the weather-god → Taru.

X

Xewioso A god of thunder and of fertility venerated in Dahomey. He is represented in the form of a ram, with the thunder-axe as his attribute.

Xhindi Invisible spirits, analogous to elves, in Albanian folk-belief and folktale. Their arrival is signalled by the creaking of doors and flickering of lights. Sometimes they are kind and helpful, but at other times they appear as a sort of oppressive → Alp.

Xian The Chinese designation for genii, spirits and immortals. The heavenly *xian*, or *tian-xian*, live on the heavenly bodies, and surpass all the others in might. Especially noteworthy are the 'Eight Immortals' (→ Ba Xian).

Xiang Yao → Gong Gong

Xipe' totec ('our lord, the flayed one') Ancient Mexican god of spring, who causes the seed to germinate in the earth. In art, he is often shown wearing a flayed human skin. The flaying of humans was a cult ritual in pre-Aztec tribes. The Aztecs regarded the god's garment as the new growth of plants covering the earth. Xipe totec was also the tutelary god of the craftsmen in gold.

Xiuhtecutli ('lord of the turquoise') Aztec fire-god, also known simply as 'old god' (*huehue teotl*). The turquoise snake provides his clothing (*nahualli*) and in manuscripts he is shown with a red or yellow face. Sacred to him is the number 3 – the number of hearth-stones on which the baking-plate and the cooking-pot sit.

Xi-Wang-mu Chinese goddess of immortality, and the embodiment of Yin. She dwells in the mythical Kun-lun mountains in the west of China and is known as 'queen mother of the western paradise'. Originally, she was thought of as a menacing figure with tiger's fangs and a leopard's tail, who sent infectious diseases. Subsequently, she changed in Taoist popular belief into a friendly being who watches over the herb of immortality, and who regales her chosen ones on the peaches of eternal life. She is accompanied by the phoenix.

Xochipilli ('flower-prince') Old Mexican god of flowers and games, and, in addition, one of the 13 watchmen of the hours of the day. The design painted on his face resembles a butterfly. In one specific form he appears under the name of Macuilxochitl ('five – flower'). He holds a staff whose point is sunk into a human heart (symbol of life).

Xochiquetzal ('upright flower') Originally this goddess had a lunar character as the wife of the Mexican sun-god. In the Aztec pantheon, she figured as the youthful goddess of love, patron of all forms of female handicrafts, and queen of plants.

Xocotl A god of fire and of the stars, originally worshipped by the Otomi and subsequently taken over by the Nahua peoples, including the Aztecs. In his honour, the 'great feast of the dead', *Xocotl vetzi*, was celebrated in August. Dead warriors were thought of as stars who stood in a special relationship to the stellar god.

Xolotl A dog-headed follower of the sun. He helps those who have died to cross the 'nine-fold stream' and enter the underworld (*mictlan*). His name means 'twin' and is understood in relation to the inverted rising and setting of the sun as perceived in the underworld. In Aztec myth he figures as the twin brother of → Quetzalcoatl.

Xrōštag and Padvāxtag Two Manichaean divinities. They are the personifications of 'call' and 'answer'. The call is uttered from above by the 'living spirit', and it is 'answered' from below by the man who is to be saved.

Xucau This is the name given by the Ossetians (in the Caucasus) to their supreme god, who rules over other heavenly spirits (e.g. → Uacilla).

Y

Yakṣas In India, semi-divine beings of a chthonic nature: they live in the Himalayas, and, as followers of → Kubera, they watch over hidden treasures. Like Kubera, they have stubby limbs and pot-bellies. Not all yakṣas are malevolent; some are benign and these are revered by ordinary people as protective spirits and bringers of fertility. The benign yakṣas were taken over by Buddhism and appear in art, for example, as supporting figures.

Yama A mythical king in Indo-Aryan times (he figures in the Avesta as → Yima) who was the first man to die, thereby path-finder into the realm of the dead and now ruler over the dead. He is accompanied by two four-eyed spotted dogs. In Hindu mythology, Yama is judge of the dead and prince of hell; he is clothed in red garments and he has a noose with which he draws the soul out of the body. He rides on a black buffalo. In Buddhism too, he figures as judge of the dead, though here he often bears a wheel on his breast as a symbol of the Buddhist teaching. In Tantric pictures he may appear standing on a bull which is copulating with a woman. In Tibet, Yama is one of the → Dharmapālas, and is represented with a bull's head, flaming hair and a club. In Japan, he is known as Emma-ten.

Yamāntaka ('he who puts an end to Yama') One of the → Krodhadevatās in Buddhism. In Tibet, he is regarded as a protective deity. He is usually dark-blue in colour, and is shown standing on a bull over the sun and a lotus. In his mandala, he is three-faced, six-armed and he is trampling on → Yama, in token of his victory over death. He is also known as Yamāri ('enemy of Yama'). As Vajrabhairava ('he who arouses fear') he has 34 arms, 16 legs and 9 heads. The central head is that of a bull.

Yan-lo (or Yan Wang)   In China the dreaded prince of the underworld, god of the dead; he corresponds to the Indian-Buddhist → Yama. Yan-lo is clad in the robes of an emperor.

Yao   Mythical primeval emperor of the Chinese; together with the heavenly archer → Shen Yi he vanquished the unruly winds. In Confucianism, he is presented as the exemplar of the good ruler.

Yao-shi-fo   The Chinese name means 'physician Buddha'. He has taken the vow to devote himself entirely to the salvation of mankind, and to cure them of mental and physical illnesses.

Yarhibol   Ancient Arabian sun-god, revered in Palmyra and Dura Europos along with the sky-god → Bel and the moon-god → Aglibol. He was also the god of the holy spring at Efka, and may have been regarded as an oracle.

Yazata ('worthy of reverence')   In old Iranian religion, a designation for 'god', along with → Baga. The Yazatas are partly protective spirits, partly personifications of abstract concepts like → Rašun ('righteousness') or → Daēnā ('religion').

Yehl (Yetl)   Creator-god in the form of a raven, among the Tlingit Indians in north-west Canada. He flew over the primeval mists and used his wings to clear them away until the dry land appeared. According to the myth, he changed himself into a blade of grass and let himself be swallowed by a chief's daughter, from whom he was then born as the first man.

Ye'loje (older name, Pugu)   The sun deity of the Yukagir people in Siberia. Ye'loje looks after those who are oppressed, and keeps an eye on behaviour and morals.

Yima   Primeval man and primeval king in Iranian mythology. He corresponds to the Indian → Yama, and in each case the name means something like 'twin'. As a king, he represents all three social functions: he is pious as a priest, strong like a warrior, and rich in herds like a husbandman. He reigned in the Golden Age, when there was no death. Yima was born in a pillar of fire as a bolt of lightning from heaven. Another version of the myth makes him the brother of the sun and the moon.

Ymir   A primeval giant in Germanic mythogy, who arose from a poisonous mixture of ice and meltwater. He drew his nourishment from the milk of the primeval cow Audhumla. Ymir was slain by the gods → Odin, → Vili and Ve, and his body was used as raw material for the creation of the world.

Yo A sort of impersonal world-spirit in the religious system of the Bambara people in West Africa. Yo created the two male elements, air and fire, and the two female elements, earth and water. Finally the world-spirit let something heavy fall on to the earth – this was the creator-god → Pemba.

Yu-di ('Jade Emperor'; also known as Yu Huang) Supreme lord of heaven in Chinese cosmogony. He has nine daughters who dwell in the nine different heavens. In certain traditions he is said to have formed the first men out of clay. Twice a year, the earthly Emperor made sacrifice to his heavenly counterpart in the Temple of Heaven in Peking. Yu-di's consort was Wang Mu niang-niang, a form of → Xi Wang-mu.

Yu-huang Shang-di During the Song Dynasty, the name given to the supreme Taoist god; sometimes abbreviated to → Yu-di.

Yu-qiang In Chinese mythology, the god of the sea and the ocean winds. As sea-god, he has a fish's body, and he rides on two dragons; as god of the winds, he has the body of a bird and a human face.

Yum Kaax The Maya god of maize, known in specialist literature as god E. He corresponds in some ways to the Aztec → Cinteotl.

Z

Zababa Ancient Mesopotamian town-god of Kiš; in the early Babylonian period he was equated with → Ningirsu or with → Ninurta. His consort is the warlike → Inanna. He himself is a war-god, and in one text he is called 'Marduk of the battle'.

Zac → Bacab

Zagreus In origin, a pre-Hellenic god of animals and of hunting; subsequently, the chief god in Orphic theology. He is said to be the son of → Zeus and the goddess of the underworld → Persephone, and at the instigation of the jealous → Hera he is torn to pieces by the → Titans. Zeus (in another version of the story → Semele) swallows the still-beating heart, thus enabling the infant → Dionysos (in an Orphic equation with Zagreus) to be reborn.

Zalmoxis The supreme god of the Thracian Getae and Dacians (Dacia being the area known today as Romania). The only solid information we have about him comes from Herodotus. The ancient Greeks interpreted Zalmoxis as the founder of a religion, while present-day scholars tend to see him rather as an earth-god, a sky-god, a ruler of the dead or as a figure in divine mysteries. The legend tells how Zalmoxis took human form and lived among his people and then vanished for three years and was mourned as dead. In the fourth year, however, he came forth again from an underworld cave (the realm of the dead).

Žaltys The ancient Lithuanians revered the grass-snake, the žaltys, and it played a special part in prophecy. In one Lithuanian folksong it is called 'envoy of the gods'. The Latvian cognate is *zalktis*.

Zam Avestan (Persian) word for 'earth', which was deified and invoked along with the heavens as an object of veneration. Zam is one of the → Yazatas.

Zana A pre-Roman goddess in the Balkans, equated by the Romans with → Diana, although there is no conclusive proof of this. She was protected by three goats with golden horns. Zana lives on in the Albanian mountains as a fairy, revered for her courage and her beauty.

Zao Jun Taoist kitchen-god, whose picture hung in virtually every Chinese kitchen until well into the present century. The image was usually placed in a niche over the hearth, and sacrifice in the shape of sweets and honey-cakes was made to him on a given day.

Zemepatis ('Lord of the earth') A Lithuanian chthonic deity, protector of the cattle and of the farm as a whole. He was supposed to be the brother of the earth-goddess → Zemyna.

Zemes māte ('earth-mother') Ancient Lettish earth- and mother-goddess. She takes an interest in man's welfare, and looks after his fields and makes them fertile. However, she also plays the part of a ruler of the dead, merging here with → Velu māte. When the Baltic lands were converted to Christianity, she changed gradually into the figure of the Virgin Mary.

Zemyna (Zemynele) Lithuanian earth-goddess, the mother of plants. In prayers she is given the poetic epithet *žiedkele*, 'she who raises flowers'. Sacrifice was made to her, as the nourisher of man and animals, especially at seed-time and harvest.

Zenenet ('the exalted one') A goddess venerated in the ancient Egyptian town of Hermonthis. She was regarded as the consort of → Month, and merged with → Rat-taui.

Zéphyros The god of the west wind, in Greek myth the son of the stellar god Astreios ('the starry one') and of the early dawn (→ Eos). As herald of spring, he is married to one of the → Horae; and at the behest of → Eros, he abducts Psyche. He was called Favonius by the Romans.

Zervan (also as Zurvan, Zrvan, = 'time') Iranian god of time, the creator of all the paths which lead to the Cinvat bridge – the crossing-point into the Beyond. In Zervanism, which was spread by magi, he figured as the supreme god, lord of light and darkness. The radiant → Ahura Mazda and the dark → Ahriman are his children. Zervan is the 'four-fold god' who comprises in his own being divinity, light, power and wisdom. As a god of fate he is related to the Greek → Chronos. In Manichaeanism Zervan is also the supreme god, 'father of greatness' and *tetraprosopos* – the god with four faces as lord of the four elements.

Zeus Supreme god of the Greeks, the son of → Kronos and of → Rheia. His name comes from the Indo-Germanic root *dei* ('to shine') and is cognate with the names of other sky-gods (→ Dyaus, Diu-pater → Jupiter). The myth of the divine child – reared by the goat → Amáltheia or by the bee Melissa, and hidden from Kronos by the armed dancers, the → Kurétes – goes back to Cretan/Mycenaean times. The grown Zeus hurls

his father and the other Titans into Tartaros, and shares world-mastery thereafter with his brothers → Poseidon and → Hades. With his wife → Hera he sits enthroned in Olympus. He has many liaisons with mortal females, and on these occasions he appears in various guises – as a golden rain (with Danae), as a bull (with Europa), as a swan (with Leda). Along with his functions as sky-god, Zeus also figures as god of weather, in which capacity his epithet is *keraunos* ('lightning'). As *katachthonios* ('the subterranean one') he is associated with the underworld, and as *meilichios* ('the gentle one') he appears as a judge. As guardian of freedom, *eleutherios*, he has pan-Hellenic significance. His symbolical creature is the eagle. It was believed that his voice could be heard in the rustling of the oak-tree (the oracle at Dodona).

Zhang Guo-lao One of the 'Eight Immortals' (→ Ba Xian). He is supposed to have been really a bat which turned itself into a man. He rides on a white ass, and his attribute is a bamboo drum with two sticks.

Zhong-Kui The Chinese god of literature and of examinations; also, a protector against evil spirits and demons. He really belongs himself to the class of demonic beings (→ Gui Xian) as he committed suicide when the authorities refused to give him the first place in the examination results which he merited. His portrait is hung up at the end of the year to drive off demons. His attribute is a sword with which he fends off the five poisonous creatures – the snake, the centipede, the scorpion, the lizard and the toad.

Zhong-li Quan One of the 'Eight Immortals'. He is recognizable by the fan with which he revives the dead.

Zhu Dian (Tian) Chinese designation for the Buddhist gods which originally came from India, as e.g. Gong De Tian or He-li Di (→ Hariti).

Zibelthiurdos → Shurdi

Zipakna and Kabrakan Earthquake-gods of the Maya. The former was the 'creator of mountains', the latter the 'destroyer of mountains'.

Zocho One of the 'heavenly kings' of Shintoism, who protect the world from the evil demons. Zocho is the guardian of the south.

Zotz Bat-god of the Maya, and still today tutelary god of the Zotzil Indians who live in Chiapas, as well as of certain Guatemaltecan tribes.

Zu (or Anzu) A demonic storm-bird in Akkadian (Babylonian) mythology. He steals the tablets of fate in order to place himself at the head of the gods, but is himself vanquished by → Ningirsu (or → Ninurta).

Appendix I
Functions, aspects, spheres of competence

Agriculture, gods of (*see also* Grain, gods of)
Ah Bolom Tzacab
Amaethon
Ao → Jw
Apóllon
Aray
Aristaíos
Balarāma
Ceres
Consus
Enbilulu
Fauna
Lactans
Mars
Ops
Renenutet
Rongo
Sabazios
Satúrnus
Satúrnus Africánus
Shang-di
Silvanus
Tellus
Ugar
Xipe totec

Ancestral gods (*see also* Progenitors)
Aenéas
Deng
Freyr
Hintubuhet
Ing
Manes
Mulungu
Nuadu

Takamimusubi
Uji-gami

Angels, *see* Messengers, divine

Animals, protective deities of
Akerbeltz
Anky-Kele
Aristeíos
Ártemis
Donbittir
Faunus
Geuš Tašan
Geuš Urvan
Hérmes
Hinkon
Inuus
Kekri
Keyeme
Kis
Lahar
Lamaria
Mal
Num
Nyrckes
Pales
Pičvu'čin
Priapos
Rudra
Sechat-Hor
Sedna
Tabiti
Tomam
Tore
Watauinewa
Zagreus
Zemepatis

Astral deities (*see also* Moon deities, Morning Star deities, Sun deities)
Allat
Astlik
Bahram
Baltis
Bṛhaspati
Budha
God C
Camaxtli
Dhruva
Dioskúroi
Inanna
Isis
Ištar
Itzpapalotl
Jyotiṣka
Kallistó
Manda
Māṅgala
Mixcoatl
Neto
Orion
Pleiades
Ṛiṣis
Shou Lao
Sothis
Šulpa'e
Tai-yi
Tiṣṭrya
Uśanas
Väinämöinen
Xolotl

Birth and protection of children, deities of
Ártemis
Disir
Eileithyia
Freyja
Guan Yin
Ḥannaḥanna
Hariti
Heket
Hera
Ixchel

Jizo
Júno
Kalteš
Lucina
Máter Matúta
Mesenet
Mokoš
Nechbet
Nona
Norns
Parcae
Sabazios
Sarpanitu
Teteo innan
Thalna
Thesan
Toeris
Volumna

Blacksmiths and forging, gods of
Goibniu
Hašam(m)eli
Hephaistos
Kinyras
Kotar
Kurdalaegon
Pērkons
Qaynān
Sethlans
Shosshu
Svarog
Teljavelik
Vulcanus

Creator deities
Ai Tojon
Akongo
Allah
Amma
Amun
Aramazd
Arebati
Awonawilona
Baiame
Brahmā
Bulaing

Buluga
Bumba
Cghene
Chnum
El
Elohim
Enki
Éros
Fidi Mukullu
Hiraṇyagarbha
Huiracocha
Hunab Ku
Imra
Isten (2)
Julunggul
Kaia
Ka Tyeleo
Koyote
Kucumatz
Kun-tu-bzan-po
Kwoth
Laima
Leza
Lisa
Lowalangi
Mahatala
Makemake
Moma
Mula Djadi
Nareau
Niamye
Nü-gua
Oriṣa Nla
Pemba
Prajāpati
Ptah
Quat
Quetzalcoatl
Rigenmucha
Sirao
Somtus
Tangaroa
Teharonhiawagon
Tiki
Tirawa
Tvaṣṭar

Umvelinqangi
Ungud
Unumbotte
Varuṇa
Vili and Ve
Wakonda
Yehl

Culture heroes, bringers of culture
  Basajaun
  Bochica
  Fu-xi
  Gluskap
  Huang-di
  Ilmarinen
  Itzamna
  Julunggul
  Koyote
  Kutkinnáku
  Marunogere
  Oannes
  Olifat
  Prometheus
  Quetzalcoatl
  Shen-nong
  Thunupa
  Wonajö

Dawning, deities of
  Aruna
  Auróra
  Eos
  Máter Matúta
  Thesan
  Uṣas

Dead, death, deities of
  Amentet
  Anubis
  Apis
  Arimanius
  Armaiti
  Astō Vidātu
  Cherti
  Chontamenti
  Citipati

Dua
Estanatlehi
Giltine
Ha
Harendotes
Hel
Heros
Hunhau
Isdes
Isis
Kalypso
Kebechet
Kebechsenef
Kṣitigarbha
Libitina
Meresger
Nantosuelta
Nehalennia
Nephthys
Nut
Odin
Orcus
Ran
Ruti
Selket
Šentait
Sokar
Sucellos
Upuaut
Velu māte
Yama
Zemes māte

Death and underworld, demons of
Ammit
Astō Vidātu
Charontes
Culsu
Elel
Harpies
Ke'lets
  Sirens
Sphinx
Tuchulcha
Vanth

Demons and spirits embodying evil (see also Enemies of gods, Sickness, demons of)
Aēšma Daēva
Ahriman
Asag
Asasel
Asmodaios
Aži Dahaka
Bolla
Cherufe
Drug
Erge
Gandarewa
Guta
Harpies
Herensugue
Imdugud
Incubus
Inguma
Iya
Kaia
Kalevanpojat
Kéres
Kingu
Kulshedra
Lamia
Lilith
Lilitu
Mahr
Mazzikin
Pēy
Psezpolnica
Puck
Rāhu
Rakṣas
Reahu
Sebettu
Strigae
Succubus
Tawiskaron
Udu(g)
Vadātājs
Vucub-Caquix

Demon-slayers
  Acala
  Bhūtadāmara
  Cāmundā
  Dharmapāla
  Hayagrīva
  Heruka
  Ihi
  Inar
  Indra
  Krodhadevatās
  Lü Dong-bin
  Mahākāla
  Michael
  Mon
  Narasimha
  Nusku
  Ogma
  Perkunas
  Rāma
  Śakra
  Tang
  Thor
  Tiṣṭriya
  Varāha
  Viṣṇu
  Zhong-Kui
  Zocho

Devils, infernal beings (see also
  Enemies of gods)
  Aatxe
  Abaddon
  Ammit
  Astō Vidātu
  Babi
  Bali
  Beelzebub
  Behemoth
  Belial
  Beng
  Dabog
  Daēvas
  Djall
  bDud
  Forneus

Galla
Gong Gong
Hiisi
Iblis
Ke'lets
Lucifer
Mammon
Marchocias
Mephistopheles
Pan
Šaitan
Samael
Satan
Velnias

Earth deities
  Aditi
  Aker
  Ala
  Ana
  Aretia
  Armaiti
  Cheng-huang
  Cihuacoatl
  Coatlicue
  Demeter
  Di-ya
  Di-zang
  Gaia
  Geb
  Hekáte
  Hlodyn
  Izanami
  Jian Lao
  Kukulcan
  Lur
  Ma
  Maía (1)
  Medr
  Nerthus
  Odudua
  Pandora
  Prithivī
  Rind
  Semele
  Semnai Theai

Spandaramet
Tailtiu
Tatenen
Tellus
Tepeyollotli
Teteo innan
Uraš
Wuru(n)šemu
Zam
Zemes māte
Zemyna

Enemies of the gods (*see also* Devils)
Ahriman
Aloádes
Apophis
Asura
Bali
Daityas
Erlik
Fenrir
Fomore
Garm
Giants
Iapetós
Jotun
Kabandha
Koyote
Kud
Leviathan
Loki
Māra
Midgard-snake
Okeus
Rahab
Rāvana
Surt(r)
Vritra

Fate, deities and spirits of
Camaxtli
Disir
Ea
Enlil
Fairy
Fatit

Gul-šeš
Hemsut
Išduštaja
Kalteš
Karta
Laima
Manat
Moires
Nabu
Namtar
Nanna (1)
Norns
Nortia
Nyame
Parcae
Šai
Sin (1)
Tyché
Urme
Vāyu

Fertility, deities of
Amun
Ana
Anahita
Aphrodíte
Apis
Armaiti
Ártemis
Ašera(t)
Astarte
Asthoreth
Atargatis
Ba (1)
Baal
Baal-Addir
Baal-Hammon
Bácchus
Bress
Ceres
Ceres Africana
Cernunnos
Curche
Demeter
Diónysos
Disir

Egres
El
Fjörgyn
Freyja
Freyr
Harpokrates
Hlodyn
Jumis
Krónos
Kybéle
Liber
Makemake
Manasa
Mars, Gallic
Men
Min
Mnevis
Mokoš
Nandin
Nehalennia
Ningirsu
Ninurta
Njörd
Nommo
Nymphs
Osiris
Pachamama
Paśupati
Poseidon
Priapos
Rauni
Reret
Rosmerta
Šentait
Serapis
Thor
Tinnit
Ukemochi
Vanir
Xewioso

Fertility demons
Baubo
Kurétes
Nāga
Rephaim

Satyr
Tu (2)
Yakṣas

Fire, deities of
Agni
Cácus
Coatlicue
Eate
Gabija
Gibil
Hephaistos
Hinokagutsuchi
Itzpapalotl
Jagaubis
Kukulcan
Li
Mahuike
Nusku
Odgan
Pāndarā
Sethlans
Svarog
Tabiti
Verbti
Vulcanus
Xiuhtecutli
Xolotl

Fortune, gifts, deities of
Benten
Bhaga
Diti
Ekajaṭā
Fortúna
Fukurokuju
Fu Shen
Gad
Garmangabi(s)
Gefjon
Gong De Tian
Hotei
Laima
Lakṣmī
Nortia
Rundas

Shichi-Fukujin
Tyché .

Ghosts and spirits of the dead
Aképhalos
Befana
Etemmu
Gui Xian
Lemures
Preta
Vampire
Vodnik

Good spirits and demons
Agathós Daímon
Amáltheia
Aralez
Bercht
Bukura e dheut
Kaukas
Kobold
Mājas gars
Metatron
Para
Pukis
Sebettu
Šedu

Grain and maize, deities
Ašnan
Chalchihuitlicue
Cinteotl
Dagan
Demeter
Gabjauja
Halki
Köndös
Neper
Nepit
Nisaba
Pellonpekko

Handicrafts, gods of
Athená
Kotar
Lug

Prometheus
Ptah
Tane
Tu (1)
Tvaṣṭar
Xochiquetzal

Healing, deities of
Aesculápius
Apóllon
Aśvins
Baal-Marqōd
Baba (1)
Bašāmum
Bhaiṣajyaguru
Borvo
Cheiron
Dian-Cecht
Endouellicus
Ešmun
Grannus
Gula
Hala
Hygíeia
Imhotep
Jizo
Jūras māte
Kamrušepa
Marduk
Meditrina
Ninazu
Nin'insina
Okininushi
Patecatl
Podaleirios
Rudra
Šadrapa
Sataran
Šauška
Yao-shi-fo

Home and hearth, deities of
Dievini
Hestia
Lamaria
Lares

Nang Lha
Nantosuelta
Penates
Portúnus
Thab-lha
Vésta
Zao Jun

Hunting, deities of
Ártemis
Artio
Diana
Hinkon
Hittavainen
Meža māte
Murukān
Onuris
Rundas
Tapio
Zagreus
Zana

Immortality, givers of
Goibniu
Gou Mang
Hah
Hébe
Idun
Jurojin
Mu Gong
Saošyant
Šesmu
Xi-Wang-Mu

Judgment, deities of (see also Justice and law)
Abat(t)ur
Aiakós
Assur
Bhagwān
Gao Yao
Hananim
Haukim
Išara
Isdes
Ištanu

Kalunga
Karuileš šiuneš
Katavul
Kṣitigarbha
Mafdet
Māmitu
Marduk
Osiris
Pugu
Rašnu
Sataran
Sin (1)
Skan
Śridevi
Yama
Zeus

Justice and law, deities of
Adrásteia
Anbay
Chenti-irti
Dharma
Díke
Eunomía
Forseti
Ḥendursanga
Maat
Nechmetawaj
Nemesis
Perkunas
Rašnu
Šamaš
Tefnut
Themis
Tyr
Ull(r)
Varuṇa
Ye'loje

Kings and rulers, deities of kingship, divine (see also State and nation, deities of
Alalu
Amun
Behedti
Enlil

Ḫanwašuit
Harpre
Ḫebat
Horus
Inmutef
Inti
Iškur
Kumarbi
Mac Gréine
Malik
Month
Nechbet
Nuadu
Qormusta
Śakra
Seth
Uto

Light, deities of (*see also* Sun deities)
Ahura Mazda
Ártemis
Balder
Belenus
Hélios
Horus
Hyperion
Júpiter
Mithras
Narisah
Nefertem
Nusku
Perses
Pūṣan
Tane
Theia
Umā
Usinš

Lightning, deities of (*see also*
Weather deities)
Aplu
Deng
Illapa
Júpiter
Pele
Perendi

Rešef
Summamus
Xolotl

Local gods, town gods
Alaunus
Alisanos
Arduinna
Assur
Athená
Baal
Baba (1)
Beelzebub
Cheng-huang
Djebauti
Dumuziabzu
Harmerti
Hemen
Ipet
Junit
Kis
Lugalbanda
Marduk
Mehit
Menhit
Nanše
Nebtuu
Nenun
Nin'insina
Quetzalcoatl
Rudianos
Šara
Tišpak
Turan
Uni
Zababa
Zenenet

Love, deities of
Alpan
Ámor
Aphrodíte
Ašera(t)
Astarte
Asthoreth
Éros

Freyja
Frigg
Hathor
Inanna
Ištar
Kadeš
Kāma
Kubaba
Nanāja
Odudua
Prende
Šauška
Tlazolteotl
Turan
Venus
Xochiquetzal

Magic, demons and spirits of
Baba-Yaga
Dākini
Daktyloi
Druden
Gullveig
Kirke
Sárkány
Šedim
Tawiskaron
Telchines
Troll

Man-eating gods; vampires
Ammit
Bolla
Cherufe
Cyclops
Dākini
Diwe
Fene
Hāriti
Iya
Kaiamunu
Kholomodumo
Kulshedra
Ljubi
Skylla
Sri

Torto
Vampire

Marriage, deities of
Airyaman
Aryaman
Bhaga
Ceres
Hera
Hymén
Júno
Pattini
Svarog
Vör

Messengers, divine; Angelic beings
Ameša Spentas
Cherubim
Gabriel
Gapn
Gou Mang
Hérmes
Hermod(u)r
Iris
Isinu
Isrāfil
Išum
Metatron
Michael
Mnevis
Namtar
Nike
Papsukkal
Raphael
Samael
Seraphim
Uriel
Valkyries

Moon deities
Aglibol
Alako
Almaqah
Amm
Arma
Ártemis

Candra
Chia
Chons
God D
Diana
Heng E
Hilal
Hina
Ilazki
Ixchel
Jarih
Joh˘
Júno Caeléstis
Kašku
Kemwer
Kušuh
Luna
Māh
Mahrem
Mani
Marama
Mawu
Men
Mēness
Menulis
Nanna (1)
Napir
Nikkal
Ouiot
Pasiphae
Persé
Quilla
Šelardi
Seléne
Si
Sin (1)
Sin (2)
Ta'lab
Tecciztecatl
Thot
Tinnit
Tsukiyomi
Wadd
Xochiquetzal

Morning/Evening Star deities
  Aruṇa
  Auróra
  Eos
  Máter Matúta
  Thesan
  Uṣas

Mother goddesses; Great Mother
  Aditi
  Amaunet
  Ammavaru
  Anahita
  Ártemis
  Atargatis
  Boldogasszony
  Cihuacoatl
  Durgā
  Gatumdu(g)
  Gaurī
  Ḥannaḥanna
  Kālī˘
  Kubaba
  Kybéle
  Ma
  Mama
  Māri (1)
  Matres
  Nammu
  Ninhursanga
  Ninmaḥ˘
  Oya
  Zemes māte

Mountain deities
  Adrásteia
  Baal-Karmelos
  Baal-Qarnain
  Baal Sapon
  Candamius
  Dercetius
  Ebech
  Elagabal
  Ḥazzi
  Himavat
  Jahwe

Kybéle
Liluri
Pele
Tork

Music, literature, dance, deities of
Apóllon
Baal-Marqod
Benten
Bragi
Dhṛtarāṣṭra
Erato
Eutérpe
Gandharvas
Gratiae
Guan Di
Gwydyon
Hathor
Hérmes
Ihi
Kalliópe
Kaménae
Kinyras
Laka
Melpoméne
Meret
Muses
Odin
Orpheus
Oya
Polyhymnia
Rongo
Śiva
Terpsichore
Thalia
Uzume
Wen-chang
Zhong-Kui

Nature demons and spirits
Centaurs
Dryads
Elben
Fairies
Gandharvas
Gnomes

Heitsi-Eibib
Jinn
Juma
K'daai
Kiskil-lilla
Kobold
Laskowice
Maahiset
Maruts
Mikal → Michael
Oreades
Perit
Ten-gū
bTsan
Typhón
Uacilla
Vili
Valkyries
Wondjina

Night deities; dark aspect of the world
Abhiyoga
Arimanius
Ármány
God D
Kuk and Kauket
Nott
Nyx
Ördög
Rātrī
Tepeyollotli
Varuṇa
Whiro

Nourishment, food, deities of (see also Grain, deities of)
Ameretāt
Chicome coatl
Durgā
Inari
Tonacatecutli
Yum Kaax

Oaths, pledges and contracts, deities
of
Dagda
Gaia
Ḥazzi
Hélios
Išara
Karuileš šiuneš
Māmitu
Mitra
Šeri and Ḥurri
Shosshu
Styx
Tomor
Ull(r)
Veles
Vör

Oracles, deities of
Ammon
Anbay
Apóllon
Baal-Hammon
Baal-Karmelos
Endouellicus
Fortúna
Hubal
Ifa
Nanše
Nereus
Proteus
Šamaš
Tages
Ta'lab
Tir
Triglav
Yarhibol

Peace, deities of
Eirene
Pax
Rongo
Salmān
Salus
Whope

Plants, deities of (see also Tree and
forest deities, Grain, deities of,
Vegetation deities)
Ameretāt
Chalchihuitlicue
Flóra
Han Xiang-zi
Haoma
Horae
Maia (2)
Nefertem
Pomona
Spes
Uneg
Xochipilli
Xochiquetzal
Zemyna

Primeval deities (see also Creator
deities)
Adibuddha
Amaunet
Ammavaru
Amun
Anšar and Kišar
Atea
Atum
Chepre
Harsaphes
Heket
Izanagi
Izanami
Kematef
Namita
Nammu
Nehebkau
Neith
Nun
Ogdoad
Pothos
Preas Prohm
Ptah
Sirao
Tatenen

Progenitors of human race
  Adam Kadmon
  Bur(i)
  Dakṣa
  Gayomard
  Kékrops
  Manu
  Martanda → Adityas
  Ouiot
  Puruṣa
  Tiki
  Yama
  Yima

Protective deities; guardians
  Acala
  Aitu
  Athená
  Ayiyanayaka
  Bhairava
  Dādimunda
  Dvārapāla
  Eranoranhan
  Grāma-devatā
  Guhyasamāja
  Harendotes
  Harsiesis
  Heimdall
  Hemsut
  Heraklés
  Hérmes
  Heruka
  He Xian-gu
  Hor-Hekenu
  Imiut
  Isis
  Iṣṭadevatā
  Ixtab
  Jānguli
  Janus
  Júno Caeléstis
  K'op'ala
  Lama (2)
  Lares
  Lhamo
  Mandah

Mbotumbo
Men Shen
Meresger
Meža māte
Nahi
Nehebkau
Pañcarakṣa
Pateke
Quiritis
Safa
Šed
Shosshu
Śridevi
Sumbharāja
Toeris
Unut
Vighnāntaka
Zotz

Protective spirits and demons
  Alardi
  Basajaun
  Bes
  Beset
  Daimon
  Elben
  Fravaši
  Fylgir
  Genii
  Ka
  Lama (1)
  Nagual
  Ora
  Raphael
  Yakṣas
  Yazata

Rain deities
  Abhiyoga
  Adad
  Afi
  Ah Bolom Tzacab
  Asurakumāra
  Chac
  Illapa
  Indra

Māri (1)
Nāgakumāra
Ngai
Nommo
Pariaćaca
Parjanya
Pērkons
Perkunas
Pon
Rongo
Sodza → So
Telipinu
Tiṣṭriya
Tlaloc

Revenge, deities of
Adrásteia
Anat(h)
Erinyes
Petbe
Rudra
Tezcatlipoca
Vidar

Riches and prosperity, deities of (see also Fortune, gifts, deities of)
Abundantia
Adad
Bab (1)
Cai Shen
Cernunnos
Daikoku (→ Shichi-Fukujin)
Dis Páter
Freyr
Gabjauja
Hades
Jambhala
Kubera
Kurukullā
Mahākāla
Mammon
Mercurius
Plutos
Rosmerta
Sucellos

Teutates
Vasudhara

River deities
Acheloos
Asopós
Gaṅgā
Hapi (2)
He Bo
Peneios
Sangarios
Sarasvati
Sequana
Styx
Tiberinus

Saviours and redeemers
Adam Kasia
Aditi
Adityas
Amida
Avalokiteśvara
Bodhisattva
Da-shi-zhi
Guan Yin
Maitreya
Manda d-Hiia
Mi-lo Fo
Orunmila
Pistis Sophia
Saošyant
Tang
Tīrthaṁkara
Yao-shi-fo

Sea deities
Achilleus
Amphitríte
Anky-Kele
Bangputys
Behēr
Glaúkos
Jamm
Leukothea → Inó
Lir
Makemake

Manannan
Melqart
Mīnākṣī
Nehalennia
Neptunus
Nereids
Nereus
Nethuns
Njörd
Okeanos
Olokun
Phorkys
Pontos
Poseidon
Proteus
Sedna
Tangaroa
Tinirau
Triton
Yu-qiang

Sickness, deities of
Apóllon
Dala Kadavara
Erra
Jarri
Lature Danö
Māri (1)
Mikal
Nergal
Rešef
Rudra
Śītalā

Sickness, demons of
Agaš
Alardi
Alp
Asag
Ays
Bilwis
Dimme
Elel
Jinn
Kukuth
Lamaštu

gNyan
Pazuzu
Thursir

Sky deities
Ākāśagarbha
Amenominakanushi
An
Arebati
Astar
Baal-Biq'āh
Baal-Šamēm
Baršamin
Bel (2)
Bhīma
Candamius
Dievs
Dyaus
Es
Faro
Hananim
Haroeris
Hathor
Horus
Inmar
Izanagi
Jabru
Juma
Jumala
Júpiter
Kamui
Mandulis
Mawu
Men
Mugasa
Ndjambi
Num
Num-Torum
Nut
Oriṣa Nla
Pon
Satúrnus Africanus
Shang-di
Singbonga
Šiuš
Skan

Tai-yi
Takamimusubi
Tengri
Tian
Tin
Tyr
Ülgän
Uranós
Urtzi
Yu-di
Zeus

Souls, guides of
Camaxtli
Charon
Charun
Cherti
Di-zang
Hermanubis
Hérmes
Ogmios
Thot
Turms
Uršanabi
We-to
Xolotl

Spirits (*see also* Demons and spirits embodying evil, Good spirits and demons, Nature demons and spirits, Protective spirits and demons)
Abgal
Aitvaras
Baba (2)
Baba-Yaga
Bardha
Bercht
Gandharvas
Hesperides
Holle
Juma
Kami
Kinnara
Laumē
Maju

dMu
Naiads
Nymphs
Sugaar
Xhindi
Xian

Spring deities
Maia (2)
Ostara
Venus
Xipe totec
Zéphyros

Star gods, *see* Astral deities

State and nation, deities of
Almaqah
Amun
Assur
Baal-Hammon
Dusares
Ḥaldi
Huitzilopochtli
Itzamna
Júno
Júpiter
Kamoš
Kataragama
Kucumatz
Mahadeo
Mahāprabhu
Mahrem
Marduk
Melqart
Milkom
Ninšušinak
Ogma
Ptah
Saxnot
Sin (2)
Tinnit
Voltumna
Wadd
Zalmoxis

Sun deities
 Ādityas
 Amaterasu
 Apóllon
 Arinna
 Aton
 Baal-Biq'āh
 Behedti
 God C
 Cath
 Chepre
 Chors
 Dabog
 Ekhi
 Elagabal
 Hammon
 Harachte
 Harmachis
 Harpokrates
 Harsaphes
 Hélios
 Horus
 Huiracocha
 Huitzilopochtli
 Hun-Hunapu
 Hvar
 Inti
 Kinich Kakmó
 Khyung-gai mGo-can
 Lisa
 Mahes
 Malakbēl
 Mandulis
 Marduk
 Mārici
 Melqart
 Mihr
 Mithras
 Mog Ruith
 Nahhundi
 Nefertem
 Osiris
 Palk
 Pugu
 Re
 Šamaš

Šams
Šapš
Saule
Savitar
Shen Yi
Simigi
Šiuš
Šiwini
Sol (1)
Sol (2)
Somtus
Suaixtix
Suchos
Sul
Sūrya
Svarog
Tawa
Tezcatlipoca
Tiwaz
Tnong
Tonatiuh
Upulevo
Utu
Vivasvat
Wi
Wunekau
Wuru(n)šemu
Yarhibol
Ye'loje

Supreme gods, supreme beings (*see
 also* State and nation, deities of)
 Abora
 Acoran
 Ahone
 Akongo
 Aramazd
 Armaz
 Baiame
 Bhagavān
 Bhagwān
 Buluga
 Bumba
 Bunjil
 Cagn
 Cghene

Devel
Hananim
Huiracocha
Hunab Ku
Imra
Io (2)
Īśvara
Kalunga
Karei
Katavul
Ka Tyeleo
Kitanitowit
Kun-tu-bzan-po
Leza
Manitu
Mayin
Mulungu
Nārāyana
Ngai
Niamye
Num
Nyame
Nzambi
Odin
Olorun
Ometeotl
Purá
Raluvhimba
Rigenmucha
Śiva
Tonacatecutli
Unkulunkulu
Viṣṇu
Viśvakarman
Watauinewa
Wele
Xucau
Zervan
Zeus

Thunder, deities of (see also Weather, deities of)
Ah Bolom Tzacab
Asurakumāra
Illapa
Júpiter

Karei
Lei-zi
Nāgakumāra
Pajonn
Pariacaca
Pērkons
Perkunas
Perun
Sango
Śusanowo
Taranis
Thor
Ukko
Urtzi
Xewioso

Time and eternity, deities of
Aetérnitas
Aión
Chons
Chronos
Hah
Kāla
Satúrnus Africánus
Tai-sui-xing
Thot
Zervan

Town gods, see Local gods

Trade, commerce, travel, deities of
Ekchuah
Guan Di
Hekáte
Hércules
Hérmes
Ilmarinen
Jizo
Lares
Mēness
Mercurius
Poseidon
Pūṣan

Treasure, demonic guardians of
Fafnir

413

Kaukas
Ladon
Pukis
Stihi

Tree and forest deities
Abellio
Artio
Diana
Fagus
Fauna
Hathor
Heléne
Hiisi
Korrawi
Lykurgos
Medeine
Meža māte
Pan
Silvanus
Tane
Tapio

Underworld, gods of
Aiakós
Alpan
Ataecina
Baal-Addir
Barastir
Bēletsēri
Belili
Bhavanavāsin
Dis Páter
Djata
Dur
Enmešarra
Epona
Ereškigal
Gestinanna
Gwydyon
Hades
Hel
Hine-nui-te-po
Hunhau
Izanami
Karuileš šiuneš

Lature Danö
Laverna
Lelwani
Māmitu
Manes
Meslamta'ea
Mictlantecutli
Moma
Morrigan
Mot
Mūtu
Nergal
Ninazu
Ningišzida
Orcus
Persephóne
Picullus
Pwyll
Šulmanu
Veles
Yan-lo

Vegetation deities (*see also* Plants, deities of)
Abu
Adonis
Ariádne
Ártemis
Attis
Balder
Disir
Duillae
Dumuzi
Egres
Heléne
Hyákinthos
Kabiroi
Malakbēl
Ningirsu
Pan
Persephóne
Sämpsä
Sif
Telipinu
Uto

Victory, deities of
  Anahita
  Korrawi
  Nike
  Vahagn
  Verthragna
  Victoria

War, deities of (*see also* Demon-slayers)
  Adraste
  Anat(h)
  Apām napāt
  Aray
  Arés
  Assur
  Astarte
  Asthoreth
  Athená
  'Attar
  Baal-Hadad
  Badb
  Beg-tse
  Bellóna (2)
  Cariociecus
  Diomédes
  Dolichénus
  Guan Di
  Gwydyon
  Hachiman
  Hadúr
  Inanna
  Indra
  Ištar
  Jarovit
  Júpiter
  Korrawi
  Laran
  Lug
  Ma
  Mahrem
  Mars
  Mars, Gallic
  Mithras
  Month
  Morrigan

Murukān
Nanāja
Neith
Neto(n)
Ningirsu
Odin
Onuris
Oro
Quirinus
Rudianos
Rugievit
Sachmet
Safa
Sajigor
Šauška
Semnocosus
Skanda
Smertrios
Šulmanu
Svantevit
Teteo innan
Teutates
Tezcatlipoca
Triglav
Tu
Tyr
Upuaut
Vestius Alonieus
We-to
Wuru(n)katte
Zababa

Watchmen, demonic
  Árgos
  Ḫuwawa
  Kérberos
  Ladon
  Nehebkau
  Python
  Stihi

Water deities (*see also* Rain, River, Sea, deities)
  Ahurani
  Apām napāt
  Apsu

Atlaua
'Attar
Chalchihuitlicue
Chnum
Donbittir
Ea
Enki
Faro
Haurvatāt
Jamm
Jūras māte
Jutúrna
Kaménae
Kukulcan
Mandah
Mehet-uret
Nāgakumāra
Nethuns
Nun
Nymphs
Satis
Tiamat
Varuṇa

Water demons and spirits
  Aegir
  Apsaras
  Egeria
  Forneus
  Harun, Haruna
  Kappa
  Katavi
  Lahama
  Mimir
  Naiads
  Ningyo
  Nixe
  Qandiša
  Ran
  Rusalka
  Vodnik

Weather deities (*see also* Lightning,
  Rain, Thunder, deities)
  Adad
  Afi

Amm
Baal-Biq'āh
Baal-Hadad
Bhīma
Dolichénus
Fjörgynn
Gebeleizis
Ilmarinen
Iškur
Perendi
Quzah
Shurdi
So
Tarhunt
Tarŭ
Tešub
Thor
Wer
Zeus

Wind and storm, deities of
  Aíolos
  Amaunet
  Amun
  Baal
  Baal-Hadad
  Boréas
  Eate
  Euros
  Fei Lian
  Fujin
  Ilmarinen
  Martu
  Notos
  Oya
  Quetzalcoatl
  Rudra
  Shen-nong
  Stribog
  Susanowo
  Tate
  Tore
  Vata
  Veja māte
  Verbti
  Yu-qiang

Breast
  Ana
  Estanatlehi
  Hatuibwari
  Lamštu
  Mīnākṣī

Breath
  Bunjil
  Selket
  Šu
  Vāyu

Bridge
  Heimdall
  Rašnu

Broom
  Baba-Yaga

Buffalo
  Lao-zi
  Yama

Bull
  Aatxe
  Acheloos
  Adad
  Almaqah
  Apis
  Baal-Hadad
  Bata
  Buchis
  Chentechtai
  Dolichénus
  Dyaus
  El
  Gurzil
  Iškur
  Kemwer
  Mars
  Mnevis
  Month
  Nandin
  Pajainen
  Parjanya

Riṣabha
Rudra
Šeri and Hurri
Sin (1)
Śiva
Tešub
Tilla
Yama
Yamāntaka
Zeus

Bull head
  Astarte
  Minotaur
  Vajrabhairava

Bull horns
  Acheloos
  Aglibol
  Baal

Bull-man
  Lama (1)
  Lamaštu
  Šedu

Bull sacrifice
  Liluri
  Mithras
  Perun
  Saošyant

Bullet
  Fortúna
  Tyché

Butter, churning
  Idā
  Imra
  Manu

Butterfly
  Fatit
  Hintubuhet
  Itzpapalotl
  Mahr
  Xochipilli

Caduceus *see* Snakes, staff of

Camel
  Arsū
  Uśanas

Candle
  Satúrnus

Cap, magic (conferring invisibility)
  Alp
  Hades
  Perseus

Cassowary
  Namita

Cat
  Aitvaras
  Bastet
  Freyja
  Para
  Utgard-Loki

Cattle (*see also* Cow, Bull)
  Aēšma Daēva
  Geuš Urvan
  Māh
  Mon
  Vohu Manah

Cave
  Amaterasu
  Anubis
  Cheiron
  Demeter
  Drug
  Mihr

Chain
  Ogmios
  Safa

Charioteer
  Aruṇa (2)
  Candra

Dievs
Eos
Hélios
Indra
Manda
Māri (2)
Mithra
Nerthus
Nott
Phaéthon
Rāhu
Savitar
Seléne
Sol (1 and 2)
Sūrya
Tešub
Thor
Ukko
Uṣas

Circle
  Adam Kadmon
  Kitanitowit

Club
  Baal-Hadad
  Buddhakapāla
  Budha
  Dagda
  Deng
  Dharma
  Iškur
  K'op'ala
  Kubera
  Māl
  Mars, Gallic
  Ogmios
  Perun
  Rešef
  Smertrios
  Sucellos
  Upuaut
  Vajrayoginī
  Viṣṇu

Cock
  Aitvaras
  Lowalangi
  Mercurius, Gallic
  Murukān
  Sraoša

Cock head
  Abraxas

Coconut
  Hainuwele

Coffin
  Nut

Coins (see also Purse)
  Cernunnos
  Charon
  Júno

Comb
  Lamaštu

Coping stone
  Atargatis
  Kybéle

Corn see Maize

Cornucopia
  Amáltheia
  Concordia
  Epona
  Fortúna
  Gaia
  Harpokrates
  Matres
  Nantosuelta
  Pax
  Plutos
  Rosmerta
  Svantevit
  Tyché

Cow (see also Cattle)
  Armaiti

Damona
Gaueko
Hathor
Hera
Hesat
Io (1)
Mehet-uret
Nerthus
Prithivī
Šentait
Uṣas
Virāj

Cow horns
  Isis
  Rat-taui

Crane
  Fukurokuju
  Jurojin
  Shou Lao

Crocodile
  Chentechtai
  Djata
  Leviathan
  Nixe
  Petesuchos
  Seth
  Suchos

Crocodile head
  Ammit

Crooked staff
  Anezti
  Osiris
  Thalia

Crow
  Badb

Crown
  Anahita
  Anat(h)
  Avalokiteśvara

Beg-tse
Bhūtadāmara
Bodhisattva
Candaroṣana
Chensit
Cundā
Geb
Metatron
Rešef
Samvara
Satis
Sumbharāja
Urthekau
Uṣṇīṣavijayā

Crown, of horns
Enlil

Cypress
Ataecina

Dance
Baal-Marqōd
Elves
Korybantes
Kurétes
Laka
Mars
Oya
Padmanarteśvara
Śiva
Uzume

Darkness (see also Appendix I:
Night deities)
Abhiyoga
Ahriman
Arimanius
Belial
Kiskil-lilla
Lature Danö
Lilith
Rāhu

Deer
Artemis

Cernunnos
Finn
Itzpapalotl
Odin

Deer head
Fei Lian

Desert
Bēletsēri
Ha
Pachet
Seth

Diadem
Anahita
Hera

Dice
Apsaras

Disc (see also Sun)
Inti

Discus
Hyákinthos
Kāmākṣī
Māl
Sūrya
Viṣṇu

Dog
Anubis
Aralez
Bhairava
Charon
Chontamenti
Epona
Garm
Gula
Hekáte
Hunhau
Ke'lets
Kérberos
Lamaštu
Legba

Nehalennia
Rakṣas
Skylla
Sucellos
Xolotl
Yama

Dog head
  Chors
  Hermanubis
  Sunmurw

Door
  Janus
  Men Shen

Dove
  Anahita
  Aphrodíte
  Astarte
  Hachiman
  Nirrti
  Shurdi
  Tinnit
  Turan

Dragon
  Confucius
  Djall
  Fafnir
  Gong Gong
  Gou Mang
  Kaukas
  Ladon
  Marduk
  Mutu
  Pukis
  Python
  Sárkány
  Satan
  Stihi
  Susanowo
  Th'uban
  Tiamat
  Vairocana
  Vritra

Yu-qiang

Dragonfly
  Tnong

Drum
  Kutkinnáku
  Votan
  Zhang Guo-lao

Duck
  Sequana

Dwarf
  Alp
  Bes
  Hayagríva
  Iwaldi
  Maahiset
  Pateke
  Troll

Eagle (*see also* Eagle, double)
  Azizos
  Bel (2)
  Dusares
  Elagabal
  Isten (2)
  Lowalangi
  Malakbel
  Nasr
  Ningirsu
  Raluvimbha
  Tomor(r)
  Tonatiuh
  Zeus

Eagle, double
  Ai Tojon
  Rundas

Eagle, lion-headed
  Imdugud

Ear of corn
  Atargatis

Demeter
Jian Lao
Jumis
Nepit
Persephóne
Serapis
Spes
Tinnit
Vasudhara

East
Akṣobhya
Bhaiṣajyaguru
Dhritarāṣtra
Duamutef
Gou Mang
Indra
Mu Gong
Nephthys
Palk
Remanta
Sopdu

Eel
Kaia

Egg
Amma
Ammavaru
Kun-tu-bzan-po
Panku
Sun Hou-zi

Elephant
Akṣobhya
Cakravartin
Dādimunda
Dala kadavara
Gaṇeśa
Indra
Murukān
Preas Eyn
Śakra
Sāmantabhadra
Viṣṇu

Elk
Alcis

Eye
Amaterasu
Árgos
Chenti-irti
Cherubim
Horus
Kemwer
Manzaširi
Midir
Mithra
Mog Ruith
Nareau
Odin
Panku
Re
Ṣango
Sirao
Sūrya
Tefnut
Thiassi
Tsukiyomi
Vanth

Falcon
Behedti
Bunjil
Chentechtai
Chenti-irti
Harachte
Harmerti
Haroeris
Hemen
Hor-Hekenu
Horus
Kebechsenef
Month
Nenun
Pariacaca
Re
Sokar

Falcon cloak
Freyja

Falcon head
  Aš

Fan
  Zhong-li Quan

Feather
  Beset
  Chensit
  Maat
  Onuris
  Oro
  Si
  Tatenen

Feather boa, Feather-snake
  Kukulcan
  Quetzalcoatl

Ferryman
  Charon
  Cherti
  Uršanabi

Fifty
  Enlil

Fig
  Tinnit

Fig-tree
  Upulevo

Finger
  Daktyloi

Fir-cone
  Satúrnus Africánus

Fire, Flame (see also Appendix I:
  Fire deities)
  Agni
  Ahura Mazda
  Ameša Spentas
  Atri
  Brigit

Lhamo
Maui
Mihr
Mīnākṣī
Olifat
Pāndarā
Perkunas
Prometheus
Qormusta
Rešef
Šrat
Sul
Vahagn
Vidyujjvālākarāli
Vivasvat

Fire-sickle
  Sugaar

Fish
  Atargatis
  Behanzin
  Dagan
  Hatmehit
  Kāma
  Kukulcan
  Manu
  Matsya
  Mīnākṣī
  Tinirau
  Yu-qiang

Five
  Nyame

Flower(s)
  Adonis
  Attis
  Chasca Coyllur
  Da-shi-zhi
  Gratiae, Graces
  Han Xiang-zi
  Hyákinthos
  Kāma
  Lan Cai-he
  Mañjuśrī

Narkissos
Spes
Turan
Vidyādhara
Xochipilli
Xochiquetzal

Flute
Eutérpe
Han Xiang-zi
Krisṇa
Lan Cai-he
Marsýas
Nü-gua
Veja māte

Footprint
Gautama

Forty
Enki

Four-headed
Brahmā
Dharmadhatuvāgīśvara
Ganeśa
Paramāśva
Porenutius
Preas Prohm
Samvara
Zervan

Fox
Inari

Fox-skin
Sabazios

Frog
Heket
Nun
Ogdoad
Para

Fruit (see also Apple, Pomegranate, Peach)

Gaia
Jumis
Matres
Nehalennia
Pomona

Garland (see also Laurel)
Hymén
Lares
Lasas
Nethuns

Gazelle
Anuket
Śiva

Gazelle's head
Rešef

Giant
Aloádes
Árgos
Bhūtas
Cyclops
Diwe
Fornjotr
Jötun
Kalevanpojat
Mimir
Puruṣa
Rephaim
Thursir
Troll
Upelluri
Utgard-Loki
Ymir

Goat (female)
Amáltheia
Chimaira
Māmitu
Veive
Zana

Goat (male)
Agni

Akerbeltz
Asasel
Ba
Diónysos
Pan
Se'irim

Goat-skin
Silvanus

Gold
Aegir
Gullveig
Jambhala
Meret

Gold rain
Zeus (*see* Perseus)

Goose
Amun
Brahmā
Geb
Kalteš

Grain *see also* Ear of corn; *see* Appendix I: Grain and maize deities

Grass, blade of
Yehl

Grass snake
Žaltys

Green
Amoghasiddhi
Larunda
Ratnapāni
Uto

Hail
Eate

Hair
Mahr

Panku

Hair sacrifice
Ártemis

Hammer
Charontes
Charun
Horagalles
Pajainen
Sucellos
Thor
Ukko

Hand
Dian-Cecht
Hetepet
Juesaes
Ka
Lug
Nyame

Hand, birth from
Ayiyanayaka
Dakṣa

Hare
Gluskap
Kalteš
Unut

Harp
Dagda

Head
Ikenga
Mimir
Ogmios
Puruṣa
Šesmu

Head, birth from
Abu
Athená
Juesaes
Thot

Headless
  Aképhalos
  Chinna-masta
  Hunapu
  Hun-Hunapu
  Vajrayoginī

Heart
  Hike
  Kucumatz
  Ptah
  Sihai → Sirao
  Xochipilli

Hearth
  Hestia
  Lamaria
  Lares
  Safa
  Thab-lha
  Vesta
  Zao Jun

Heel
  Achilleus
  Kriṣṇa

Helmet
  Armaz
  Laran
  Maruts
  Menrva
  Virtus
  We-to

Herald's staff
  Hermanubis
  Hérmes
  Iris
  Turms

Heron
  Djebauti

Hippopotamus
  Behemoth

Ipet
Reret
Seth
Toeris

Honey
  Aśvin
  Kvasir

Horn (see also Bull horns)
  Amáltheia
  Asthoreth
  Chors
  Diwe
  Heimdall
  Hýpnos
  Ikenga
  Lares
  Paśupati

Horse
  Apām Napāt
  Aśvin
  Bhútas
  Cakravartin
  Candra
  Charon
  Dievs
  Dioskúroi
  Eos
  Hvar
  Isten (2)
  Kalki
  Nott
  Pirwa
  Poseidon
  Remanta
  Sárkány
  Seléne
  Svantevit
  bTsan
  Víly

Horse head
  Hayagríva
  Kalki

Paramāśva

Horse-rider
Arsū
Epona
Heron
Heros
Indra

Human sacrifice
Adraste
Ártemis
Baal-Hammon
Coatlicue
He Bo
Kulshedra
Moloch
Olokun
Tezcatlipoca
Tu (1)

Humming bird
Huitzilopochtli

Hunt, hunters *see* Appendix I:
Hunting deities

Ibex
Almaqah
Ta'lab

Ibis
Chons
Thot

Ice-block
Bur(i)

Ichneumon
Atum

Ivy
Thalia

Jackal
Ammavaru

Anubis
Duamutef
Upuaut

Jewels
Akāśagarbha
Anahita
Aparājitā
Armaz
Aśokakāntā
Avalokiteśvara
Cakravartin
Ratnapāni

Judge *see* Appendix I: Judgment
deities

Jug
Nymphs
Olokun

Kerykeion *see* Herald's staff

Kettle
Baba-Yaga
Dagda
Hymir

Key
Janus
Kybéle
Portúnus
Vanth

Knife
Bes
Buddhakapāla
Ekajaṭā
Sajigor
Unut

Ladle
He Xian-gu

Lamp
Nusku

Ran-deng
Upulevo

Lance
  Laran
  Libertas
  Mars
  Menrva
  Onuris
  Virtus

Lapis lazuli
  Bhaiṣajyaguru

Laurel
  Apóllon
  Dáphne

Laurel wreath
  Aplu
  Nike
  Veive

Left
  Daktyloi
  Es
  Fidi Mukullu
  Kemwer
  Laverna
  Panku
  Sirao

Lemon
  Jambhala

Leopard
  Tore

Lettuce
  Min

Light (see also Appendix I: Light
  deities)
  Amida
  Amitābha
  Lucifer

Mārici
Pūṣan

Lightning (see also Appendix I:
  Lightning deities)
  Kucumatz
  Lucifer
  Ngai
  Poseidon
  Preas Eyn
  Semele
  Tirawa
  Yima

Lightning flashes, cluster of
  Adad
  Almaqah
  Amm
  Baal-Hadad
  Bel (2)
  Dolichénus
  Iškur
  Taranis
  Tešub
  Tin

Lingam
  Paśupati
  Preas Eyssaur
  Śiva

Lion
  Arsnuphis
  Ártemis
  Atargatis
  Bastet
  Budha
  Dedun
  Ḥebat
  Kadeš
  Kybéle
  Mahāvīra
  Mahes
  Mañjughoṣa
  Mehit
  Pachet

Pekar
Ratnasambhava
Ruti
Satúrnus Africánus
Šauška
Triphis
Urthekau
Vairocana

Lion head
Aión
Aker
Chnubis
Ḍākinī
Imdugud
Šu

Lion skin
Bes
Heraklés

Liver
Imset
Prometheus

Lizard
Išara
Kukulcan
Olokun

Lotus
Amitābha
Arapacana
Brahmā
Cundā
Dharmadhatuvāgīśvara
Gaṅgā
Harpokrates
Kāmākṣī
Khasarpana
Kurukulla
Lakṣmī
Nārāyaṇa
Nefertem
Padmanarteśvara
Padmasambhava
gShen-rab

Somtus
Sūrya
Tārā
Vasudhara
Viṣṇu
Viśvapāni

Lungs
Hapi

Lyre
Apóllon
Hérmes
Kinyras
Terpischore

Maize
Chicome coatl
Kukulcan

Maize meal
Estanathlehi

Mango
Pattini

Mare
Loki

Mask
Melpoméne
Thalia

Mead
Goibniu
Hymir
Kvasir
Valkyries

Mermaid, merman
Abgal
Ningyo
Nixe
Oannes
Olokun
Triton

Metals (*see also* Gold)
  Ameša Spentas
  Gayomard
  Illmarinen

Milk
  Amáltheia
  Boldogasszony

Milk ocean
  Ammavaru
  Kūrma
  Nāga

Milk sacrifice
  Acoran
  Idā
  Manu

Milky Way
  Gwydyon
  Heimdall
  Labbu
  Wondjina

Millipede
  Sepa

Mirror
  Amaterasu
  Išduštaya
  Kubaba
  Kybéle

Mistletoe bough
  Balder

Mongoose
  Jambhala

Monk
  Akṣobhya
  Fo
  Mi-lo Fo

Monkey
  Hanuman
  Hapi (1)
  Hez-ur
  Isten (1)
  Mbotumbo
  Ogdoad
  Sun Hou-zi
  Thot

Moon (*see also* Appendix I: Moon
    deities)
  Ahura Mazda
  Amoghapāśa
  Aśokakāntā
  Avalokiteśvara
  Baal-Šamēm
  Bhṛkuti
  Horus
  Lature Danö
  Nyame
  Osiris
  Ratnapāni
  Silewe Nazarata
  Vasudhara

Moon, sickle
  Aglibol
  Arma
  Chons
  Mah
  Saptākṣara
  Si
  Sin (1)
  Śiva
  Tīrthaṁkara

Morning and Evening Star *see*
  Appendix I: Morning/Evening Star
    deities
Mountain (*see also* Appendix I:
    Mountain deities)
  Assur
  Ehlil
  Huang Fei-hu
  Júpiter

Mercurius, Gallic

Mountain ash
  Alisanos
  Raudna

Mouse
  Pičvu'čin

Mule
  Seléne
  Sipe gyalmo
  Śridevi

Musical instruments (see also Flute,
  Harp, Lyre)
  Dhṛtarāṣṭra
  Erato
  Hathor
  Hérmes
  Ihi
  Israfil
  Jānguli
  Kinyras
  Korybantes
  Pan

Mussel
  Cakravartin
  Mal
  Nareau
  Nymphs
  Tangaroa
  Viṣṇu

Mussel-shell vehicle
  Amphitríte

Myrrh tree
  Adonis

Myrtle
  Quirinus

Nail
  Nortia

Navel
  Aditi
  Nārāyana
  Puruṣa

Net
  Maui
  Ran

Noose
  Acala
  Amoghapāśa
  Astō Vidātu
  Varuṇa
  Vighnāntaka
  Yama

North
  Amoghasiddhi
  Ani
  Hapi (1)
  Kubera
  Pekar
  Tezcatlipoca
  Thunupa
  Vaiśravaṇa

Nose
  Susanowo

Oak
  Perkunas
  Thor
  Zeus

Obelisk
  Re

Ointment
  Bastet
  Hor-Hekenu

Olive-branch
  Pax

Ostrich feathers
  Anat
  Maat

Owl
  Athená
  Cāmundā
  Lilith

Owl's head
  Hunhau

Ox
  Kwoth

Palm
  Endouellicus
  Hathor
  Nike

Palm-leaf, frond
  Hah
  Thot

Palm-tree
  Lao-zi

Panther
  Dusares
  Hebat
  Kybéle
  Šarruma

Parrot
  Kāma

Peach
  He Xian-gu
  Shou Lao
  Sun Hou-zi
  Xi-Wang-Mu

Peacock
  Amitābha
  Anahita
  Hera

Murukan
Sarasvatī
Skanda

Pearl
  Allah
  Virūpākṣa

Phallus (*see also* Lingam)
  Dionysos
  Freyr
  Isten (2)
  Min
  Mutunus Tutunus
  Satyr
  Tu (2)

Phoenix
  Aetérnitas
  Xi-Wang-Mu

Pickaxe
  Marduk

Pig
  Aśokakāntā
  Bjūtas
  Demeter
  Endouellicus
  Kirke
  Lamaštu
  Lowalangi
  Mārici
  Nang Lha
  Nut
  Pryderi
  Pwyll
  Reret
  Seth
  Vajravārāhi

Pillars
  Hérmes
  Inmutef
  Irmin
  Junit

Kamui
Num-Torum
Yima

Pine
Attis
Silvanus

Pine-cone
Demeter

Pipe
Whope

Plough
Balarāma
Mac Gréine

Pole Star
God C
Dhruva
Mixcoatl

Pomegranate
Hariti
Kubaba
Persephóne
Tinnit

Pomegranate blossom
Anahita

Poppy
Hýpnos

Potter's wheel
Chnum
Ptah

Protractor
Fu-xi

Purse
Kubera
Mercurius, Gallic
Mi-lo Fo
Sucellos

Rain *see* Appendix I: Rain deities

Rainbow
Binbeal
Iris
Julunggul
Mari (2)
Rauni
Rongo
Ungud

Rainbow snake
Julunggul
Wondjina

Ram
Agni
Ammon
Amun
Ba
Cherti
Chnum
Gao Yao
Harsaphes
Hérmes
Mari (2)
Mercurius, Gallic
Ṣango
Xewioso

Ram horns
Hommon
Tatenen

Rat
Gaṇeśa

Rattle
Chalchihuitlicue
Chicome coatl

Raven
Kutkinnáku
Lug
Manda
Mihr
Odin

Yehl

River *see* Appendix I: River deities

Rays
Ariádne
Aton
Baal-Šamēm
Cath
Chnubis
Ekhi
Inanna
Lug
Mārici
Mummu
Šamaš

Rock
Díke
Eranoranhan
Kumarbi

Rosary
Allah
Avalokiteśvara
Bhṛkuti
Brahmā
Bṛhaspati
Mi-lo Fo

Red
Amitābha
Arapacana
Aṣṭabhuja-Kurukulla
Cāmundā
Kataragama
Lature Danö
Murukan
Padmanarteśvara
Paramāśva
Thab-lha
Virūpākṣa

Rose
Saules meitis

Rudder
Fortúna
Isis
Tyché

Reeds
Inanna

Sack
Fujin

Reindeer
Horagalles
Num

Salt
Gabija

Scales
Abat(t)ur
Ammit
Anubis
Michael
Moires
Rašnu

Rhinoceros bird
Lowalangi
Mahatala

Right
Daktyloi
Es
Ha
Panku
Sirao

Scarab
Atum
Chepre

Scissors
Culsu

Scorpion
Ekchuah

Hedetet
Išara
Šadrapa
Selket

Semen
Gayomard
Skanda

Sexual organs (*see also* Phallus, Womb)
Agdistis
Amma
Baubo
Hine-nui-te-po
Marunogere
Prajāpati
Priapos
Sheila-na-gig

Shield
Anat(h)
Astarte
Budha
Hemsut
Mars
Menrva
Neith
Rešef

Ship, boat
Dionysos
Nehalennia
Re
Shichi-fukujin
Sin (1)

Sickle
Bilwis
Chronos
Marduk
Mari (2)
Psezpolnica
Satúrnus Africánus
Uranós

Skeleton
Citipati

Skull
Bhūtadāmara
Buddhakapāla
Ekajaṭā
Kālī
Krodhadevatās
Samvara

Smith, *see* Blacksmiths, gods of in Appendix I

Snail
Coatlicue
God D
Tecciztecatl

Snake
Acheloos
Aetérnitas
Agathós Daímon
Ahriman
Aión
Aparājiṭa
Apóllon
Apophis
Asklepiós
Athená
Atum
Aži Dahaka
Bhairava
Bhūtadāmara
Bolla
Bulaing
Candaroṣana
Chepre
Chnubis
Demeter
Djata
Echidna
Erinyes
Genius
Glykon
Harun
Hatuibwari

Ḫedammu
Herensugue
Heron
Huitzilopochtli
Hygíeia
Illujanka
Jānguli
Kadeš
Kaia
Kematef
Keyeme
Krodhadevatās
Labbu
Lature Danö
Leviathan
Mahākāla
Maju
Midgard-snake
Nāga
Nehebkau
Nepit
Ningišzida
Nirah
Nü-gua
Ogdoad
Pārśva
Quetzalcoatl
Rahab
Renenutet
Sabazios
Šadrapa
Šai
Salus
Satan
Smertrios
Somtus
Sugaar
Susanowo
Tefnut
Thab-lha
Tuchulcha
Uto
Väinämöinen
Vanth
Virūpākṣa
Vritra

Wadd
Wonajö
Wunekau

Snake-dress
  Coatlicue

Snake hair
  Charun
  Gorgons
  Hekáte

Snake legs
  Abraxas
  Tages

Snake-staff (caduceus)
  Aesculápius
  Asklepiós
  Mercurius, Gallic
  Rosmerta

South
  Huitzilopochtli
  Imset
  Li
  Rapithwin
  Ratnasambhava
  Virūdhaka
  Zocho

Spear
  Anat
  Astarte
  Izanagi
  Lug
  Murukan
  Odin
  Skanda
  Tin
  Tyr

Spear-point
  ʿAttar

Spindle
  Išduštaya
  Lamaštu
  Moires

Spinning and weaving
  Ixchel
  Laume
  Moires
  Nommo

Spittle, spitting
  Bumba
  Julunggul
  Kvasir
  Nainuema
  Thot

Spoon
  Durgā
  He Xian-gu

Spring *see* Appendix I: Spring deities

Springs and wells
  Borvo
  Chac
  El
  Goibniu
  Grannus
  Jutúrna
  Kaménae
  Mimir
  Muses
  Nethuns
  Nymphs
  Yarhibol

Staff (*see also* Herald's staff, Crooked staff, Snake-staff)
  Aplu
  Bṛhaspati
  Cakravartin
  Dionysos
  Ištanu
  Janus

Jizo
Nechbet
Tlaloc
Uśanas
Xochipilli

Stake
  Ašera(t)
  As (Aesir)
  Cghene

Star (*see also* Appendix I: Astral deities)
  Ištar
  Šamaš
  Xian

Stomach
  Duamutef

Stone (*see also* Rock)
  Allat
  Deive
  Dusares
  Elagabal
  Empung Luminuut
  Éros
  Grāma-devatā
  du-l Halasa
  Hubal
  Kybéle
  Papas
  Preas Eyssaur
  Ullikummi

Stones, heap of
  Heitsi-Ebib
  Hérmes

Stupa
  Gautama
  Maitreya

Stylus
  Nabu
  Nisaba

Summer
  Auxo
  Horae
  Huitzilopochtli
  Rapithwin

Sun (see also Appendix I: Sun deities)
  Ahura Mazda
  Akāśagarbha
  Aker
  Akṣobhya
  Allah
  Aṣṭabhuja-Kurukulla
  Atri
  Baal-Šamēm
  Lowalangi
  Nyame
  Ostara

Sun-disc (see also Winged sun)
  Apis
  Arinna
  Aton
  Behedti
  Cath
  Hathor
  Isis
  Rat-taui
  Suchos

Sun, eye of
  Haroeris
  Horus
  Sachmet
  Uto

Sunshade
  Aparājita

Swallow
  Makemake
  Mula Djadi
  Tang

Swan
  Brahmā
  Sarasvatī
  Turan
  Víly
  Zeus

Swastika
  gShen-rab
  Sipe Gyalmo
  Supārśva

Sword
  Acala
  Akāśagarbha
  Arapacana
  Armaz
  Budha
  Cakravartin
  Caṇḍaroṣaṇa
  Dievs
  Ekajaṭā
  Ikenga
  Kalki
  Lü Dong-bin
  Mal
  Mañjuśrī
  Michael
  Mot
  Perseus
  Rugievit
  Sárkány
  Saxnot
  Sipe Gyalmo
  Surt(r)
  Ukko
  Virūdhaka
  We-to
  Zhong-Kui

Tears
  Eos
  Freyja
  Tārā

Ten
 Iškur

Thirty
 Kušuh
 Sin (1)

Three
 Ouiot
 Viṣṇu
 Xiuhtecutli

Three-eyed
 Acala
 Bhūtadāmara
 Ekajaṭā
 Heruka
 Krodhadevatās
 Mahākāla
 Saptākṣara
 Śiva
 Sumbharāja

Three-headed, three-faced
 Amoghasiddhi
 Guhyasamāja
 Mārici
 Nzambi
 Sarasvati
 Triglav
 Uṣṇīśavijayā
 Vairocana
 Yamāntaka

Throne
 Allah
 Atargatis
 Cherubim
 Ḥanwašuit
 Ḥebat
 Isis
 Šamaš

Thumb
 Dakṣa

Thunder (see also Appendix I:
 Thunder deities)
 Baiame
 Buluga
 So

Thunderbolt (see also Vajra)
 Amoghasiddhi
 Niamye
 Saptākṣara
 Vighnāntaka

Thyrsos staff
 Dionysos

Tiger
 Cai Shen
 Li

Tiger-skin
 Candaroṣana
 Ekajaṭā
 Mahākāla
 Parṇaśavari

Toad
 Heng E
 Tawiskaron

Toe
 Namita
 Nārāyana

Tongue
 Hike
 Ptah

Torch
 Amor
 Cautes and Cautopates
 Culsu
 Dionysos
 Erinyes
 Hekáte
 Hymen
 Kukulcan

Phosphóros
Thanatos
Toeris
Vanth

Tortoise
Fukurokuju
Jurojin
Kaśyapa
Kūrma
Mercurius, Gallic
Prajāpati

Tree (see also Appendix I: Tree deities)
Dryads
Fagus
Gautama
Hašam(m)eli
Hathor
Heléne
Hun-Hunapu
Isten (2)
Kalteš
Lao-zi
Mahatala
Māl
Murukan
Nareau
Ningišzida
Pemba
Sirao
Teharonhiawagon
al-Uzza

Tree, birth from
Bestla

Triangle
Tinnit

Trident
Agni
Harihara
Poseidon
Sipe Gyalmo

Śiva

Triple staff
Bhṛkuti

Turnip
Egres

Turquoise snake
Huitzilopochtli

Two-headed, two-faced
Ani
Harihara
Janus

Ūrṇa
Fo
Gautama

Uṣṇīṣa
Fo
Gautama

Vajra (see also Thunderbolt)
Acala
Akṣobhya
Indra
Śakra
Vajrapāni
Vajrasattva
Vajravārāhi

Vessel (see also Bowl, Water-pot)
Sucellos

Vine
Gapn
Geštinanna

Vulture
Manda
Mut
Nechbet

Vulture-crest
Rat-taui

Water (*see also* Appendix I: Water
demons, Water deities)
Amitābha
Amoghasiddhi
Marama
So

Water-buffalo
Lao-zi

Water-pot (*see also* Jug)
Agni
Anahita
Bhṛkuti
Brahmā
Bṛhaspati
Ea
Gaṅgā
Okeanos
Uśanas

West
Amentet
Amitābha
Chontamenti
Estanatlehi
Ha
Isdes
Kebechsenef
Ru Shou (→ Gou Mang)
Varuṇa
Virūpākṣa
Xi-Wang-Mu

Wheel
Avalokiteśvara
Cakravartin
Fortúna
Gautama
Harihara
Locana
Mog Ruith
Taranis
Tyché
Vairocana
Yama

Whip, scourge
Anezti
Osiris

White
Amoghapāśa
Aparājitā
Arapacana
Buchis
Candra
Cundā
Dhṛtarāṣtra
Faro
Gaurī
Giltine
Khasarpana
Locana
Mawu
Ora
Singbonga
Uṣṇīśavijayā
Vairocana

Wind, storm (*see also* Appendix I:
Wind deities)
Adro
Buluga
Empung Luminuut
Enlil
Gaueko
Harpies
Iya
Kwoth
Psezpolnica
Sachmet
Sun Hou-zi
Tirawa
Tomor(r)
Typhón
Verethragna
Wunekau

Wings
Alardi
Alpan
Ámor

Arma
Ártemis
Charun
Éros
Genii
Gorgons
Hatuibwari
Hymén
Hýpnos
Lasas
Marchocias
Orcus
Phosphóros
Šauška
Seraphim
Tabiti
Turan
Vidyādhara

Winged shoes
Hérmes
Perseus
Turms

Winged sun
Ahura Mazda
Assur
Behedti
Horus
Ištanu
Šamaš

Winter
Akṣobhya
Vairocana

Wolf
Fenrir
Laskowice
Lupercus
Mani
Mars
Odin
Romulus
Upuaut

Womb
Aditi
Hathor
Śakti

Wood
Brahman

Woodpecker
Mars
Picus

Wool
Ariádne

Yellow
Aparājitā
Aśokakāntā
Bhṛkuti
Ratnasambhava
Vaiśravaṇa
Vasudhara

Zodiac, Signs of
Aión
Narisah